LIFE
APPLICATION®
BIBLE
COMMENTARY

PHILIPPIANS
COLOSSIANS
PHILEMON

Bruce B. Barton, D.Min.
Mark Fackler, Ph.D.
Linda K. Taylor
Dave Veerman, M.Div.

Series Editor: Grant Osborne, Ph.D.
Editor: Philip Comfort, Ph.D.

Tyndale House Publishers, Inc.
Wheaton, Illinois

Contributing Editors: James C. Galvin, Ed.D. and Ronald A. Beers

Life Application is a registered trademark of Tyndale House Publishers, Inc.

Scripture quotations marked NIV are taken from the *Holy Bible,* New International Version®. Copyright © 1973, 1978, 1984 by International Bible Society. Used by permission of Zondervan Publishing House. All rights reserved. The "NIV" and "New International Version" trademarks are registered in the United States Patent and Trademark Office by International Bible Society. Use of either trademark requires permission of International Bible Society.

Scripture quotations marked NKJV are taken from The New King James Version. Copyright © 1979, 1980, 1982, Thomas Nelson Inc., Publishers.

Scripture quotations marked NRSV are taken from the New Revised Standard Version of the Bible, copyrighted, 1989 by the Division of Christian Education of the National Council of the Churches of Christ in the United States of America, and are used by permission. All rights reserved.

(No citation is given for Scripture text that is exactly the same wording in all three versions—NIV, NKJV, and NRSV.)

Scripture quotations marked NASB are taken from the *New American Standard Bible,* © 1960, 1962, 1963, 1968, 1971, 1972, 1973, 1975, 1977 by The Lockman Foundation. Used by permission.

Scripture verses marked TLB are taken from *The Living Bible,* copyright © 1971 owned by assignment by KNT Charitable Trust. All rights reserved.

Scripture quotations marked RSV are taken from the *Holy Bible,* Revised Standard Version, copyright © 1946, 1952, 1971 by the Division of Christian Education of the National Council of the Churches of Christ in the United States of America, and are used by permission. All rights reserved.

Scripture verses marked NEB are taken from *The New English Bible,* copyright © 1970, Oxford University Press, Cambridge University Press.

Scripture verses marked TEV are taken from *The Bible in Today's English Version,* copyright © 1976, American Bible Society.

Library of Congress Cataloging-in-Publication Data

Philippians, Colossians, and Philemon / Bruce B. Barton . . . [et al.].
   cm. — (Life application Bible commentary)
   Includes bibliographical references and index.
   ISBN 0-8423-2974-9 (pbk.)
   1. Bible. N.T. Philippians—Commentaries. 2. Bible. N.T.
Colossians—Commentaries. 3. Bible. N.T. Philemon—
Commentaries.
I. Barton, Bruce B. II. Series.
BS2705.3.P48   1995
227—dc20   95-6670

Printed in the United States of America

05   04
8   7   6

CONTENTS

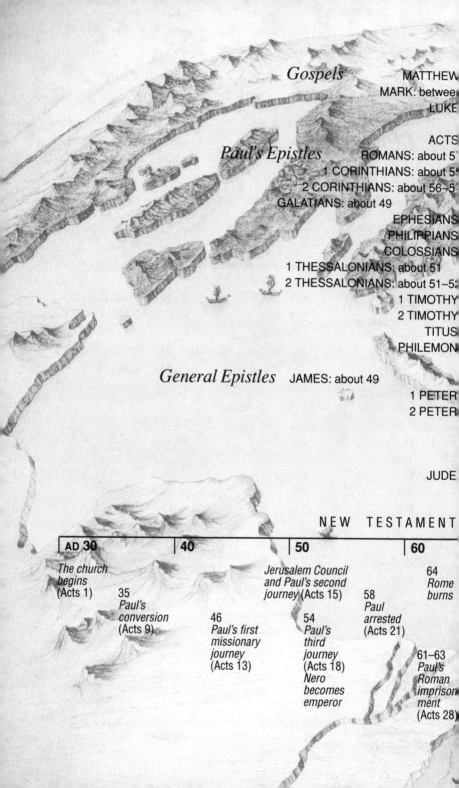

Gospels MATTHEW
MARK: between
LUKE

ACTS
Paul's Epistles ROMANS: about 5
1 CORINTHIANS: about 5
2 CORINTHIANS: about 56–5
GALATIANS: about 49

EPHESIANS
PHILIPPIANS
COLOSSIANS
1 THESSALONIANS: about 51
2 THESSALONIANS: about 51–5
1 TIMOTHY
2 TIMOTHY
TITUS
PHILEMON

General Epistles JAMES: about 49

1 PETER
2 PETER

JUDE

NEW   TESTAMENT

AD 30	40	50	60

The church begins (Acts 1)

35 Paul's conversion (Acts 9)

46 Paul's first missionary journey (Acts 13)

Jerusalem Council and Paul's second journey (Acts 15)

54 Paul's third journey (Acts 18) Nero becomes emperor

58 Paul arrested (Acts 21)

64 Rome burns

61–63 Paul's Roman imprisonment (Acts 28)

between 60–65
5–65
about 60

about 63–65

JOHN: probably 80–85

about 61
about 62
about 61

about 64
about 66–67
about 64
about 61

HEBREWS: probably before 70

about 62–64
about 67

1 JOHN: between 85–90
2 JOHN: about 90
3 JOHN: about 90

about 65

REVELATION: about 95

TIMELINE

| 70 | 80 | 90 | 100 |

7–68
Paul and
Peter
executed

Jerusalem
destroyed

79 Mt. Vesuvius
erupts in Italy

68
Essenes hide
their library
of Bible
manuscripts
in a cave
in Qumran
by the
Dead Sea

About 75
John begins
ministry in
Ephesus

75
Rome begins
construction
of Colosseum

About 98
John's
death
at Ephesus

FOREWORD

The *Life Application Bible* Commentary series provides verse-by-verse explanation, background, and application for every verse in the New Testament. In addition, it gives personal help, teaching notes, and sermon ideas that will address needs, answer questions, and provide insight for applying God's Word to life today. The content is highlighted so that particular verses and phrases are easy to find.

Each volume contains three sections: introduction, commentary, and reference. The introduction includes an overview of the book, the book's historical context, a timeline, cultural background information, major themes, an overview map, and an explanation about the author and audience.

The commentary section includes running commentary on the Bible text with reference to several modern versions, especially the New International Version and the New Revised Standard Version, accompanied by life applications interspersed throughout. Additional elements include charts, diagrams, maps, and illustrations. There are also insightful quotes from church leaders and theologians such as John Calvin, Martin Luther, John Wesley, A. W. Tozer, and C. S. Lewis. These features are designed to help you quickly grasp the biblical information and be prepared to communicate it to others.

The reference section includes a bibliography of other resources and an index.

GENERAL INTRODUCTION

Letters of all sizes and purposes flood our homes and businesses, filling our mailboxes and lives with envelopes, paper, and requests for urgent responses. Written, stamped, deposited, collected, sorted, routed, bundled, and delivered, millions of these epistles travel daily from senders to receivers with hi-tech efficiency. These days, most of our mail falls into the "junk" category: ads, contests, political endorsements, polls, newsletters, insurance and credit card enticements, and financial appeals for a variety of causes. Monthly bills also march in the postage parade, and occasionally "official" correspondence, business letters, and checks are in the mail. Most of these envelopes are quickly dispatched, with their contents relegated to the appropriate places (often the "circular file").

Personal letters break through this stack of unwanted paper. Enthusiastically grasping these grand exceptions, we rip open the envelopes and eagerly read each line (and between the lines). Birthday cards, postcard vacation notes, annual family reports, letters from camp, encouragements from friends and relatives, and love letters all receive our full attention.

Twenty centuries ago, before computer labels, color separations, zip and bar codes, high-speed presses, electronic sorting, and photocopy and fax machines, people wrote to each other. Hand delivered by friends or special couriers, these letters carried greetings, instructions, encouragements, and personal words. With no flood of junk mail competing for attention, the epistles were received with joy and were shared with others.

As Paul traveled throughout the Roman Empire preaching the gospel, teaching new converts, and establishing churches, he developed close relationships. To keep in touch with these dear friends and to instruct them further in biblical theology and Christian living, he would write letters—personal epistles. Paul even wrote to believers in cities that he had not yet visited, but whom he knew needed a word of instruction, encouragement, or correction. God used Paul and many of his letters, now contained in the New Testament, to communicate his message to those first-century believers and beyond—reaching to us today.

The three of these epistles in this volume, Philippians, Colossians, and Philemon, provide an interesting collection of Paul's writings. Although widely divergent in purposes and content, each one comes from Paul's heart—for Christ, for the church, and for individual believers. And imagine the joy with which these letters were received—personal words from their beloved teacher, mentor, and friend.

AUTHOR

Paul: apostle of Christ, courageous missionary, gifted teacher, articulate apologist, and Christian statesman.

Having received an excellent secular and religious education (Acts 22:3), Paul was destined for leadership in Jerusalem Judaism. We first read of Paul in Acts at the stoning of Stephen, a courageous and outspoken deacon in the Jerusalem church. Paul collected the coats of the executioners (Acts 7:58) and approved of Stephen's death (Acts 8:1). Soon afterward, Paul persecuted followers of Christ, capturing them and throwing them into prison (Acts 8:3; 22:4; Galatians 1:13-14). A Pharisee and influential member of the Jewish ruling council (the Sanhedrin), he voted to have these followers of "the Way" put to death (Acts 26:5, 10). As a zealous defender of the faith, Paul found great favor among the religious establishment. But his fast track took a U-turn on the road to Damascus, where he was confronted by the Lord (Acts 9:1-6; 22:5-10; 26:12-18).

Following his conversion, Paul immediately began to publicly proclaim Jesus as the Son of God, and he used his tremendous, now Spirit-filled, intellect to prove Jesus to be the Messiah (Acts 9:22). This enraged the Jewish leaders, Paul's former compatriots, causing them to conspire to kill him (Acts 9:23). Paul escaped and went to Arabia, where he probably studied the Word and preached to the Gentiles (Galatians 1:15-17). Three years later, he traveled to Jerusalem with his "sponsor," Barnabas (Acts 9:27). When Grecian Jews threatened to kill him there, Paul returned to his hometown of Tarsus (Acts 9:30). Soon Barnabas brought Paul to Antioch where they ministered together for a year in the church there (Acts 11:25-26).

In approximately A.D. 46, the believers in Antioch commissioned Barnabas and Paul to take the gospel to both Jews and Gentiles in other lands (Acts 13:1-3). Stops on this first missionary journey included Paphos (on Cyprus), Perga, Attalia, Pisidian Antioch, Iconium, Lystra, and Derbe (Acts 13:4–14:28). When word came to Jerusalem of the ministry among the Gentiles, a controversy arose over whether non-Jewish converts had to be circumcised and had to obey the law of Moses (Acts 15:1). So Paul and Barnabas, along with other believers, were sent to Jerusalem to see the apostles and elders in order to settle the dispute (Acts 15:2-4). After hearing their testimony, the Jerusalem Council affirmed the ministry to the Gentiles (Acts 15:12-35).

A few months later, in approximately A.D. 50, Paul and Barnabas discussed a second trip, to visit the churches they had established on their first missionary journey (Acts 15:36). But because of a disagreement over Mark, they went separate ways: Barnabas and Mark sailed for Cyprus, while Paul and Silas went through Syria and Cilicia (Acts 15:37-41). On this trip, Paul and Silas visited the believers at Derbe, Lystra, and Iconium. Then, passing through the region of Phrygia and Galatia, they journeyed to Troas. There, through a vision, God told Paul to travel to Macedonia (Acts 16:1-10). Obeying the Holy Spirit, Paul and Silas sailed to Samothrace and then to Neapolis. From there they traveled to Philippi, where they ministered for several days (Acts 16:11-40). Upon leaving Philippi, Paul and Silas traveled through Amphipolis and Apollonia to Thessalonica. Next they went to Berea, and then to Athens and Corinth, where they stayed for some time (Acts 17:1–18:18). Leaving Macedonia, they traveled to Ephesus. Then they sailed to Caesarea and made their way back to Antioch.

On his third missionary journey, in approximately A.D. 53, Paul concentrated on the region of Galatia and Phrygia. Then he returned to Ephesus where he ministered for two years (Acts 18:23–19:41). Continuing his trip, Paul revisited the believers in Macedonia and Greece. His itinerary included Troas, Neapolis, Philippi, Amphipolis, Thessalonica, Berea, and Athens (Acts 20:1-2). Determined to go to Jerusalem, Paul retraced his steps through Macedonia (Acts 20:3-12). Then he sailed to Assos, Mitylene, Kios, Samos, and Miletus, where he met with elders from Ephesus who tried to dissuade him from continuing on to Jerusalem. But Paul was determined (Acts 20:13-37). Leaving Miletus, he sailed to Cos, and then to Rhodes, Patara, and, finally, Tyre, in Phoenicia (Acts 21:1-3). From there he traveled through Ptolemais and Caesarea to Jerusalem (Acts 21:4-17).

At the temple in Jerusalem, Paul was recognized by Asian Jews who stirred up the crowd against him. Seizing Paul, they dragged him from the temple and would have killed him if the Roman commander had not intervened (Acts 21:18-36). Paul attempted to state his case to the assembled mob. They listened for a while until he spoke of his ministry to the Gentiles; then they called for his death (Acts 21:37–22:21). After revealing his Roman citizenship to the commander, Paul was taken into protective custody (Acts 22:25–23:11). Eventually, after a transfer from Jerusalem to Caesarea, trials before Felix and Festus, and an audience with Agrippa, Paul appealed to the emperor (his right as a Roman citizen) (Acts 23:12–26:32). On the way to Rome, the ship broke apart in a violent storm, but everyone was miraculously saved on the island of Malta (Acts 27:1–28:10). Finally, Paul, in chains, reached Rome. There he remained awaiting trial under guard in a rented house. During this time, Paul was allowed to have many visitors and to preach and teach (Acts 28:11-31).

Although the Bible makes no mention of this, scholars believe that after two years Paul was released, whereupon he probably left on another missionary journey. This trip took him through Ephesus, Colosse, and Macedonia. He may also have realized his goal of going to Spain (Romans 15:24, 28). After a while, Paul probably journeyed east and visited Crete (Titus 1:5). Eventually, however, he was arrested a second time and returned to Rome, this time to await execution (2 Timothy 4:9-18). Paul was martyred in the spring of A.D. 68.

From the moment he met Christ on the dusty road to Damascus, Paul was committed to telling everyone the Good News. Despite imprisonments, stonings, beatings, life threats, danger, hunger, slander, and shipwreck, he courageously proclaimed God's message throughout the Roman Empire (see 2 Corinthians 11:23–12:10 for a summary of Paul's struggles and hardships). Taking every opportunity, he preached in synagogues, on the beach, in a school, aboard ship, in prison, at a philosophical roundtable, and in court—wherever he had an audience. And he told *everyone:* Jews and Gentiles, men and women, old and young, healthy and sick, wealthy and poor, free and slave, Roman soldiers, God fearers, idol worshipers, prison guards, and magistrates.

Not content to merely preach and spread the Word, Paul was also committed to see the new converts grow strong in their relationship with Christ. So he established churches, trained leaders, and wrote letters—those precious letters, his epistles. Three of these letters—Philippians, Colossians, and Philemon—provide a clear picture of Paul's commitment to the spread of the gospel, his uncompromising stand for the fundamentals of the faith, and his strong love for the lost and for his brothers and sisters in Christ.

In contrast, today many Christians will not walk across the street to tell a neighbor about the Lord because of the inconvenience, or they remain silent about their faith, even when asked, for fear of social embarrassment. May we renew our commitment to Christ and depend on the Holy Spirit for power and courage to spread the Word. May we be like Paul.

PHILIPPIANS

INTRODUCTION TO PHILIPPIANS

Picture a baby, rested, fed, and lying in his mother's arms. Looking down with unspeakable love into those precious eyes, Mommy begins to talk to her son and gently strokes his cheek, evoking a sudden smile.

Or imagine a three-year-old playing with his father on the living room floor. With Dad's wrestling moves transformed into tickles, the little boy begins to giggle, and both end up laughing hysterically.

That's joy—contentment, security, and unbridled laughter.

But joy can also be discovered in the pain and struggles of life—at a funeral, knowing, through tears, that your loved one now lives with God; in a hospital bed, knowing that the Lord stands near; at the unemployment office, knowing that God will provide for all your needs. True joy runs deep and strong, flowing from confident assurance in God's loving control. Regardless of your life's situation, you can find joy, true joy, in Christ.

Joy dominates this letter to the believers at Philippi. In fact, the concept of "rejoicing" or "joy" appears sixteen times in four chapters. The pages radiate the positive, triumphant message that because of Christ's work for us (2:6-11; 3:12), because of the Holy Spirit's work in and through us (1:6, 12-14, 18-26; 2:12-13; 4:4-7, 10-13), and because of God's plan for us (1:6, 9-10; 3:7-14, 20-21; 4:19), we can and should REJOICE!

As you read Paul's letter from prison to his beloved friends in Philippi, note all that you possess in Christ, and find your joy in him.

AUTHOR

Paul (See the introduction to this volume.)

Evidence for Paul's authorship of Philippians comes from the letter itself, as the very first sentence states: "Paul and Timothy, servants of Christ Jesus, To all the saints in Christ Jesus at Philippi, together with the overseers and deacons" (1:1 NIV).

Although Timothy's name also appears in the greeting, it soon becomes obvious that Paul alone is writing since he uses the first person throughout the letter. In addition, the personal references in 3:4-11 and 4:10-16 clearly apply to Paul. The early church fathers Polycarp, Irenaeus, Clement of Alexandria, Eusebius, and others affirmed Paul's authorship.

▨ SETTING

Written from prison in Rome in approximately A.D. 61 Paul wanted to get to Rome (Acts 19:21), not only to teach and fellowship with the believers there (Romans 1:8-13), but also because Rome stood as the center of the civilized world. It was a strategic city for the spread of the gospel. To reach the Roman Empire, the gospel had to reach Rome.

In God's sovereign plan, Paul did sail to Rome, but not as a prominent citizen, missionary statesman, or even itinerant preacher. He arrived, rather, as a prisoner, in chains (Acts 28:11-16). Even as a prisoner, however, Paul was free to teach, preach, and write (Acts 28:17-31). During these years of house arrest, Paul wrote what have come to be known as the "Prison Epistles"—Ephesians, Philippians, Colossians, and Philemon.

It is clear that Paul was a Roman prisoner when he wrote this letter because of his words in 1:12-17. He wrote of being "in chains" (1:13, 17) and of being a witness for Christ to the "whole palace guard" (1:13 NIV). Some scholars, however, have proposed sites other than Rome as the setting for these letters.

Some have surmised that Paul wrote this letter to the Philippians during his imprisonment in Caesarea (Acts 23:23–26:32). After all, Paul was imprisoned there for about two years (A.D. 57–59), interrupted by hearings before Felix, Festus, and Agrippa. He would have had the freedom and the time to write. The uncertain and menacing situation in Caesarea seems to fit Paul's indication that death was an imminent possibility (1:20-23, 30; 2:17). And references to a "palace guard" (NIV) or "praetorian guard" (RSV) could fit this location.

Some have even proposed that this letter may have been written from Ephesus, even though the Bible makes no mention of Paul being imprisoned in that city. The main reason for this theory is the distance between Philippi and Rome (or Caesarea). In his letter, Paul implies that several trips have been made to and from the place of his confinement:

■ Timothy traveled to Paul. Although not mentioned in the trip to

Rome (Acts 26–28), Timothy was with Paul when this letter was written (1:1).

- Someone sent a message to Philippi informing the believers of Paul's imprisonment (4:14).

- Epaphroditus brought the love gift from Philippi to Paul (4:18).

- News of Epaphroditus's sickness was sent back to Philippi (2:26).

- Paul received word that the Philippians had received the news of Ephaphroditus's condition (2:26).

Paul also implies the following future journeys:

- Epaphroditus will bring the letter to Philippi (2:25, 28).

- Timothy will travel to Philippi (2:19).

- Then Timothy will return to Paul (2:19).

- Paul will travel to Philippi after his release (2:24).

According to this theory, it is more likely for these journeys to have occured to and from Ephesus, which is much closer to Philippi than either Rome or Caesarea. But even if all these statements refer to actual trips, there would have been enough time for them to have been taken to Rome, even if the travel time had been seven or eight weeks—Paul was imprisoned for two years. Certainly travel to Rome was both common and convenient, along the Egnatian and Appian Ways.

Despite these alternate proposals, Rome still stands as the most likely location for the writing of the Prison Epistles. Paul's imprisonment at that time and place fits the statement about his needs (4:17-18), allows time for the trips to and from Philippi, and makes sense of his references to the palace guard (1:13) and Caesar's household (4:22).

All that is known of Paul's place of confinement in Rome at this time is that it was his own rented house. Thus Paul's prison was considerably more comfortable than the environment in which he wrote 2 Timothy. In that prison, the Mamertine dungeon, Paul was suffering and chained like a criminal (2 Timothy 2:9). He had been deserted (2 Timothy 4:10, 16), he was cold (2 Timothy 4:13), and he was expecting to die (2 Timothy 4:6-7, 18). In this setting, however, although guarded constantly, Paul enjoyed great freedom to welcome visitors (Acts 28:17-30) and to preach and teach (Acts 28:31).

Paul was imprisoned in Rome for two years—approximately A.D. 60–62. He wrote Philippians in about A.D. 61. Evidently this was the last letter written from prison—1:21-28 seems to indicate that Paul was expecting a decision about his fate very soon. (See also note on 1:1 in the commentary section.)

AUDIENCE

The believers in Philippi

The Macedonian (northern Greece today) city of Philippi was named after Philip of Macedon (the father of Alexander the Great). Surrounded by mountains and close to the sea, Philippi became a strategic city in the Greek empire. In 167 B.C. it became part of the Roman Empire, but it did not achieve real importance until after 31 B.C. when Octavian defeated Antony at the battle of Actium. After that decisive battle, Philippi received a number of Italian colonists who had favored Antony and had been dispossessed of their property. The colony was then renamed Colonia Iulia Philippensis to honor Julius Caesar. Later, in 27 B.C., when Octavian was designated Augustus, the colony's name was changed again to Colonia Augusta Iulia (Victrix) Philippensium, equating the cause of Augustus with that of Caesar. At that time, Philippi was given the right to the Law of Italy together with many rights and privileges, including immunity from taxation. The residents of Philippi were very conscious and proud of their Roman citizenship and heritage (see Acts 16:20-21). Philippi also boasted a fine school of medicine.

Paul visited Philippi on his second missionary journey, in A.D. 51, about ten years previous to this letter. By the time of Paul's visit, Philippi had become a thriving commercial center because of its strategic location as the first city on the Egnatian Way, an important ancient highway linking the Aegean and Adriatic Seas. Travelers to Rome would cross the Adriatic and then continue up to Rome on the Appian Way. Thus, Philippi was the gateway to the East. Although thoroughly colonized by the Romans after 31 B.C., Philippi was still more Greek in culture than Roman. Luke refers to Philippi as "a Roman colony and the leading city of that district of Macedonia" (Acts 16:12 NIV). Although Philippi was not the capital city of the region (sub-province of Macedonia), it certainly was the "leading city." Luke's statement also reflects civic pride in his hometown.

The church at Philippi in ancient Macedonia was the first European church founded by Paul. Thus, it represents the first major penetration of the gospel into Gentile territory (see Philippians 4:14-15).

Acts 16:9-40 tells how the church began. On the second missionary journey in about A.D. 51, prevented by the Holy Spirit from preaching in Asia and in Bythynia, Paul and Silas traveled to Troas, the farthest Asian port on the Aegean Sea. While there, God spoke to Paul through a vision, telling him to take the gospel to Europe. In this vision, a Greek man begged, "Come over to Macedonia and help us" (Acts 16:9 NIV). Immediately, Paul and his traveling companions set sail for Samothrace and Neapolis, continuing on to Philippi.

In every city, Paul and his party would go to the synagogue to share the gospel with the Jews. So on their first Sabbath in Philippi, Paul and Silas probably looked for a synagogue. Instead, they found a group of women who had gathered outside the city on the banks of a river. The fact that Philippi had no synagogue indicates that there were few Jews in that city. Therefore, from its inception, the church at Philippi consisted mainly of Gentiles. Acts 16:14-34 tells of two of the first converts in Philippi: Lydia, a businesswoman who may have been a Jew or a Jewish proselyte; and a Roman jailer. The response of these three provided clear demonstration that God's Good News was for all classes, sexes, races, and nationalities.

Luke also mentions that when Lydia responded to Paul's message, so did the members of her household (Acts 16:15). The same was true for the jailer—his family responded with him (Acts 16:34). No other specific converts are mentioned in this account in Acts, but the chapter concludes with: "After leaving the prison they [Paul and Silas] went to Lydia's home; and when they had seen and encouraged the brothers and sisters, they departed" (Acts 16:40 NRSV). "Brothers and sisters" seems to indicate that a small but vital group of believers had been forged. Clement, Euodia, and Syntyche may have been won to Christ during this time (see 4:2-3).

When Paul and Silas departed from Philippi, they left Luke there, in his hometown, to carry on the ministry. A few years later, at the end of his third missionary trip, Paul visited Philippi prior to spending the winter in Corinth. When Paul wrote this epistle, the church in Philippi was thriving, and he felt very close to the believers there.

OCCASION AND PURPOSE FOR WRITING

To thank the Philippians for their gift and to strengthen the believers in their faith

This is a very personal epistle. It is obvious from Paul's opening comments that he enjoyed a close friendship with the Philippian believers: "I thank my God every time I remember you. In all my prayers for all of you, I always pray with joy because of your partnership in the gospel from the first day until now" (1:3-5 NIV). During their visit to Philippi, Paul and Silas had witnessed immediate and dramatic response to their message. And despite the fact that they were attacked and imprisoned, they had seen the church begin and then grow into a strong core of believers (Acts 16:40). During the course of Paul's ministry, the Philippian believers had continually come to his assistance through their gifts (4:15-18). At this time, nearly ten years later, the Philippians had again sent a gift to Paul to help him in his time of need: "I rejoice greatly in the Lord that at last you have renewed your concern for me. . . . It was good of you to share in my troubles" (4:10, 14 NIV). Perhaps their donated funds were helping to pay for the rented house to which Paul was confined (Acts 28:30). In response to this gift and to their relationship over the years, Paul wrote to express his deep appreciation for their love, faithfulness, and generosity.

Paul also took the opportunity of this letter to deal with important issues in the church. He had heard of divisive rivalry and selfish ambition (2:3-4), so he gave strong counsel and even named names (4:2). Paul knew that the Judaizers could be a problem, so he gave clear instructions to avoid those men (3:2-3). He also warned of those who would go to the opposite extreme and live totally without the law or any personal discipline (3:17-19). None of these issues were full-blown problems that were threatening the life of the church, but Paul knew their destructive pattern. So he warned his beloved Christian brothers and sisters, encouraging and challenging them to continue to stand strong and united and to live for Christ (1:27; 4:1, 4-9).

Paul's sensitivity to the needs at Philippi stands as a great example. He didn't wait for a crisis; instead, he confronted potential problems early, before they could fester and infect the whole body. When we see a fellow believer begin to struggle or stray, we should follow Paul's example and lovingly confront that person, urging him or her to stay on track.

MESSAGE

Joy, Humility, Self-Sacrifice, Unity, Christian Living

Joy (1:3-6, 12-26; 2:1-4, 17-18; 3:1; 4:4-13). Although Paul had suffered much for the cause of Christ and was writing this letter as a prisoner of Rome, still he was filled with joy because of what God had done for him, because of his hope in God's plan for the future, and because of the faithfulness of the Philippian believers. Paul knew that his beloved brothers and sisters in Christ would be tempted and tested, so he urged them to stay strong in their faith, to be content, and to "rejoice in the Lord always" (4:4 NIV). Regardless of the circumstances, believers can have profound contentment, serenity, and peace. This joy comes from knowing Christ personally, depending on his strength, and trusting in his plan for our lives.

Importance for Today. Far from content, people today truly believe that they need every new product, toy, or appliance. Or they think that they will find happiness and personal fulfillment through relationships, travel, adventure, or something else. Thus, most people are discontent and continually seeking meaning and peace. But true, lasting contentment comes only through knowing Christ. With sins forgiven, our future secure, and our lives in God's control, we can be content . . . and have joy. Yes, we can have joy, even in hardship. Joy does not come from outward circumstances but from inward strength.

In addition to discontent, Paul highlights other joy stealers: selfish ambition (1:17; 2:3), complaining and arguing (2:14), self-centeredness (2:21), hedonism (3:18-19), anxiety (4:6), and bad thoughts (4:8). What steals your joy?

Rely on Christ within you to give you joy, not on what you own, who you know, or what you experience.

Humility (1:15-18; 2:5-11; 3:7-14). If anyone had the right to boast, it was Paul. Yet he continued to lay aside personal ambition and glory in order to know Christ (3:7-11) and to glorify him (3:12-14). Paul knew that Jesus had left glory to come to earth in order to live as a man and to die on the cross. Paul held up Jesus as the example to follow, urging the Philippians to humble themselves as Christ had done.

Jesus showed true humility when he laid aside his rights and privileges as God to become a human being (2:5-11). He poured out his life to pay the penalty that we deserve. Laying aside self-interest is essential to being Christlike.

Importance for Today. We naturally worry about ourselves first, making sure that we are comfortable and that we get the credit and glory we deserve. But as Christ's representatives, we should live as he would. This means putting others first and renouncing personal recognition. It also means serving others and looking out for their best interests. When we give up our self-interest, we can serve the Lord with joy, love, and kindness. True humility is a by-product of seeing ourselves from Christ's perspective and recognizing that we are nothing without him.

What can you do to see yourself and the world from Christ's point of view? What can you do to give your life for others?

Self-Sacrifice (1:15-26; 2:4, 17, 25-30; 3:7-14; 4:14-19). Christ suffered and died so that all who believe might have eternal life. Following Christ's example, with courage and faithfulness, Paul sacrificed himself for the ministry, taking every chance to tell others God's Good News, preaching and teaching even while in prison. For Paul, living meant opportunities for serving the Lord, but dying would mean going to live with the Lord (1:20-24). So Paul lived with his goal always before him, motivating him to forget the past and press on to win the prize (3:13-14).

Importance for Today. "Sacrifice" seems like a dirty word these days. Instead, people want to indulge themselves and do everything they can to have a comfortable and easy life. Unfortunately, this cultural attitude can carry into the church. For example, many believers are more concerned about not having padded pews than the fact that people are headed for hell. But reaching people for Christ, helping those in need, and changing our world will involve personal sacrifice. Christ gives us the power to do that. We must follow the example of Jesus and of godly leaders like Paul who demonstrate self-denying concern for others.

What will it take—what sacrifices will you have to make—for you to be an effective witness for Christ in your neighborhood? at work? What will it take for your church to make a difference for Christ in your community?

Unity (1:15-18, 27-30; 2:1-4, 14-16; 4:2-3). In every church, in every generation, controversial issues, personality conflicts, and other divisive issues arise. The tendency toward arguments and division intensifies during hard times, when people can turn against each other. Although the church at Philippi was strong, it was not immune to these problems and, in fact, had experienced some internal conflicts. Paul encouraged the Philippians to get along, agree with one another, stop complaining, and work together.

Importance for Today. Christians should contend against their common enemy—Satan and his work in the world—and not against each other. We need all our resources, focus, and energy for the battle. When we are unified in love, Christ works through us, and we can make a difference for him. We need to keep before us the ideals of teamwork, consideration of others, and unselfishness.

What tends to break your unity with other believers? What issues threaten to divide your church? Keep your focus on Christ and his mission in the world; don't be sidetracked by petty jealousies, competition, hurt feelings, or minor irritations. Work together with your brothers and sisters in Christ to make a difference in the world.

Christian Living (1:6, 9-11, 21-29; 2:12-13; 3:12-21; 4:4-13). Paul could not stay in Philippi, teaching the new believers, encouraging them to live for Christ, and holding them accountable. When he was with the Philippians, they were careful to obey the Lord (2:12) because they were aware of Paul's powerful example and strong encouragement. But now, in his absence, they should be even more careful to live the Christian life (work out their own salvation—2:12). They could be confident that God was with them and in them, changing them from the inside out (2:13). Certainly God would complete his good work in them (1:6).

Paul also explained the steps these believers could take to live for Christ: be unified with other Christians (1:27-30), remember Christ's work on the cross (2:5-11), rejoice in God's work for them and in them (3:1), keep focused on the goal (3:12-14), guard their thoughts (4:8-9), be content with what they have (4:10-13), and help those in need (4:14-19).

Importance for Today. In this day of media evangelists, celebrity Bible teachers, and articulate preachers, it can be easy to depend on others for our spiritual nourishment and motivation. Yet the Christian life always depends on the relationship an individual believer has with the Lord Jesus. Instead of relying on others for our "faith," we must depend on Christ and the Holy Spirit working within us. And instead of expecting growth to happen because we have a strong Christian environment, we must keep our focus on Christ, discipline ourselves to pray and to read the Bible, and apply God's Word to our lives.

On whom do you depend for your motivation to live for Christ? Where do you find your spiritual nourishment? Christian living depends on Christ living in you and you then living in obedience to him.

VITAL STATISTICS

Purpose: To thank the Philippians for the gift they had sent Paul and to strengthen these believers by showing them that true joy comes from Jesus Christ alone

Author: Paul

To whom written: All the Christians at Philippi and all believers everywhere

Date written: About A.D. 61, from Rome during Paul's imprisonment there

Setting: Paul and his companions began the church at Philippi on his second missionary journey (Acts 16:11-40). This was the first church established on the European continent. The Philippian church had sent a gift with Epaphroditus (one of their members) to be delivered to Paul (4:18). Paul was in a Roman prison at the time. He wrote this letter to thank them for their gift and to encourage them in their faith.

Key verse: "Rejoice in the Lord always. I will say it again: Rejoice!" (4:4 NIV).

OUTLINE OF PHILIPPIANS

1. Joy in suffering (1:1-26)
2. Joy in serving (1:27–2:30)
3. Joy in believing (3:1–4:1)
4. Joy in giving (4:2-23)

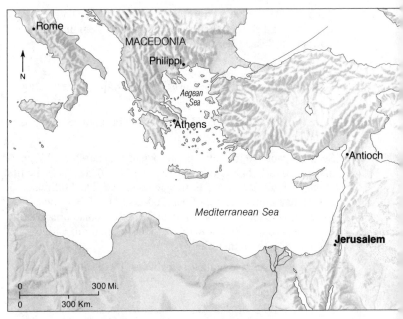

LOCATION OF PHILIPPI
Philippi sat on the Egnatian Way, the main transportation route in
Macedonia, an extension of the Appian Way, which joined the eastern
empire with Italy.

Philippians 1:1-26

As Paul wrote this letter, he was under house arrest in Rome. When the Philippian church had heard about Paul's imprisonment, they had sent Epaphroditus (who may have been one their elders) to Rome to visit and encourage him. Epaphroditus had arrived with words of affection from the church, as well as a financial contribution that would help make Paul's confinement more comfortable. Paul wanted to thank the believers for helping him during his time of need. He also wanted to tell them why he could be full of joy despite his imprisonment and upcoming trial. He wanted them to remain strong in the faith, realizing that although he was in chains for the gospel, God was still in control and the truth of the gospel remained unchanged. In this uplifting letter, Paul counseled the Philippians about humility and unity and warned them about potential problems they would face.

1:1 **Paul.** The undisputed author of this letter is the apostle Paul, missionary to the Gentiles, imprisoned in Rome for preaching the gospel. Paul had founded the church in Philippi, so the recipients of the letter were his dear friends and children in the faith. Paul filled his letter with joy and love as he sought to dispel the Philippians' fears regarding his imprisonment, to thank them for their financial support, and to encourage them in their faith.

"Paul" is the Greek version of the Hebrew name Saul (Acts 13:9). From the tribe of Benjamin (3:5), Paul was born in Tarsus, was raised as a strict Pharisee, and was educated in Jerusalem under Gamaliel (Acts 22:3). Though born to Jewish parents, Paul was also a Roman citizen (Acts 22:27-28).

Out of this diverse background, God formed and called a valuable servant. God used every aspect of Paul's upbringing to further the spreading of the gospel. God called him: "This man is my chosen instrument to carry my name before the Gentiles and their kings and before the people of Israel" (Acts 9:15 NIV). Paul fulfilled his calling. So far, he had taken three missionary journeys, covering thousands of miles as he carried the gospel from Jerusalem, across Asia, and into Europe. His ultimate goal had

always been to take the gospel to Rome itself—capital of the vast
Roman Empire that had spread over most of Europe, North
Africa, and the Near East. The fact that all roads led to Rome
made Rome a perfect center for the gospel message to spread
across the known world.

Paul wrote this letter from Rome. He had arrived there through
a series of unusual circumstances. He had been arrested in Jerusalem by the Romans for seemingly inciting a riot. A plot to kill
Paul caused the Romans to take Paul to Caesarea (on the coast of
the Mediterranean Sea). There Paul gave the gospel message to
Governor Felix and his wife Drusilla (Acts 23:24; 24:1-26). Felix
didn't make a decision in the case, leaving Paul in prison for two
years until Festus became the new governor. Then Paul was able
to present the gospel to Festus, and then to King Agrippa and Ber-
nice (Acts 25:1–26:32). Paul did indeed carry God's name to
Israel, and to the Gentiles and to their kings, just as God had said
(Acts 9:15).

Every Roman citizen had the right to appeal to Caesar. This
didn't mean that Caesar himself would hear the case, but that the
citizen's case would be tried by the highest courts in the empire.
As a prisoner being unjustly tried, Paul used the opportunity to
get to Rome by appealing his case to Caesar (Acts 25:12). Paul
had wanted to preach the gospel in Rome, and he eventually got
there—in chains, through shipwreck, and after many trials (Acts
27–28).

In Rome, Paul was under house arrest. This meant that he
could receive visitors and write and receive letters. Paul had to
finance his imprisonment. Acts 28:30 states that Paul had to pay
for his own rented apartment in Rome; plus he had to pay for the
guards as required by Rome. Although Paul's normal policy was
not to accept support from the churches so that he could not be
accused of having a "profit motive," he did accept a gift from the
Philippians for his support in prison (see 4:10-18).

Paul wrote several letters during this imprisonment. These are
called the Prison Letters, or Prison Epistles, and Philippians is
one of those (the others being Ephesians and Colossians). Paul
also wrote personal letters, such as the one to Philemon. Luke
was with Paul in Rome (2 Timothy 4:11). Timothy was a frequent
visitor, as were Tychichus (Ephesians 6:21), Epaphroditus (4:18),
and Mark (Colossians 4:10). Paul witnessed to the imperial guard
(that is, the Roman soldiers, 1:13) and was involved with the
Roman believers.

Paul had arrived in Rome around A.D. 59 and had spent two
years under house arrest. The letter to the Philippians was proba-

bly written toward the end of Paul's imprisonment there, in
A.D. 61. The reasons for a late dating of this letter include the following:

- Paul expressed expectation of an impending decision on his
  case (2:23).

- Enough time had gone by for the Philippians to have heard of
  Paul's imprisonment, send Epaphroditus, hear back of Epaphroditus's sickness, and then send back words of concern. (Some
  scholars contend that travel back and forth between Rome and
  Philippi could not have occurred during this short time period,
  and so they say that Paul was writing from either Caesarea or
  Ephesus, not Rome. See the introduction to Philippians for a
  full discussion.)

- Philippians must have been written after Colossians, Ephesians,
  and Philemon because Paul says in Philippians that Luke was no
  longer with him (2:20), and Luke had been there when Paul
  wrote Colossians (Colossians 4:14) and Philemon (Philemon 24).

And Timothy. Timothy was a frequent visitor during Paul's
imprisonment in Rome (Colossians 1:1; Philemon 1) and was
with Paul in Rome when he wrote this letter. Then Timothy went
as Paul's emissary to the church in Philippi (2:19). Timothy had a
special interest in the Philippians (2:20), for he had traveled with
Paul on his second missionary journey when the church at Philippi had begun (Acts 16:1-3, 10-12). Although he is mentioned in
the salutation, Timothy is not considered a coauthor. Paul wrote
in the first person throughout this letter.

Timothy grew up in Lystra, a city in the province of Galatia.
Paul and Barnabas had visited Lystra on Paul's first missionary
journey (Acts 14:8-21). Most likely, Paul had met the young Timothy and his mother, Eunice, and grandmother Lois (2 Timothy
1:5) on this journey, perhaps even staying in their home.

On Paul's second missionary journey, he and Silas returned to
several cities that Paul had already visited, including Lystra.
There Paul invited Timothy to accompany them. Timothy would
travel the empire with Paul, preaching and teaching the Good
News, traveling with Paul as his assistant and sometimes for him,
as his emissary.

Paul and Timothy had developed a special bond, like father
and son (2:22). Paul had led Timothy to Christ during his first
missionary journey. Timothy would become an important leader
in the early church and, like Paul, eventually would be imprisoned for his faith. The writer of Hebrews mentioned Timothy at

the end of that letter: "I want you to know that our brother Timothy has been released. If he arrives soon, I will come with him to see you" (Hebrews 13:23 NIV).

Servants of Christ Jesus.^{NRSV} While Paul usually used the designation "apostle" in the beginning of his letters, here he referred only to his and Timothy's role as *servants of Christ Jesus.* The Philippians had been an encouragement to Paul, readily accepting his position and message. Apparently, Paul did not feel the need to mention his apostleship or to present his credentials as in some of his other letters.

The word *doulos,* translated "servant," means "slave," one who is subject to the will and wholly at the disposal of his master. Paul expressed his and Timothy's absolute devotion and subjection to Christ Jesus. In Greek culture, the custom of manumission enabled a slave to be set free but remain devoted to a master for life as a bondservant. Paul may have had that in mind as he wrote to this audience. More likely, he was using the Old Testament concept of "servant of *Yahweh,"* as used of Moses (Exodus 14:31) and other prophets (Jeremiah 25:4; Daniel 9:6-10; Amos 3:7). This concept conveyed their dignity as authoritative messengers of the Lord.

The pattern of ancient letters was for the writer to first identify himself or herself (as opposed to letters today that are signed at the end). Paul always declared his Christian faith from the very start. Paul and Timothy were not mere servants, they were servants of the divine Lord, Christ Jesus himself.

SERVING
The work that servants perform benefits both their masters and those whom their masters wish to help. When we serve others, as Paul did, we can call ourselves servants of Christ Jesus. We serve Christ by serving them. Jesus made our servant job description very clear during his last evening with his disciples. After washing their feet, he said, "Now that I, your Lord and Teacher, have washed your feet, you also should wash one another's feet" (John 13:14 NIV). What can you do to serve others this week?

To all the saints in Christ Jesus.^{NKJV} The word "saints" was a common term designating believers. It did not mean those who were without sin. The Greek word is *hagioi,* meaning "those set apart." Like Paul and Timothy, these believers were also *in Christ Jesus* because of their faith; they had accepted Jesus as their Savior and had joined God's family. Only through faith in Christ and our union with him in his death and resurrection can we be set apart from evil and for service to God.

The first "saint" or convert in Philippi was a woman named Lydia. Because few Jews lived in the city, there was no synagogue for Paul to visit. Thus in Philippi, Paul did not face the problem of false teaching from the Judaizers as he had faced in so many other areas with significant Jewish populations. The Romans tolerated religious practices other than their state religion, but often relegated them to territory outside the city. Thus, these people were outside the city gates beside the river (Acts 16:11-15). From those humble beginnings began the faithful Philippian church.

The church at Philippi was about twelve years old when Paul wrote this letter. It had been a significant source of financial support for Paul (4:15-16; 2 Corinthians 11:9). Paul had often commended the church, holding it up as an example of generosity (2 Corinthians 8:1-2).

Who are in Philippi.[NKJV] The city of *Philippi* had a rich history. The site of the city was northern Greece (called Macedonia). The city of Philippi, with mountains on every side, and its port city of Neapolis on the Aegean Sea, had originally been strategic sites in the Greek empire. Gold was discovered at Mount Pangaeum to the west, tempting settlers from the Aegean island of Thasos to seize the area. They founded a city near the site of Philippi, naming it Krenides (meaning "spring" for the spring-fed marshlands in the valley).

When Philip II of Macedon (the father of Alexander the Great) ascended the throne of the Greek empire, he captured the city in about 357 B.C., enlarged and strengthened it, and gave it his name. Philip used the yield of the gold mines to outfit his army.

In 168 B.C., the Romans conquered Macedonia. The mountain's gold was exhausted, and the city declined. But in 42 B.C., the city became a Roman colony (see Acts 16:12). On the plains surrounding the city, Augustus had defeated Brutus and Cassius (assassinators of Caesar). He then gave the city the status of a "colony" to celebrate his victory. A colony was considered a part of Rome itself. Its people were Roman citizens (a standing that carried high privilege), had the right to vote, were governed by their own senate, and had Roman law and Latin language. Later the city was given the right to the Law of Italy, giving it many privileges and immunities—most significantly immunity from taxation. Philippi was also a "garrison city" with a Roman garrison stationed there to keep it secure. The Philippians were proud of their Roman heritage and standing (Acts 16:20-21).

At the time of Paul's visit, Philippi was a thriving commercial center at the crossroads between Europe and Asia. During Paul's second missionary journey, he tried to continue his ministry northward into Bithynia and Mysia, only to be stopped by the Spirit. In Troas, "Paul had a vision of a man of Macedonia standing and begging him, 'Come over to Macedonia and help us'" (Acts 16:9 NIV). Thus in about A.D. 50, Paul, Silas, Timothy, and Luke crossed the Aegean Sea from Troas and landed at Neapolis, the port of Philippi (Acts 16:11-40).

At Troas, Paul received the Macedonian call, so he, Silas, Timothy, and Luke boarded a ship. They sailed to the island of Samothrace, then on to Neapolis, the port for the city of Philippi.

Paul certainly had a memorable experience in Philippi. While he didn't face Judaizers, he did find opposition of another kind. Paul cast a demon out of a young slave girl who had been earning a great deal of money for her owners through fortune-telling. When the demon was released, the girl's fortune-telling powers disappeared, so the girl's owners were furious. Paul and Silas were arrested, stripped, beaten, flogged (the Roman punishment that Jesus also received—a punishment so severe it sometimes killed the receiver), and thrown into prison, where they were put in an inner cell with their feet fastened in stocks (Acts 16:16-24). Paul later wrote to the Thessalonians, "We had previously suffered and been insulted in Philippi, as you know" (1 Thessalonians 2:2 NIV).

But Paul and Silas praised God and sang hymns in their prison cell. "Suddenly there was such a violent earthquake that the foundations of the prison were shaken. At once all the prison doors flew open, and everybody's chains came loose" (Acts 16:26 NIV). As a result, the jailer and his family believed, and Paul and Silas were released to continue their journey.

It seems that Luke remained in Philippi, because the "we" account in Acts ends in chapter 16 and picks up again in 20:5 when Paul again leaves Philippi on his return to Jerusalem. Luke's presence could account for the growth and strengthening of the church in Philippi. Luke would have been a logical choice to remain there, for Philippi may have been Luke's home. The city had a famous school of medicine, where Luke, a medical doctor, may have studied.

Together with the overseers and deacons.[NIV] While Paul greeted all the "saints," meaning the entire church, he singled out the church's leadership for greetings as well. *Overseers* (also called elders) were in charge of the church, "overseeing" it—watching over, nourishing, and protecting the spiritual life of the

believers. The church in Philippi had several overseers drawn
from the church membership. Paul had appointed overseers in
various churches during his journeys: "Paul and Barnabas
appointed elders for them in each church and, with prayer and
fasting, committed them to the Lord, in whom they had put their
trust" (Acts 14:23 NIV). In Acts 20:28, Paul spoke to the "elders"
in the Ephesian church: "Keep watch over yourselves and all the
flock of which the Holy Spirit has made you overseers" (NIV).
The sheer number of churches meant that neither Paul himself,
his companions, nor all the apostles could administer the day-to-
day workings of each church. So Paul wisely set up groups of
leaders, allowing church members to govern themselves with
guidance from the apostles. The new churches needed strong spiritual leadership. The men and women chosen were to lead the
churches by teaching sound doctrine, helping believers mature
spiritually, and equipping them to live for Jesus Christ despite
opposition. The qualifications and duties of the overseers are
explained in detail in 1 Timothy 3:1-7 and Titus 1:5-9. (See Philippians 1:1-5 for Paul's view of partnership.)

TEAM SPIRIT
Paul knew that God had given him unusual spiritual gifts and a
special mission, but he also knew that he was not a one-man
band.
  Right away, before his teaching and doctrine and pastoral
words, Paul displayed his team spirit, referring to Timothy, the
deacons, the elders, and all the Christian brothers and sisters
near and far.
  We who are "in Christ Jesus" need each other. A one-person
team will not stay in the game for long. Neither will your team if
you drop out. Christians need to work together, side by side, to
see God's kingdom grow.

Deacons were selected to handle the church's external concerns.
In the secular culture, the *diakonoi* handled certain welfare-type
duties such as distributing food or other gifts. Some scholars think
that the office of deacon first arose in response to a need in the Jerusalem church. Distributing food and caring for widows was drawing
the apostles away from preaching and teaching, so seven men were
carefully chosen to care for the physical needs of the congregation
(Acts 6:1-6). These men, though they were not called "deacons,"
functioned as deacons because they were responsible for specific
administrative details of the church. The qualifications and duties of
deacons are spelled out in 1 Timothy 3:8-13.

1:2 Grace to you and peace from God our Father and the Lord Jesus Christ.^{NKJV} Paul used *grace* and *peace* as a standard greeting in all his letters. *Grace* and *peace* were the typical Greek and Hebrew greetings (respectively) utilized by Paul to express God's desire for the believers' well-being. "Grace" is God's undeserved favor—his loving-kindness shown to sinners whereby he saves them and gives them strength to live for him; "peace" refers to the peace that Christ made between sinners and God through his death on the cross. "Peace" also refers to that inner assurance and tranquility that God places in the heart, producing confidence and contentment in Christ. Only God can grant such wonderful gifts. Paul wanted his readers to experience God's grace and peace in their daily living.

The world offers a temporary and counterfeit version of grace and peace. Grace might be considered luck; peace might be seen as the absence of conflict. But for believers in Philippi and today, God's blessings are not the result of luck, but because of God's grace; peace is not a fragile calm, but an inner security. Grace and peace are abundant and available even in troubles, conflicts, and turmoil. Paul was in prison and the Philippians were experiencing persecution (1:28-30), yet Paul greeted them with the assurance of grace and peace.

UNOPENED GIFTS

We get upset at children who fail to appreciate small gifts, yet we undervalue God's immeasurable gifts of grace and peace. Instead, we seek the possessions and shallow experiences the world offers. "Grace" and "peace" easily become common religious words rather than names for very real benefits that God offers to us. Compared to the big and bright "packages" of our culture, grace and peace appear insignificant. But when we unwrap them, we discover God's wonderful personal dealings with us. Not a single heartbeat or breath occurs outside of God's grace. We live because of his divine favor. His favor cannot be earned by effort or bought with money. Jesus calmly spoke of "peace" as a personal possession that he gladly left to those who would follow him (John 14:27). Inside the tiny package marked "Grace and Peace," we find an inexhaustible treasure of God's daily presence in our lives. Using these two words in his greeting to the churches, Paul wasn't offering something new. He was reminding his readers of what they already possessed in Christ. Thank God for his grace, and live in his peace.

The phrase *God our Father* focuses on the family relationship among all believers as God's children. By using the phrase *Lord*

Jesus Christ, Paul was pointing to Jesus as a full person of the Godhead and he was recognizing Jesus' full deity. God the Father and Christ the Lord are coequal in providing the resources of grace and peace.

PAUL'S PRAYER FOR THE PHILIPPIAN BELIEVERS / 1:3-11

Following the convention of first-century letter writing, Paul extended his greeting by expressing thanksgiving and saying a prayer for the believers. Paul's words in this section are tender and sincere; he was genuinely thankful for the Philippians' gifts and partnership in the gospel, and he was confident that they would continue in the faith. Paul truly loved these believers, as expressed in these gentle words; and they truly loved Paul, as expressed by their concern and support. Paul's prayer for this church gives us an example for a prayer we can pray for our church and for believers around the world.

1:3 I thank my God upon every remembrance of you.NKJV In these words, Paul expressed his love for the Philippian believers. Every time he thought about the Philippians, he thanked God for them. Paul's love for these believers had not diminished; nor had theirs for him, evidenced by their generous support (4:10-20). The Philippian church had brought Paul much joy and little pain. Some of the churches had developed severe problems, and Paul's letters had focused on dealing with the problems. For example, the churches in Rome and Galatia were threatened by Judaizers, who wanted the believers to return to obeying the Jewish law; the church in Corinth was plagued by internal strife; the church in Ephesus was being plagued by false teachers; the church in Colosse was turning away to a heresy all its own; the church in Thessalonica was dealing with false rumors about Paul, disrespect toward leaders, laziness among the members, and false teaching about the resurrection. Paul's letter to the Philippians, while mentioning some concerns and giving some advice, could be considered a beautiful thank-you note for their unwavering support.

Paul probably visited Philippi on three separate occasions: (1) on the second missionary journey, when the gospel was planted (Acts 16:12); (2) on his journey from Ephesus through Macedonia on his way to Greece, where he stayed for three months; and (3) on his way back to Jerusalem (Acts 20:6). While the length of time of each stay is uncertain, his time with the Philippians had cemented a strong relationship.

Some Bible versions expand *you* to read "you all," and correctly so. At the start of his letter, Paul focused on the unity of the fellowship, thanking God for all the believers.

CLASS REUNION
Assemble a group of old classmates, or army buddies, or teammates, and memories become so vivid you can almost reach out and touch them. Paul hinted that such memories can put new energy into prayer. Try this:
- Today when a bank clerk reminds you of a friend from long ago, pause for a moment to pray.
- When a kid on a bike reminds you of a grandchild, take a minute to pray.
- When a song reminds you of an old boyfriend or girlfriend, pray for that person you once couldn't get out of your mind.
- When a different dialect jogs your memory of a foreign friend, pray for Christians in his or her country (and for your friend too).

Let your memories spark the engine of prayer. And let people know that you thank God when you think of them.

1:4-5 **In all my prayers for all of you, I always pray with joy because of your partnership in the gospel from the first day until now.**[NIV] Here again, Paul focused on unity in the fellowship. He prayed for *all of you,* referring to all the believers in the church. The words *I always pray* are in the present tense, meaning that Paul was praying for them continually. Paul planted churches and then kept those churches in prayer as he continued in his ministry.

When Paul prayed for the Philippians, he thanked God for them, and he prayed *with joy.* This is the first of many times that Paul used the word "joy" in this letter. The focus on joy sets this letter apart from all of Paul's other letters; the word "joy" (in its various forms: joy, rejoice) is found fourteen times in this short epistle (see the chart on page 14). Coming from an itinerant preacher imprisoned for his faith, joy would be the last attitude one would expect. Paul had joy despite his imprisonment and the uncertain decision on his case. Paul's life was on the line, yet he could rejoice and encourage others.

> We today might take the lesson to heart that the sign of our professed love for the gospel is the measure of sacrifice we are prepared to make in order to help its progress.
> *Ralph P. Martin*

A standard dictionary equates joy with happiness, but in Scripture the two words are quite distinct. For example, when life is going well, we may feel happy; but when hard times come, we lose that feeling and become unhappy or sad. True joy, however, rises above the rolling waves of circumstance; true joy keeps us on an even keel no matter how happy or sad we might feel because of our situation. Happiness reflects a horizontal perspective, focusing on circumstances on one's plane of experience. We are happy when events are going our way. Joy reflects a vertical perspective centering on God. We can feel joy in trials because we know that God is still in control (as stated in Romans 8:26-28). True joy is found only in relationship with Jesus Christ. Joy is the gladdening of the heart that comes from knowing Christ as Lord, the feeling of relief because we are released from sin; it is the inner peace and tranquility we have because we know the final outcome of our lives; and it is the assurance that God is in us and in every circumstance. In his final words to his disciples, Jesus promised, "These things I have spoken to you, that My joy may remain in you, and that your joy may be full" (John 15:11 NKJV). Jesus said these words as he faced crucifixion. Clearly, for Jesus and for Paul, joy was separate from their circumstances.

REMEMBERED WITH JOY
The Philippians were willing to be used by God for whatever he wanted them to do. When others think about you, what comes to their minds? Are you remembered with joy by them? Do your acts of kindness lift up others?

One reason for Paul's joy was the Philippians' *partnership* (in Greek, *koinonia*) *in the gospel*. The Philippians were partners through their generous and valuable contribution to Paul's ministry of spreading God's message. They contributed through their practical help when Paul was in Philippi and through their financial support over the years, even when he was in prison. By helping Paul, they were helping Christ's cause to bring the gospel to all nations (Matthew 28:19-20). This partnership had never wavered; Paul mentioned that their support had been constant from the very first time they heard the gospel right through to the day that he was writing this letter (a span of about twelve years). These people did not just sit back and applaud Paul's efforts; instead, they got actively involved in his ministry through their fellowship with him and their financial support. As we help our ministers, missionaries, and evangelists through prayer, hospitality, and financial donations, we become partners with them.

Not only did the Philippians help Paul, but they also got involved in other ministry needs. During his third missionary journey, Paul collected money for the impoverished believers in Jerusalem. The

PRAYER IN PAUL'S LIFE AND LETTERS
(verses quoted from NIV)

For Opportunities to Minister

Romans 1:10 | "I pray that . . . the way may be opened for me to come to you."

Colossians 4:3 | "Pray for us, too, that God may open a door for our message."

1 Thessalonians 3:10 | "Night and day we pray most earnestly that we may see you again."

For Knowledge and Insight for Believers

Ephesians 1:18-19 | "I pray also that the eyes of your heart may be enlightened in order that you may know the hope to which he has called you, the riches of his glorious inheritance in the saints, and his incomparably great power for us who believe."

Philippians 1:9 | "And this is my prayer: that your love may abound more and more in knowledge and depth of insight."

Colossians 1:9 | "Since the day we heard about you, we have not stopped praying for you and asking God to fill you with the knowledge of his will through all spiritual wisdom and understanding."

For Progress and Growth for Believers

2 Corinthians 13:9 | "Our prayer is for your perfection."

1 Thessalonians 3:13 | "May he strengthen your hearts so that you will be blameless and holy."

For the Believers to Live Holy Lives

2 Corinthians 13:7 | "Now we pray to God that . . . you will do what is right."

Colossians 1:10 | "We pray this in order that you may live a life worthy of the Lord and may please him in every way."

2 Thessalonians 1:11 | "We constantly pray for you, that our God may count you worthy of his calling."

churches in Macedonia—including Philippi, Thessalonica, and Berea—were not wealthy, yet they gave joyfully and generously. Paul held these churches up as examples of generosity:

- *We want you to know, brothers and sisters, about the grace of God that has been granted to the churches of Macedonia; for during a severe ordeal of affliction, their abundant joy and their extreme poverty have overflowed in a wealth of generosity on their part. For, as I can testify, they voluntarily gave accord-*

For the Believers to Persevere

Romans 12:12	"Be joyful in hope, patient in affliction, faithful in prayer."
Colossians 4:2	"Devote yourselves to prayer, being watchful and thankful."
Colossians 4:12	"Epaphras . . . is always wrestling in prayer for you, that you may stand firm."

For the Believers to Be Encouraged

Ephesians 1:16	"I have not stopped giving thanks for you, remembering you in my prayers."
Ephesians 3:16, 19	"I pray that out of his glorious riches he may strengthen you with power . . . [and] that you may be filled to the measure of all the fullness of God."
Colossians 1:3	"We always thank God . . . when we pray for you."
1 Thessalonians 1:2	"We always thank God for all of you, mentioning you in our prayers."

For the Spread of the Gospel

Romans 10:1	"My heart's desire and prayer to God for the Israelites is that they may be saved."
Ephesians 6:19	"Pray also for me . . . that I will fearlessly make known the mystery of the gospel."
2 Thessalonians 3:1	"Pray for us that the message of the Lord may spread rapidly and be honored."
Philemon 1:6	"I pray that you may be active in sharing your faith."

For Others

Philippians 1:4-5	"In all my prayers for all of you, I always pray with joy because of your partnership in the gospel."
1 Timothy 2:1	"I urge, then, first of all, that requests, prayers, intercession and thanksgiving be made for everyone."
2 Timothy 1:3	"Night and day I constantly remember you in my prayers."
Philemon 1:4	"I always thank my God as I remember you in my prayers."

ing to their means, and even beyond their means, begging us earnestly for the privilege of sharing in this ministry to the saints (2 Corinthians 8:1-4 NRSV).

1:6 Being confident of this, that he who began a good work in you will carry it on to completion until the day of Christ Jesus.NIV The verb tense indicates that Paul had been confident (that is, he had full assurance) from the first, and he was still confident to that very day, of God's continued work to transform the lives of the Philippian believers. *He* refers to God; the *good work* refers to God's salvation and continued perfecting of the believers. God's goal for believers is that they be "conformed to the likeness of his Son, that [Jesus] might be the firstborn among many brothers" (Romans 8:29 NIV).

NO "INCOMPLETES"
Do you sometimes feel as though you aren't making progress in your spiritual life? When God starts a project, he completes it! As with the Philippians, God will help you grow in grace until he has completed his work in your life. When you are discouraged, remember that God won't give up on you. He promises to finish the work he has begun. When you feel incomplete, unfinished, or distressed by your shortcomings, remember and be confident in God's promise and provision. Don't let your present condition rob you of the joy of knowing Christ or keep you from growing closer to him.

God who began a good work of redemption in us *will carry it on to completion* throughout our lifetime and then finish it when we meet him face-to-face. God's work *for* us began when Christ died on the cross in our place. His work *in* us began when we first believed. Now the Holy Spirit lives in us, enabling us to be more like Christ every day. God not only initiates our salvation, he guarantees its fulfillment (Ephesians 1:13-14). Paul was describing the process of Christian growth and maturity that began when we accepted Jesus and continues until *the day of Christ Jesus* (see also 1:10), that is, when Christ returns. Nothing in this life or after death can stop God's good work in us (Romans 8:28-39). Despite any persecution the church in Philippi might face, Paul was confident that God would continue his good work in them. Paul didn't know when the "day of Christ Jesus" would arrive, but he lived as though it could come at any moment.

Variations of the phrase "day of Christ Jesus" occur only six times in the New Testament; three of those times are in Philippians (see 1 Corinthians 1:8; 5:5; 2 Corinthians 1:14; Philippians 1:6, 10; 2:16). The phrase emphasizes the future day when Christ will return for his church, complete believers' salvation, and give believers their rewards. The phrase "day of the Lord" (Amos 5:18-20; 1 Thessalonians 5:2) has more of an emphasis on judgment.

WHO'S IN CHARGE?
If your God is second fiddle to some higher power, then your
God is too small. The God of the Bible is "sovereign," an old
word used to describe a king—and nobody has more power
than a king.
   God's sovereign action is the Christian's belief that all of life,
the good and the ugly, happens under the eyes and loving will
of the universal ruler. Nothing happens that God does not know
about. And while God does not approve of the evil people do,
God controls even that and will judge it one day, as befits a righteous king.
   Be confident today that your life is fully in the hands of the
sovereign God, who doesn't miss anything and who loves you
with the same boundlessness with which he rules all of creation.

**1:7 It is right for me to feel this way about all of you, since I have
you in my heart.**[NIV] Paul knew that his feeling of confidence in the
Philippians was *right* and appropriate because of his personal relationship with them and knowledge of their sincere faith in Christ.
The Greek word translated *to feel (phronein)* is used by Paul
twenty-three times in this letter. This word means more than simply
affection or an emotional reaction; it goes deeper, showing special
concern based on others' best interests. These Philippian believers
held a special place in Paul's heart (see also 1:8; 4:1).

   The Greek structure of the sentence makes it possible to translate the last part "because you hold me in your heart" (as in
NRSV) and could refer back to Paul's thankfulness for their support. In either translation, Paul and the Philippians had mutual
affection: Paul in his constant prayers for them and concern for
their faith; and the Philippians in their constant and generous support of Paul's ministry.

**For all of you share in God's grace with me, both in my
imprisonment and in the defense and confirmation of the gospel.**[NRSV] Notice again Paul's emphasis on *all of you.* If there were
any divisions in the church, Paul made it clear that all the believers shared *in God's grace* (see 1:2). As Paul sat imprisoned in
Rome, he knew that the Philippians suffered as well because of
their deep concern and love for him. Paul knew that the church
was constantly praying on his behalf. As Paul received God's
grace in his struggles, so the Philippians would share in that
grace as they faced persecution for their faith. The Philippians
also shared *in the defense and confirmation of the gospel* through
their support of Paul's ministry across the world and during his
imprisonment. The words "defense" and "confirmation" could

refer to Paul's preaching ministry, as he continued to defend (maintain and uphold the truth of) and confirm (establish the truth and validity of) the gospel message. Or the words could be looking forward to Paul's upcoming trial, where he would defend and confirm his faith in the gospel before the Roman court. In either case, the believers in Philippi shared with Paul through their prayers and support. Wherever Paul was, even in prison, he faithfully preached the Good News. Remember Paul's inspiring example when hindrances, small or large, slow down your work for God.

IN THE HEART
You've heard sermons on the duty to serve others selflessly. Now go one step further: put those people in your heart.

Doctors take an oath, a symbol of their duty to heal. Judges promise to render decisions "without fear or favor," a duty to fairness. Christians are to share the gospel and minister to people's needs, but in this case, duty alone isn't enough.

Do you have anyone in your heart? With that person, you don't calculate costs or punch a time clock. The energy you exert is borne on wings of love; the times you give are the happiest moments of your day.

Open your heart to another person today. Turn duty into love, a job into joy.

1:8 For God is my witness, how greatly I long for you all with the affection of Jesus Christ.^{NKJV} Paul, separated by his imprisonment from his dear friends in Philippi and uncertain of whether he would see them again during his life on earth, experienced intense longing for fellowship with them. He called God as his witness to the truth of his statement; Paul's *affection* for the Philippians was so strong that it was deeper than human emotion; it was the selfless affection *of Jesus Christ* himself.

The word "affection" is literally "inward parts" or "viscera," such as the inward parts of an animal sacrifice (heart, liver, kidneys). It conveys very strong internal feelings. How could Paul say that he loved the Philippians with the affection of Jesus Christ? Just as Jesus loved them, so Paul loved them. Although Christ is the originator of this love, it was expressed through Paul.

1:9 And this I pray, that your love may abound still more and more in knowledge and all discernment.^{NKJV} While Paul's travels were hindered by his imprisonment, his prayers were not. And Paul prayed with joy for the Philippians (1:4). Here he explained what he prayed for them. He asked that their *love* for God and for

LONGING TO SEE
Have you ever longed to see a friend with whom you share fond memories? Paul had such a longing to see the Christians at Philippi. His love and affection for them was based not merely on past experiences, but also on the unity that comes when believers draw upon Christ's love. All Christians are part of God's family and thus share equally in the transforming power of his love. Do you feel a deep love for fellow Christians, friends and strangers alike? Let Christ's love motivate you to love other Christians and to express that love in your actions toward them.

one another *may abound* (that is, overflow). But Paul wasn't talking about gushing sentimental or emotional affection. He was praying that their love would overflow, first in the *knowledge* of God and his ways. As each believer learned more and more about God and his ways, the entire congregation would experience a stronger fellowship and love for one another.

Paul also prayed that the Philippians' love would overflow in *discernment* (also translated "depth of insight" or "perception"). The church in Philippi was experiencing several problems in its fellowship, such as pride and faultfinding (see 2:1-18 and 3:10–4:1). Before giving any admonition, Paul tactfully revealed that he was praying that the believers would have discernment in their words and actions. Certainly this would affect their relationships. Relationships must not be based on changeable emotions; spontaneity must be tempered by self-restraint and tactfulness. If there were a problem, it should be prayed about and then dealt with in loving discernment.

Often the best way to influence others is to pray for them. Paul's prayer for the Philippians was that they would be unified in love (see also Colossians 3:14). Their love was based, not on feelings, but on what Christ had done for them. As you grow in Christ's love, your heart and mind must grow together. Is your love and insight growing?

1:10 So that you may be able to discern what is best and may be pure and blameless until the day of Christ.^{NIV} The Philippians should have both knowledge and discernment so that, in their Christian lives and in their dealings with one another, they would be able to *discern what is best*. They should have the ability to differentiate between right and wrong, good and bad, healthy and dangerous, vital and trivial; but they should also have the discernment to decide between acceptable and right, good and best, and important and urgent—in other words, to know what really matters. We ought to pray for moral discernment so we can maintain our Christian morals and values (see Hebrews 5:14). A lot of Christians get involved in peripheral pursuits and neglect the most important priority: to know Christ and live for him (3:8).

Their ability to discern (that is, to test and approve) should cause them to focus on what really matters as a body of believers. Paul prayed that the Philippians would be *pure*. The Greek word is *eilikrineis,* used only here and in 2 Peter 3:1. The word derives from the Greek words for "sunlight" and "judgment." The Philippians' transformation should be so thorough that the resulting purity could pass the toughest scrutiny—the light of God's judgment (see 2 Corinthians 5:10).

Paul also prayed that they would be *blameless*. The Greek word is *aproskopoi,* which also means "not causing others to stumble." Believers ought to be blameless with God (keeping their relationship with him up-to-date and personal) and with people (that their behavior would not lead others into sin).

The *day of Christ* refers to the time when God will judge the world through Jesus Christ. We should live each day as though he could return at any moment—expectant, ready, and eager to be in his presence.

1:11 Filled with the fruit of righteousness that comes through Jesus Christ—to the glory and praise of God.^{NIV} Finally, Paul prayed that the believers would be *filled with the fruit of righteousness,* that "fruit" being all of the character traits flowing from a right relationship with God. "Righteousness" means a right relationship with God as a result of justification from sin. Paul expounds on this in 3:9, wherein he says that he does not want to have a righteousness of his own that comes from the law, but "that which is through faith in Christ—the righteousness that comes from God and is by faith." Being made right with God through Christ enables us to live rightly before him. There is a parallel between what Paul prayed for the Philippians and what he himself pursued (as clarified in 3:7-15).

The phrase, "fruit (or harvest) of righteousness" is found in Isaiah 32:17 in the Old Testament, and in Hebrews 12:11 and James 3:18 in the New. It refers to the righteousness of God implanted in us, causing acts of practical righteousness to flow out of us. There is no other way for believers to gain this fruit than through a personal relationship with Jesus Christ. Only his life through us can help us live in ways that often go against our human nature. See Galatians 5:22-23 for a listing of this fruit of righteousness or "fruit of the Spirit."

Such infilling and the results revealed as "fruit" in people's

lives are always *to the glory and praise of God.* Believers' lives
ought to glorify and praise God, for it is by his grace alone that
sinful human beings can obtain righteousness. See Ephesians
1:12-14 for more on how our lives bring praise to God.

HONOR CHRIST BY LIFE OR DEATH / 1:12-26

Paul explained to the Philippians that they shouldn't despair over
his imprisonment because what had happened to him was helping
to spread the gospel. Paul's example encouraged many believers
to willingly take a stand for Christ and preach the Good News
regardless of the consequences. Paul himself never stopped
preaching, even in his confinement. The soldiers guarding Paul
heard the gospel, and they learned that he was in prison not for
being a criminal, but for being a Christian. Despite the differing
circumstances of Paul's life, his goal never changed—the gospel
of Christ was to be preached to as many people as possible. This,
too, should be our goal. While we go about the busyness of daily
living, we should remember that we are to tell others about Christ
and represent him in every situation.

**1:12 I want you to know, beloved, that what has happened to me
has actually helped to spread the gospel.**NRSV Paul called the
Philippians *beloved,* again emphasizing his fatherly love for
them, and he turned his attention to a concern expressed by the
Philippian church through Epaphroditus. The Philippians were
certainly concerned for Paul's well-being (expressed by their
financial gift), but they were also concerned that Paul's imprisonment had slowed down the spread of the gospel. By the time of
this writing, Paul had been in prison about two years. Paul even

---

PIONEERS
Missionaries of the past who boarded ships to go to foreign
lands did not expect to see their homeland shores again. Their
good-byes were final, in terms of earth time. Some early missionaries (from Europe to the New World) actually sold themselves into slavery in order to preach to slaves. There was no
turning back for them.

Pioneering requires a high sacrifice. Paul's passion was for
others to discover the Good News of eternal life through Jesus
Christ. No matter what.

Pressing through frontiers of spiritual darkness still requires
pioneers today—people who will reach neglected people or
new people groups. Pray for missionaries, support them, join
them.

may have questioned God's reason for his lengthy imprisonment, for it effectively put him out of commission for further traveling and preaching. But Paul had come to understand, and he wanted the Philippians to *know* beyond any doubt, that *what has happened* (that is, Paul's imprisonment) *has actually helped to spread the gospel.* Although one of Christianity's most tireless missionaries had been imprisoned, God's work could not be slowed down. In fact, God was using Paul's imprisonment to actually help spread the gospel to Europe. "Helped to spread" is also translated "furtherance" and comes from the Greek word meaning "to cut the way before." The picture is of pioneers cutting through uncharted territory. Paul's arrest and subsequent lengthy imprisonment had resulted in the gospel moving in new directions. Paul went on to explain this in the following verses.

1:13 So that it has become known throughout the whole imperial guard and to everyone else that my imprisonment is for Christ.NRSV Paul's long arrest had allowed him to share the gospel with the very soldiers who guarded him. As a result, *the whole imperial guard* (the Praetorian guard, elite troops housed in the emperor's palace) and *everyone else* (others in the palace, other believers, those who came to visit Paul, those in power, and members of the Jewish community—see Acts 28:17-23) knew that Paul was in prison only because of his belief in Christ and teaching of the gospel, not for being a criminal. Paul's example, fervent love for Christ, and manner of life, even in prison, had allowed others to see the gospel in a whole new light. The custom of the time was for a prisoner to be guarded by a soldier who would be replaced every four hours. These soldiers certainly heard Paul's words to those who visited, as well as his message spoken to them personally. Paul was confident that the message of the gospel was infiltrating the Roman army and the palace itself (see comments on 4:22).

How did Paul end up in chains in a Roman prison? While he was visiting Jerusalem, some Jews caused a riot and had him arrested. Eventually, Paul appealed to Caesar to hear his case (Acts 21:15–25:12). Paul was then escorted by soldiers to Rome, where he was placed under house arrest while awaiting trial—not a trial for breaking civil law, but for proclaiming the Good News of Christ. At that time, the Roman authorities did not consider this to be a serious charge. A few years later, however, Rome would take a different view of Christianity and make every effort to stamp it out of existence. Paul's house arrest allowed him some degree of freedom. He could have visitors, continue to preach, and write letters such as this one. A brief record of Paul's time in Rome is found in Acts 28:11-31. The Jews certainly hoped that Paul's arrest would silence his teaching; the Romans hoped the arrest would keep the peace (Paul's teaching sometimes infuriated his audiences to the point of rioting). However, locking up Paul only served to spread the gospel through new preachers to new audiences.

A NICE REFLECTION
Being imprisoned would cause many people to become bitter or to give up, but Paul saw it as one more opportunity to spread the Good News of Christ. He realized that his current circumstances weren't as important as what he did with them. Turning a bad situation into a good one, Paul reached out to the Roman soldiers who made up the palace guard and encouraged those Christians who were afraid of persecution. We may not be in prison, but we still have plenty of opportunities to be discouraged—times of indecision, financial burdens, family conflict, church conflict, or the loss of our jobs. How we act in such situations will reflect what we believe. Like Paul, look for ways to demonstrate your faith, even in bad situations. Whether or not the situation improves, your faith will grow stronger.

1:14 And most of the brothers and sisters, having been made confident in the Lord by my imprisonment, dare to speak the word with greater boldness and without fear.[NRSV] Not only was the gospel being spread by Paul through his contacts in prison, but his efforts were being multiplied outside the prison. Paul's faith, confidence, and patience in spite of his imprisonment helped his fellow believers become more *confident in the Lord.* Whatever the reason for their lack of confidence before— whether they had been afraid to speak up, whether they left all the mission work to Paul because they lacked his boldness, or whether they wondered if faith in God was worth the price—they saw Paul's faith and it strengthened their own. They began to tell the gospel *with greater boldness and without fear.* With more and more believers gaining boldness in telling the gospel of Jesus Christ, more and more people heard the message and had the opportunity to accept it. This gave Paul great joy. He passed this good news on to his friends in Philippi, that they might know how God was working through his difficult situation.

1:15 It is true that some preach Christ out of envy and rivalry, but others out of goodwill.[NIV] Paul had been made aware that some of the brothers and sisters who had been newly emboldened to speak about Christ were doing so *out of envy and rivalry.* But others were preaching Christ *out of goodwill*—that is, with pure motives. They wanted to help others to faith and they wanted to glorify God.

ON THE FRONT LINES
On Omaha Beach, June 6, 1944, when regiments of men were pinned down in fear, desperate for confidence, a brigadier general who could have sent written orders took charge by roaming the beaches like a coach along the sidelines. His language was coarse but his courage was unmistakable. He moved the beachhead uphill, turning a disaster into victory.

Paul's battle was spiritual, and he carried no rank except "servant of Jesus Christ." But his bold leadership inspired many others to share the gospel. His courage dissolved others' fear. *See,* his life told them, *it can be done!*

How can you become less inhibited about witnessing for Christ? First, watch those who do it. Second, do it yourself. And third, lead others in doing it. Your confidence will sit still as long as you do and grow as fast as you step out from behind your cover.

This comment by Paul provides an interesting look into people's motives. All of those who preached Christ were sincere believers—they had the right doctrine and they acted upon it by sharing it with others. While the end result might be the same (people hearing the Good News), some actually had wrong motives in their preaching. Their motives stemmed from *envy and rivalry.* Now that the great missionary Paul had been virtually silenced in prison, some of these brothers were hoping to make a name for themselves in the vacuum that Paul left. Perhaps they hoped for great notoriety, trying to turn people's eyes away from Paul and toward themselves. These people had no personal love for Paul. They even hoped that their planting churches and gaining converts would upset Paul and make his imprisonment even more frustrating.

CHRISTIAN COMPETITION
These Christian preachers were driven by envy and rivalry. They saw the authoritative position Paul enjoyed, and that painful awareness drove them to desire the same advantage. They were striving to equal or excel Paul's position. Christian leaders today can fall for this same temptation: to gain leverage over another or to compete for status or position. God gives us what we really need, so Christian leaders must learn to be content with what God has given (see 4:11). Our eternal life in Christ is our greatest asset, so we should not compete against or strive with others.

1:16 The latter do so in love, knowing that I am put here for the defense of the gospel.^{NIV} Those who preached Christ "out of goodwill" (1:15) did so *in love,* spreading the Good News of Christ with pure motives. They knew Paul was in prison, not because of any criminal act, but simply for his *defense of the gospel* (see also 1:7). Paul had landed in prison because of his devotion to Christ and his zeal to spread the gospel. Yet his fellow believers in Rome, some of whom may have been his spiritual children, fearlessly picked up where he left off, continuing and expanding his ministry.

FOR A PURPOSE
Paul could have become depressed, discouraged, or disillusioned. He could have wallowed in self-pity and despair. Instead, he regarded his imprisonment as being appointed or destined. He considered, "I am put here to fulfill God's greater purpose." God had used Paul's imprisonment in Rome to bring the gospel to the Roman emperor. Do you have difficulty accepting your station in life? Do you resent where God has placed you? Although education and focused effort may enable us to take a new role or get a new job, often God puts us in a place to serve. Whether it is an actual prison or a place that feels like one, God wants you to serve him faithfully and joyfully.

1:17 The former preach Christ out of selfish ambition, not sincerely, supposing that they can stir up trouble for me while I am in chains.^{NIV} Those who were preaching Christ "out of envy and rivalry" (1:15) were doing so because of their own *selfish ambition,* making their motives less than pure. These preachers were not so much interested in their message as they were in their reputation. Apparently their doctrine was sound—these were not false teachers—Paul never tolerated any kind of false teaching (see 2 Corinthians 11:4; Galatians 1:6-9). The error was in motive, not in content. These self-seeking opportunists hoped that Paul would be angered at the notoriety of new and powerful preachers who took his place while he was in prison. Little did these men understand Paul's sincere love for God and his single-minded focus on spreading the gospel.

1:18-19 But what does it matter? The important thing is that in every way, whether from false motives or true, Christ is preached. And because of this I rejoice.^{NIV} Paul had an amazingly selfless attitude. He knew that some were preaching to build their own reputations, taking advantage of Paul's imprisonment to try to make a name for themselves. Regardless of the motives of these preachers, Paul rejoiced that *whether from false motives or true, Christ is preached.* Some Christians serve for the wrong reasons. Paul wouldn't condone, nor does God excuse, their motives, but we should be glad if God uses their message, regardless of their motives. Paul had no concern for his own reputation or success; he had dedicated his life to glorifying God. He understood that God was being glorified even as he sat in chains; thus, Paul could rejoice.

> That is the way it is in the church. It never lives by its deeds, not even by its deeds of love. Rather it lives by what it cannot see and yet believes. It sees affliction and believes deliverance.
> *Dietrich Bonhoeffer*

Yes, and I will continue to rejoice, for I know that through your prayers and the help given by the Spirit of Jesus Christ, what has happened to me will turn out for my deliverance.[NIV] Paul had been able to rejoice during his two years in prison, could rejoice that good results could come from preachers with bad motives, and would *continue to rejoice* no matter how long he would remain in prison or how long he would live. Paul knew that all that had happened (resulting in his imprisonment, see also 1:12) would end in his *deliverance.*

DELIVERANCE
Paul, the prisoner, expected to be delivered, but not by a daring raid. In fact, the means of his escape are downright curious: prayer and the help of the Holy Spirit. What kind of talk is this?

Prayer—his own, no doubt, and the prayers of many Christians. Paul counts them as part of his life's treasure.

The help of the Holy Spirit—the calm assurance that God is present and potent.

Paul may never escape detention; his shackles may never be loosened. So what? He is delivered.

Today, try prayer, and whatever your circumstances, accept the help of the Holy Spirit, the key to real freedom.

What kind of deliverance did Paul envision? While most scholars agree that Paul was quoting from Job 13:16, "Indeed, this will turn out for my deliverance" (NIV), they disagree on what Paul meant. Some scholars argue that Paul was referring to his upcoming trial, believing that he would be acquitted and freed (which did happen). However, this is unlikely because of Paul's words in the next verse that reveal his uncertainty about the outcome of his trial. Others believe that, like Job, Paul was focusing on his relationship with God—that whether he lived or died, his stand for

Christ would be vindicated. Still others think Paul was referring to his apostleship in the face of the envious preachers. As Job sought to prove his integrity, so Paul was seeking to vindicate his standing, despite his chains. A final option, and most likely, is that Paul was referring to his ultimate deliverance in salvation. That is, whether or not he would be delivered by the Roman court, he would be delivered from God's judgment.

Paul's confidence came from two sources: human and divine. Paul knew that the Philippians' constant prayers had sustained him. As Paul consistently prayed for the churches (1:4-5), so he petitioned their prayers on his behalf (Romans 15:30; 2 Corinthians 1:11; Colossians 4:3; 1 Thessalonians 5:25; 2 Thessalonians 3:1-2). In addition, Paul depended upon *the help given by the Spirit of Jesus Christ.* The word "help" *(epichoregias)* carries the meaning of "support." The "Spirit of Jesus Christ" refers to the Holy Spirit, who makes Christ's presence real in true believers. The prayers of the church and the support of the Holy Spirit sustained Paul through a difficult trial and, in the end, no matter what the outcome, Paul would ultimately be "delivered."

1:20 **It is my eager expectation and hope that I will not be put to shame in any way, but that by my speaking with all boldness, Christ will be exalted now as always in my body, whether by life or by death.**NRSV The Greek word *apokaradokia,* translated "eager expectation," pictures a person straining his neck to see what is ahead. In Romans 8:19, Paul used the same word as he described looking forward to the revelation of God's children, as

> Perish all things, so that Christ be magnified. *Lord Shaftesbury*

God had planned from the beginning of creation. Hope and expectation are linked together. Paul looked forward to the final fulfillment. He was not concerned about the verdict of his trial, but for the testimony he would leave. Paul hoped and expected to *not be put to shame in any way.* He was not worried about his own humiliation, but he prayed for courage to present the gospel. When standing trial, Paul wanted to speak God's truth courageously and not be timid or ashamed. The word "boldness" means with "sufficient courage" (NIV). Paul wanted to have openness and fearlessness when he spoke out for Christ. *Whether by life or by death,* he wanted only to exalt Christ. "Exalt" means to raise in status, to give dignity and honor. Paul did not say, "I will exalt Christ"; instead, he said, "Christ will be exalted." Paul did not rely on his own boldness, but rather on the help of the Holy Spirit to produce that exaltation of Christ through Paul. Paul wanted his witness to heighten the effect of God's power and plan. Early Christians would remember the death of Stephen (a death Paul himself witnessed), the first martyr for the faith, who died bravely, and whose death glorified Christ and resulted in an incredible spread of the gospel (Acts 7:1–8:1).

This was not Paul's final imprisonment in Rome, but he didn't know that. Awaiting trial, Paul knew that he could either be released or executed; however, he trusted Christ to work it out for his deliverance. If the verdict were to go against him, Christ would be glorified in Paul's martyrdom. If Paul was to be released, he would welcome the opportunity to continue serving the Lord. As it turned out, Paul was released from this imprisonment but arrested again two or three years later. Only faith in Christ could sustain Paul in such adversity.

1:21 For to me, to live is Christ, and to die is gain.^{NKJV} To those who don't believe in God, life on earth is all there is, and so it is natural for them to strive for this world's values—money, popularity, power, pleasure, and prestige. For Paul, however, to live meant to develop eternal values and to tell others about Christ, who alone could help them see life from an eternal perspective. *For to me* indicates Paul's firm resolve and unshaken faith. Paul used the present tense when he said *to live is Christ,* thus emphasizing the process of living. For Paul, the essence of life was Christ and having a vital spiritual union with him. Everything Paul desired or attempted was inspired by his devotion for Christ. The meaning is not quite the same as Colossians 1:27: "Christ in you, the hope of glory" (NIV), or Galatians 2:20: "I no longer live, but Christ lives in me" (NIV). Paul wrote not so much of the indwelling Christ here as of Christ being the motive and goal for living and doing worthwhile work for the benefit of others.

Paul's whole purpose in life was to speak out boldly for Christ and to become more like him. Those who wished to "stir up trouble" for Paul (1:17 NIV) might have thought that his anticipation of death would bring shame and fear. Instead, Paul knew that both his living and dying were the decision of God's sovereign will. *To die* would not be a tragedy but, instead, a realization of Paul's hope and expectation (1:20). On one hand, death would be a release from the toils and troubles of this life; on the other, death was the gateway to Christ's presence. To live would continue Paul's ministry of spreading the gospel; to die would be *gain* because Paul's martyrdom would glorify Christ and bring him face-to-face with the Savior. Paul's faithful and fearless witness even unto death would enhance the reputation of the gospel. Christ would be magnified as much as in Paul's death as he had been in Paul's life. In addition, Paul could confidently say that dying would be even better than living because he would be with God whom he had served and loved (1 John 3:2-3).

A LIFE-AND-DEATH SITUATION
Some people hold tightly to this life. Afraid to lose or let go, they in effect become slaves to their mortality. In contrast, those who do not fear death, seeing it as merely the door to eternal life, are free to live with purpose, meaning, and commitment to a cause. Because Paul was ready to die, he was ready to live. He belonged to Christ and was confident of his eternal destination, so he could donate his life on earth to living for Christ. Where is your hope—is it in this life or in the next? Until you are ready to die, you won't be ready to live.

1:22 **If I am to go on living in the body, this will mean fruitful labor for me. Yet what shall I choose? I do not know!**NIV Paul poured out his heart to his friends in Philippi. If the verdict should go for Paul and he should be released, that would mean more *fruitful labor*—further missionary travels, more churches planted, more converts, the strengthening of fellow believers, more opportunities to serve Christ. (Paul used this expression elsewhere; see Romans 15:18; 2 Corinthians 10:11; Philippians 2:30.) Certainly that would be a happy result; yet the opposite might happen—he could be sentenced to death. Yet that would not be bad, for Paul states that death would be preferred to life if more glory could be given to Christ. Paul was not saying, "What a burden; if I am alive I must do my toilsome work." Instead, he seems to be saying, "Being alive is a gift; I'm responsible to use it. Fruitful labor is a must."

Yet what shall I choose? I do not know! reveals Paul's inner dilemma. He did not have a "choice" to make, for the decision was in God's hands. Yet if the decision were up to him, he wouldn't know what to choose. How many of us are so dedicated to God that if the choice were given, we would choose to be in God's presence?

1:23 **For I am hard-pressed between the two, having a desire to depart and be with Christ, which is far better.**NKJV If Paul had to choose between these two options, he would be unable to do so. The two choices were equally compelling: (1) the desire to die and be with Christ himself and (2) the desire to stay alive and so continue his fellowship with and service to the believers. While Paul lived in intimate communion with Christ during his (Paul's) service on earth, being *with Christ* in heaven would be even closer and more intimate than any human could imagine.

These words reveal Paul's understanding of death—believers not waiting in purgatory or in a "soul-sleep," but being immediately present with the Lord (2 Corinthians 5:2-8). Paul had no question that death would be *far better* because in death he would reach his ultimate goal (to be with Christ) and finally have eternal fellowship in God's presence.

Although the choice wasn't Paul's to make, he knew in his heart that it would be *far better* to depart and be with Christ because death would remove him from the trials of the world and bring him face-to-face with his Savior. There is absolute certainty in Paul's words. He had seen Jesus on the road to Damascus upon his conversion. After a life of faithful service, Paul knew that he would go to heaven to live forever with Christ.

1:24 But it is more necessary for you that I remain in the body.^{NIV} Paul was prepared and ready to die at any moment for his faith, and he actually looked forward to death because of the certainty of heaven. But he knew that his personal desires had to be subordinated to God's will. Paul felt that his ministry on earth was not yet complete and that he needed to *remain in the body* to help the churches grow and solidify. Paul placed his fellow believers' needs above his own desires.

MAKING THE MOST
Paul knew that heaven would be better than this life, and he looked forward to it. Yet in obedience to Christ, Paul would work and serve as Christ saw fit. We must avoid two errors: (1) to work and lose sight of our ultimate home with Christ and (2) to desire only to be with Christ and neglect the work he has called us to do. So we must work hard now, live at our peak, serve and love those around us, help the church grow, heal someone's wounds, write a good poem, clean up our yard, do our best at school, but we always know there's a better day coming!

Always with one eye toward heaven, Paul made the most of each day. So should we.

1:25 Since I am convinced of this, I know that I will remain and continue with all of you for your progress and joy in faith.^{NRSV} This verse seems to reveal a new confidence. At times, Paul felt that death was certain (1:20; 2:17). At times, he was convinced that God still had work for him to do. In this verse, Paul expressed confidence that this imprisonment, at least, would not end in his death. Paul would remain alive, would return to Philippi (Philemon 22), and would work among them for their *progress and joy in faith*. The "progress" Paul envisioned involved a deepening of the Philippians' joy and a strengthening and stretching of their faith. Perhaps Paul wrote these words thinking that if he was released, their joy would know no bounds (1:26) and their faith would certainly be strengthened.

1:26 **So that through my being with you again your joy in Christ Jesus will overflow on account of me.**[NIV] Paul's return would reassure the Philippians as they saw God answering their prayers for Paul's safety (1:19). The word used for "joy" in this verse is different from the many other usages in this letter (even from the word in 1:25). Here it means "exulting in Jesus Christ," boasting in Jesus Christ as the grounds or basis for overflowing joy. Paul's safe return would cause the congregation that loved him so much to exult in Christ Jesus because of answered prayer.

Philippians 1:27–2:30

While Paul focused his letter to the Philippians on his thankfulness for their partnership and gifts to him, he also focused on problems that were brewing in the congregation. Paul encouraged the believers to be unified and to always remember that Christ is their example. We must follow Christ because of who he is and what he has done for us.

1:27-28 Whatever happens, conduct yourselves in a manner worthy of the gospel of Christ.^{NIV} While Paul felt confident that God still had work for him on earth, he did not know for sure the outcome of his trial. So he urged the Philippians that whether he would return to them, or whether he would be martyred, they would live worthy of the gospel. The words translated *conduct yourselves* literally mean "live as citizens." Philippi was a Roman colony, and its citizens were proud of all the privileges gained by their Roman citizenship (see Acts 16:20-21). While the Philippians enjoyed the privileges and fulfilled the responsibilities of their Roman citizenship, Paul asked the Philippian Christians to remember that they were also citizens of another kingdom and that they ought to "live as citizens" of heaven, with all the responsibilities their status entailed.

> When spider webs unite, they can tie up a lion.
> *Ethiopian proverb*

Paul, joyful throughout his imprisonment, would be deeply saddened if for some reason his Philippian friends were to fail to maintain the honor of the gospel in their lives. They must not disappoint Paul by becoming lax in their faith or morals, lowering their standards, or refusing to live up to the calling they had received. The gospel of Christ must never be slandered or put to shame by the lax conduct of those who claim to follow it.

What does it mean to live *worthy of the gospel?* Paul used this phrase in other letters (Roman 16:2; Ephesians 4:1; 1 Thessalonians 2:12), but the answer is best revealed in an extended command to the church in Colosse (verses quoted from NIV, list setup is ours):

And we pray this in order that you may live a life worthy of the Lord and

- *may please him in every way*
- *bearing fruit in every good work*
- *growing in the knowledge of God*
- *being strengthened with all power according to his glorious might*
- *so that you may have great endurance and patience*
- *and joyfully giving thanks to the Father*

who has qualified you to share in the inheritance of the saints in the kingdom of light (Colossians 1:10-12).

This is what Paul meant when he told the Philippians to live worthy of the gospel (a further explanation of this verse is found in the Colossians section of this commentary).

Being a believer is indeed a high calling. To live worthy of the gospel does not mean that one must live perfectly before being accepted into God's family—for such a life is impossible outside of the Holy Spirit's help. Instead, believers ought to live differently because of the grace they have received. When we believe, we become God's children, heirs of his promises, and members of Christ's body. And this privilege was bought at a price—the precious blood of Jesus Christ. Believers ought to reflect humility, gentleness, patience, understanding, peacefulness, strength, endurance, and gratitude to God in every aspect of their lives on earth.

WORTHY CONDUCT
Paul warned that disputes and grudges would drive a wedge into the church. And churches cannot survive when relationships rub like sandpaper.

You must always work for unity, no matter what splitting headaches tend to drive your church apart. Work hard for healing and work to mend offenses.

If someone steps on your toes, and before you give in to the impulse to stomp back, ask: "Am I worthy of the gospel?"

Whether I come and see you or am absent and hear about you, I will know that you are standing firm in one spirit, striving side by side with one mind for the faith of the gospel, and are in no way intimidated by your opponents.[NRSV] News got around, and Paul kept tabs on the churches:

- To the church in Rome, Paul wrote, "I thank my God through Jesus Christ for all of you, because your faith is being reported all over the world" (Romans 1:8 NIV).

- To Corinth he exclaimed, "It is actually reported that there is sexual immorality among you" (1 Corinthians 5:1 NIV).

- About Galatia, Paul had heard, "that you are so quickly deserting the one who called you by the grace of Christ . . . Evidently some people are throwing you into confusion" (Galatians 1:6, 7 NIV).

- To Thessalonica, Paul reported, "Timothy has just now come to us from you and has brought good news about your faith and love" (1 Thessalonians 3:6 NIV).

Whether by letter or personal contact through key people (such as Timothy, Silas, Epaphroditus, and Luke), Paul knew what was happening in the churches. Sometimes questions sparked a response (as in the case of 1 Thessalonians); at other times, reports of unrest or heresy prompted Paul to fire off a letter to stop anything that would hinder the truth of the gospel (as was the case with 1 Corinthians and Galatians).

Thus, even though Paul hoped to return to the Philippian church, if he didn't, he would inevitably hear about the believers there, and he wanted to hear that they were unified in the Spirit.

- The believers were to be *standing firm in one spirit*. This is an exhortation to spiritual solidarity; the believers should share an esprit de corps. The Holy Spirit unites Christians into one spiritual group. If they can stand firm in the Spirit, they can overcome small differences among individual members and work forcefully toward a common goal—to withstand external persecution (see also commentary on 4:1).

- The believers were to be *striving side by side with one mind for the faith of the gospel*. Like athletes on a team, they were to work together with one mind focused on one goal—to help advance the faith that comes through the preaching of the gospel. In order to face opposition, they needed to be of "one mind," unhindered by internal dissension, jealousies, and rivalries (2:1-18).

- The believers were to be *in no way intimidated by [their] opponents*. Paul had faced severe opposition in many cities, including Philippi. If he was persecuted for his faith, the Christians ought to expect like treatment. Jesus himself had told his disciples, "If the world hates you, you know that it hated Me before it hated you" (John 15:18 NKJV). Christianity's opponents included the Roman Empire, the pagan Philippian populace (whom Paul had encountered, Acts 16:16-24), and false teachers who had infiltrated many Christian circles and whom Paul blasted in many of his letters. False teachers might attempt to undermine Paul's authority because of his suffering, or entice the believers into thinking that a loving God would not allow suffering. The church would need to be strong within the fellowship in order to live out the three attributes Paul listed and to stand firm against false teaching.

How sad that much time and effort are lost in some churches by people's fighting against one another instead of uniting against the real opposition! It takes a courageous church to resist infighting and to maintain the common purpose of serving Christ.

For them this is evidence of their destruction, but of your salvation. And this is God's doing.[NRSV] The opposition the believers faced at that time and would face in the future gave them proof of two things: (1) the destruction of their opponents and (2) the salvation of the believers (see 2 Thessalonians 1:5-10). Doom would be sealed for those who persecuted the believers; salvation is assured for God's people. Like Paul, whether the believers witnessed through their lives or through their deaths, they would ultimately be saved because of God's control of the entire situation. Again Paul focused on the assurance of eternal salvation for those who believe.

THE PRIVILEGE
We do not by nature consider suffering a privilege. Yet when we suffer for Christ's sake, if we faithfully represent Christ, our message and example will affect us and others for good. Suffering has these additional benefits: (1) it takes our eyes off of earthly comforts; (2) it weeds out superficial believers; (3) it strengthens the faith of those who endure; and (4) it serves as an example to others who may follow us. When we suffer for our faith, it doesn't mean that we have done something wrong. In fact, it may achieve the opposite effect by verifying that we have been faithful. Use suffering to build your character. Don't resent it or let it tear you down.

All that would happen *is God's doing.* The salvation of the believers is God's doing; the destruction of evildoers is God's doing; but does Paul dare say that persecution itself is also God's doing? It would be tempting for a church facing severe persecution to begin to doubt God's goodness, love, and mercy. If the key proponent of the gospel, Paul himself, had landed in prison for two years, did that signify some wrongful teaching from Paul? Had God abandoned Paul? Was persecution a sign of wrongdoing, or a revelation that God wasn't really as powerful as the Roman gods?

Paul knew all these questions might plague the Philippian church, so he argued beforehand that, whether they understood God's doings or not, God controlled everything that occurred. Already Paul had explained how his imprisonment had actually helped spread the gospel; here Paul assured the Philippian believers that persecution also would work for God's glory and the spread of the gospel. They had to trust in that fact alone, knowing that whatever happened on this earth, their eternal destiny in heaven was secure. Indeed, suffering ought to be seen as a privilege, as Paul went on to explain.

1:29 **For it has been granted to you on behalf of Christ not only to believe on him, but also to suffer for him.**NIV The believers had received a high calling (1:27-28). By God's grace alone and by the sacrifice of Jesus Christ, they had been *granted* the privilege of believing. The Greek word translated "granted" is derived from a word meaning "grace" or "favor." Both believing and suffering were to be associated with God's grace toward his people. Paul wrote, "For by grace you have been saved through faith, and that not of yourselves; it is the gift of God" (Ephesians 2:8 NKJV). They also had another privilege: that of suffering for Jesus Christ. Indeed, the apostles understood this right from the beginning of their ministry: "The apostles left the Sanhedrin, rejoicing because they had been counted worthy of suffering disgrace for the Name [that is, for Jesus Christ]" (Acts 5:41 NIV). Christ had endured great suffering on their behalf; they felt honored to be worthy to suffer for him.

WHEN LIFE IS COMFORTABLE
Not every Christian suffers. Plenty of Christians prosper in business or career, enjoy excellent health care, and are not targets of political injustice. Many have heard about but do not personally experience hunger or oppression. Is something wrong?

Paul never urges Christians to seek suffering, as if there were virtue in pain. Neither should we forget those who suffer. If your cupboard is full, share your food. If you control the wheels of state power, work for justice and mercy. If you are wealthy, give generously to the poor.

When life is comfortable, willingly take a share of someone else's pain, and so tell the world that the gospel is true.

Paul also considered it a privilege to suffer for Christ. Paul wanted the believers in Philippi to understand that suffering persecution was not punishment for their sins, nor was it accidental (that somehow God had gotten sidetracked and had forgotten to protect them). Instead, suffering for the faith was to be considered a high honor. While suffering has its temporal benefits (see application box), it simply is a gift of God's grace (see 3:10; Colossians 1:24; 1 Peter 3:13–4:19).

1:30 Since you are having the same struggle that you saw I had and now hear that I still have.NRSV Paul and the Philippians faced the same basic struggle—suffering for spreading the gospel. The Philippian believers had encouraged Paul through his struggle; Paul wanted to encourage them in the same manner. Paul had faced that struggle in Philippi on his first visit there (Acts 16:12, 19; 1 Thessalonians 2:2), and he still faced it in his imprisonment.

> We shall overcome, we shall overcome,
> We shall overcome some day.
> Oh, deep in my heart I do believe
> We shall overcome some day. *Albert Tindley*

Like the Philippians, we are in conflict with anyone who would discredit the saving message of Christ. All true believers are in this fight together, uniting against the same enemy for a common cause.

2:1 If you have any encouragement from being united with Christ, if any comfort from his love, if any fellowship with the Spirit, if any tenderness and compassion.NIV Verses 1-18 continue the thought from 1:27-28, "Whether I come and see you or am absent and hear about you, I will know that you are standing firm in one spirit, striving side by side with one mind for the faith of the gospel, and are in no way intimidated by your opponents" (NRSV). Paul wanted unity in the Philippian church so they could carry on the ministry of the gospel; but such unity would only be possible by being united with Christ so that there would be harmonious relationships among the believers themselves. Thus Paul used four "if" clauses here that can actually be rendered "since." Paul had no doubt that, for the most part, these conditions existed in the Philippian church. They had some problems to deal with, but the church had proven itself to be strong and unified. Paul gave four results of being unified:

(1) Paul knew the believers experienced *encouragement from being united with Christ*. The word translated "encouragement" is *paraklesis,* also translated "exhortation" (which can mean either comfort or rebuke). Jesus used a form of the same word

when he spoke of the Holy Spirit (the Paraclete) as the Counselor or Comforter (John 14:16). Every believer has received encouragement, exhortation, and comfort from Christ. That common experience ought to unite the Philippians.

(2) The Philippian believers had *comfort from his love*. The common experience of Christ's love should unite believers (Ephesians 5:25). In turn, their common love for Christ should cause them to love one another. This love that is available to us more than compensates for the pain and trouble we face.

> Two cities have been formed by two loves: the earthly by the love of self, even to the contempt of God; the heavenly by the love of God, even to the contempt of self.
>
> *St. Augustine, The City of God*

(3) The Philippian believers had *fellowship with the Spirit*. When a person believes in Jesus Christ as Savior, he or she receives the Holy Spirit. This might be better translated, "The Spirit has brought you into fellowship with one another." Each believer has personal fellowship with the Holy Spirit in his or her private life; all the believers are united by the same Spirit in times of fellowship. This is the fellowship of the Spirit—the common participation of all believers in the Spirit (see 1 Corinthians 12:13). Because there is only one Spirit, there can be only one body (Ephesians 4:4); factions or divisiveness have no place in the body of Christ. (See also 2 Corinthians 13:14.)

(4) Paul combined *tenderness and compassion*—as if he were saying, "tender compassion." When the Holy Spirit works in a believer's life, fruit is produced (Galatians 5:22-23). Paul pointed out two particular "fruits" of true concern for one another that help build unity among believers. "Tenderness" refers to sensitivity to others' needs or feelings; "compassion" means feeling the sorrow of another person and desiring to help alleviate it. Such concern for one another unifies a body of believers.

2:2 Then make my joy complete by being like-minded, having the same love, being one in spirit and purpose.NIV The Philippians had given Paul great joy (1:4). Yet Paul was aware of a lack of unity in the Philippian church. For example, believers were demonstrating a false sense of spiritual superiority over others (2:3), and some were not working harmoniously with others (4:2). Paul knew that even the beginnings of divisiveness could cause major problems unless the "cracks" were repaired quickly. Even as he listed above four results of being unified with Christ and described those results as if they were already present in the church, he asked the Philippians to make his joy in them *com-*

plete by responding to any problems and making any needed adjustments so that they would be truly and completely unified.

The four results of unity listed above are here joined by four goals for harmony in the church. Paul wanted the Philippians to understand the importance of a unified outlook.

(1) Because of their common experience in Christ and their common fellowship with the Holy Spirit, the believers should then be *like-minded*. This does not mean that the believers have to agree on everything; instead, each believer should have the mind (or attitude) of Christ, which Paul describes at length in 2:5-11. The word translated "like-minded" in this verse is the same word translated "attitude" in 2:5.

MIND YOUR MIND
Why did Paul focus on the mind ("like-minded") during times of conflict and trouble? Because the mind has analytic abilities. It creates reasons and justifies actions. It harbors suspicions and catalogs offenses against us. It advocates fighting for our rights.
   A bad attitude fosters resentment. The remedy is twofold: keep the proper attitude with a wholehearted love for others, and keep unified with fellow believers. Make peacemaking a top priority.

---

(2) Paul also wanted the church to have *the same love*. Paul described the mind of Christ in 2:5-11, and these verses also describe the love of Christ. Christ's love sent him from heaven, into humble humanity, to death on a cross on behalf of sinners. Although believers cannot do what Christ did, they follow Christ's example when they express the same love in their dealings with others (see Galatians 5:22). Because the believers had received comfort from Christ's love (2:1), they ought to have that same love toward one another. They should also love like Christ as they reach out to a lost world.

(3) Jesus had prayed for future believers, "that they may be one" (John 17:22 NIV). The church ought to be *one in spirit*. Paul's thought was the same as he wrote in 1:27. The Holy Spirit should unite the believers into one body.

(4) As they stand firm in the Spirit, they overcome small differences and work forcefully toward *one purpose*—a common goal (3:14-15). The church's goal was to spread the gospel. While its members could do that in various ways, they should be unified in reaching it.

If the Philippian believers sought these goals, they would maintain harmony. Paul's joy would be complete—he would have no more need to worry about them. A unified church is a formidable fortress for any enemy. The very unity of the Philippian church would ensure that it could stand against any persecution or false teaching that might come its way.

Paul would likely be horrified at the fragmentation and lack of unity among believers and churches today. While legitimate differences of doctrine must be examined, we as Christians should have more unity than division.

2:3 Do nothing from selfish ambition or conceit, but in humility regard others as better than yourselves.[NRSV] Here Paul identifies the problems grating on the Philippian church. The words *do nothing* could just as easily be rendered "think nothing." Both actions and thoughts need to be guarded against ambition and conceit.

> Where there is charity and wisdom, there is neither fear nor ignorance. Where there is patience and humility, there is no greed.
> *St. Francis of Assisi*

Members in the Philippian church were causing discord by their attitudes or actions. They desired recognition or distinction, not from pure motives, but merely from *selfish ambition* (see also 1:17). They were creating factions based on personal prestige, drawing away members and creating parties. Their *conceit,* that is, their excessively favorable opinion of themselves or their abilities, caused them to place themselves above others. They were conceited about their own opinions, without reason or basis. When a group of such people gets together, looking down on everyone else for one reason or another, factions form and divisions occur. The result is an absence of any encouragement, comfort, fellowship in the Spirit, or tenderness and compassion (2:1). Those kind of people cannot work with others in the church in

---

LASTING IMPRESSIONS
Many people—even Christians—live only to make a good impression on others or to please themselves. But self-centered living, selfish ambition, or conceit brings discord. Paul therefore stressed spiritual unity, asking the Philippians to love one another and to be one in spirit and purpose. When we work together, caring for the problems of others as if they were our problems, we demonstrate Christ's example of putting others first, and we experience unity. Don't be so concerned about making a good impression or meeting your own needs that you strain relationships in God's family. Let the Spirit of God work through you to attract others to himself.

---

like-mindedness and love (2:2). When people are conceited and selfishly ambitious, they ruin a church's unity. We should not tolerate arrogant leaders who are willing to split a church into factions in order to gain power and followers.

While selfish ambition and conceit can ruin unity, genuine *humility* can build it. Being humble involves having a true perspective about ourselves in relation to God (see Romans 12:3), which in turn gives us a correct perspective on our relationships with others. Being humble does not mean that we should put ourselves down, tell everyone how bad we are at everything, and refuse to acknowledge any good in ourselves. Instead, humility is a healthy respect for who God is, and then a healthy respect for ourselves because of what God did on our behalf. We are sinners, saved only by God's grace, but we *are* saved and therefore have great worth in God's kingdom. We are to lay aside selfishness and treat others with respect and common courtesy.

Regarding others as better than ourselves means that we are aware of our own failings and are thus willing to accept failings in others without looking down on them. It means that we can look for and point out the good in others, rather than just looking for and pointing out our own good qualities. It also means that we consider others' interests as more important than our own. This selfless attitude links us with Christ, who was a true example of humility. It is the very opposite of conceit and selfish ambition, and it allows believers to work together, to have tenderness and compassion, and to have the attitude and love of Christ Jesus himself.

COMPARISONS
People often compare themselves to others to excuse their behavior or to bolster their pride. They may think, for example, "What I did wasn't so bad. After all, look at what she did." They may look at people who are worse off and think that they are pretty good in comparison. Or they may think the worst of people and quickly judge them. Those kinds of comparisons can only lead to pride and self-centeredness. Paul wrote that instead we should assume that others are better than we are, giving them the benefit of the doubt. In so doing, we will build others up and develop humility. We need to show consideration to others.

Paul wrote to the Romans, "Do not think of yourself more highly than you ought, but rather think of yourself with sober judgment. . . . Be devoted to one another in brotherly love. Honor one another above yourselves" (Romans 12:3, 10 NIV). Selfish conceit has no place in a believer's life. Such pride undermines the oneness vital to the church. Instead, we ought to give other believers the value and respect they deserve. While people are different, and although we may really dislike some other believers, there is no room for pride. We must acknowledge fellow believers as valuable members of God's kingdom.

Like Paul, Peter also counseled humility. Peter had been greatly humbled in his experience of denying his Lord. He wrote: "All of you, clothe yourselves with humility toward one another, because, 'God opposes the proud but gives grace to the humble.' Humble yourselves, therefore, under God's mighty hand, that he may lift you up in due time" (1 Peter 5:5-6 NIV, see also 1 Peter 3:8).

2:4 Let each of you look not to your own interests, but to the interests of others.^{NRSV} The word translated *look* is *skopein,* used by Paul to mean "regard as your aim." Each believer should not be completely absorbed in his or her own concerns and spiritual growth, but should also look at others, noting their good points and qualities. A sure cure for conceit and ambition is appreciative recognition of others' good qualities and their walk with the Lord.

In 2:21, Paul pointed out that people look to their own interests, not those of Jesus Christ. It is easy to get caught up in competition, aggressive acquiring, and vying for our own rights and needs. But compared to knowing Christ, those interests seem shallow. We need Christ's attitude of self-sacrifice to look beyond ourselves to the needs of others. Ultimately, all believers must look to the one supreme Example and follow in his footsteps, which Paul will describe in 2:5-11. Paul wrote to the Romans, "We who are strong ought to bear with the failings of the weak and not to please ourselves. . . . For even Christ did not please himself" (Romans 15:1, 3 NIV).

INTEREST RATES
Philippi was a cosmopolitan city. The composition of the church reflected great diversity, with people from a variety of backgrounds and walks of life. Acts 16 gives us some indication of the diverse makeup of this church, which included Lydia, a Jewish convert from Asia and a wealthy businesswoman (Acts 16:14); perhaps a slave girl (see Acts 16:16-17), probably a native Greek; and the jailer serving this colony of the empire, probably a Roman (Acts 16:25-36). With so many different backgrounds among the members, unity must have been difficult to maintain. Paul encourages us to guard against any selfishness, prejudice, or jealousy that might lead to dissension. Showing genuine interest in others is a positive step forward in maintaining unity among believers.

2:5 Your attitude should be the same as that of Christ Jesus.[NIV] If anyone didn't understand what Paul meant by acting out of humility (2:3) and looking first to others' concerns (2:4), then Paul made it clear by giving an example to follow. The believers should adopt the same attitude or frame of mind that was found in Jesus Christ, their Lord. Paul was speaking to the Philippian church as a whole, describing the church's attitude, that each believer, as part of the whole, was to have Jesus' attitude of service so that the entire church would be thus characterized.

Many people feel that they can't control their moods or attitudes. But Paul doesn't accept the fact that Spirit-filled Christians are slaves to their attitudes. Christ had this attitude; so must we. "Those who live according to the sinful nature have their minds set on what that nature desires; but those who live in accordance with the Spirit have their minds set on what the Spirit desires" (Romans 8:5 NIV). One of the great myths of popular psychology that has drifted into the church today deals with impulsive behavior based on emotions. In an attempt to get in touch with our feelings, this myth advocates that we must do what our feelings indicate. Christians are able to be in touch with their feelings but still do what following Christ requires. Those who accept Jesus Christ as Savior enter a community of believers, the church. Believers are to obey their Savior because of who he is and what he has done on their behalf. Paul eloquently describes this in the following verses.

CAN'T IMAGINE?
Imagine Jesus as a grump, so negative by midday that people cross the street to avoid eye contact.

Or imagine Jesus waking in the morning and making statements like, "What a dull day. I'm sleeping in."

If Jesus doesn't fit these scenes, neither should you. In the morning, get up with the zest Jesus had, sure that God the Father will guide each hour. As dusk approaches, refresh yourself in the tender mercies of the Lord, and don't let the day's pressures make you a grump. Live your day like Jesus lived his.

2:6 Who, being in very nature God, did not consider equality with God something to be grasped.[NIV] Most scholars believe that verses 6-11 are from a hymn sung by the early Christian church. Paul was using this hymn to show Jesus as a model of servanthood. Like Jesus, we are to seek and fulfill our place of service, even if it is lowly (2:6-8), and leave the glory to God (2:9-11) rather than seeking glory for ourselves (2:3). The passage holds many parallels to the prophecy of the Suffering Servant in Isaiah 53. As a hymn, it was not meant to be a complete statement about the nature and work of Christ. It is not known if Paul wrote it or merely quoted it. The celebrated passage 1 Corinthians 13 demonstrates Paul's ability to write poetic pieces. Several key characteristics of Jesus Christ are praised in this passage:

■ Christ has always existed with God.

■ Christ is equal to God because he *is* God (John 1:1-14; Colossians 1:15-20).

■ Though Christ is God, he became a man in order to fulfill God's plan of salvation for all people.

■ Christ did not just have the appearance of being a man—he actually became human to identify with us.

■ Christ voluntarily laid aside his divine rights and privileges out of love for his Father.

■ Christ died on the cross for our sins so we wouldn't have to face eternal death.

■ God glorified Christ because of his obedience.

■ God raised Christ to his original position at the Father's right hand, where he will reign forever as our Lord and Judge.

This verse describes the status of Christ as he existed before the creation of the world—that is, his preincarnate state. The words *who being* in Greek are a present participle indicating continuing existence from the beginning (Genesis 1:1). Jesus Christ was not merely a human who lived for thirty-three years on this earth; instead, he existed with God before time began. In Jesus' prayer before his death, he said, "And now, Father, glorify me in your presence with the glory I had with you before the world began" (John 17:5 NIV).

Jesus Christ is *in very nature God*. The Greek word translated "nature" (or "form"; Greek *morphe*) appears in the New Testament only here, in 2:7, and in Mark 6:12. It was generally used to describe the way objects appear to the human senses. Yet scholars attest that Paul must have used it with a deeper meaning to describe the outward manifestation corresponding to and expressing the inward essence. Having the form of God means Christ expressed the very nature and character of God. In Jesus, we see what God is like.

In 2:7 there is a parallel to the meaning of *morphe*; it is expressed in the words "taking the form of a slave." Jesus took on more than just the appearance of a slave, he took on servant-hood. He became the ultimate expression of humility and service to others. God, in Jesus, dwelt among his people. It was this true claim made by Jesus that infuriated the religious leaders and ultimately caused Jesus to be sentenced to death (John 5:18; 10:33; Mark 14:63-64). But Jesus' death was all part of God's plan.

Jesus has *equality with God*. Everything God is, Christ is; the equality is in essential characteristics and divine attributes. But Jesus did not consider this equality *something to be grasped*. There are two schools of thought regarding these words about Jesus' equality with God: (1) Christ did not have to seize or grasp his equality, it was already his, or (2) Christ did not consider his equality with God as something which he had to hold on to and not let slip from his grasp. Actually both ideas are true.

(1) Christ did not have to wrest equality from God. Scholars compare this attitude to Adam and Eve's, who were tempted by Satan to become like God (Genesis 3:5). Using the analogy from Romans 5, the "first Adam" disobeyed God and yielded to a temptation to be like God. In disobedience, he grasped at something that was not rightfully his, and his pride caused him to lose the glory God had given. The "last Adam," Jesus Christ, obeyed God. He willingly shed his glory in order to take on the form of fragile humanity. He endured hatred and horror; and when he had completed his task, he returned to his place of honor at God's right hand.

(2) Christ did not cling to his equality, but set it aside for a time in order to become human. When Christ was born, God became a man. Jesus was not part man and part God; he was completely human and completely divine. Before Jesus came, people could know God partially. Afterward, people could know God fully, because he became visible and tangible. Christ is the perfect expression of God in human form. As a man, Jesus was subject to place, time, and other human limitations. He did not give up his eternal power when he became human, but he did set aside his glory and his rights. In response to the Father's will, he limited his power and knowledge. What made Jesus' humanity unique was his freedom from sin. In his full humanity, we can see everything about God's character that can be conveyed in human terms.

As Christians, we must take Christ's example to heart. No one must flaunt his or her rights or authority, but instead should seek a life of service. The church also must serve, not promoting its own power, survival, or security. The church must not hoard its resources of people and treasure but should make them available to God's worldwide mission.

THE PLOT NO ONE EXPECTED
Two plotlines fill the world with stories. The first tells of bottom-up progress: pauper to magnate, scavenger to CEO, log cabin to White House. In the Bible, the stories of Joseph, Ruth, and David provide exciting examples of how people held in low esteem rose to power and blessing.

Another plotline tells of top-to-bottom change: height to depth, glory to shame, power to weakness, monarch to slave. One Bible person really fits this story line, and he urges all who follow him to consider its meaning for them. He is the living Christ, God incarnate, who died as a criminal on a Roman cross for you. He laid aside his rights as son of God to enter our world to find us.

Our life stories should parallel his. We must become servants (slaves) of God for a needy world. It is a plotline few people will understand until *we* live it for them.

2:7 But made himself nothing, taking the very nature of a servant, being made in human likeness.^{NIV} The NRSV translates *eauton ekenosen* as "emptied himself." The word *ekenosen* was used by scholars to elaborate the "kenosis" theory of Christ's incarnation. The theory attempted to explain what Christ emptied himself of. What did Christ relinquish, divest, or renounce on becoming human? Much debate led to various proposals: (1) he emptied himself of his divine preincarnate glory; (2) he gave up the rights and authority of his deity; (3) he relinquished the independent use of his power and authority; (4) he limited the use of some of his attributes of deity—omniscience, omnipresence, omnipotence. Other views differentiate and combine elements of this argument.

Recently, scholars say that this passage teaches nothing about what Christ gave up. Instead, a better interpretation would be that Christ voluntarily gave of himself, poured himself out, put himself on the line. So he made himself lowly. *Taking the very nature* (or form) *of a servant* was not an exchange, but an addition to his essential nature. The Incarnation was the act of the preexistent Son of God voluntarily assuming a human body and human nature. He did not give up his deity to become human.

Jesus was in very nature *(morphe)* God (2:6) and, upon his birth as a human being, he took the form *(morphe)* of a slave. What appeared on earth was not a prince in a palace, or a royal king, or a wealthy and scholarly teacher; instead, Jesus' form or nature on this earth was best wrapped up in the social position of one whose entire life is devoted to serving others—a slave: "For even the Son of Man did not come to be served, but to serve, and to give his life as a ransom for many" (Mark 10:45 NIV). He was born in human likeness. He didn't look any different from anyone else, certainly not like a god. Isaiah had predicted, "He had no form or majesty that we should look at him, nothing in his appearance that we should desire him" (Isaiah 53:2 NRSV). He was born subject to the Jewish law (Luke 2:21; Galatians 4:4) and to his parents (Luke 2:51). He did not have great wealth, breeding, privilege, or position. He was, instead, a poor carpenter living in a dusty town in the Roman-occupied territory of Galilee. He got tired, hungry, and thirsty. While Jesus was fully human, his humanity was a "likeness." The similarity stopped at the human nature's inborn tendency to sin. Jesus, though fully human, was without sin (Hebrews 4:15).

Jesus didn't take on the form of just a human, but of a slave. He went far beyond any of us in any act of service. He made servanthood his essential mission: "For even the Son of Man did not come to be served, but to serve, and to give his life as a ransom for many" (Mark 10:45 NIV). This is the strongest theology of the Incarnation found anywhere in the New Testament (even beyond John 1:1-18).

Jesus' glory and divinity were veiled by his humanity and mortality. While he walked as a human on this earth, Jesus Christ never ceased to be God.

2:8 And being found in appearance as a man, he humbled himself and became obedient to death—even death on a cross![NIV] The Greek word for *appearance* here is not *morphe* as in 2:6-7; it is *schema,* meaning an outer appearance, rather than "nature" or "essence." When Jesus took on a human body (that is, after he grew to manhood), he then humbled himself to accomplish that task for which he had come—to die for sinful humanity in order that they might have eternal life. All humans must die, but Jesus, as the divine Son, accepted death in obedience to the Father's will. This does not mean that he was obedient "to death" as if death had any power over him; instead, Jesus obeyed the will of God to the point of death.

Jesus died the worst possible torture—death by crucifixion. *Death on a cross* was the form of capital punishment that Romans used for notorious criminals. It was excruciatingly painful and humiliating. Prisoners were nailed or tied to a cross and left to die. Death might not come for several days, and it usually came by suffocation when the weight of the weakened body made breathing more and more difficult. Jesus died as one who was cursed (Galatians 3:13). The writer to the Hebrews

THE GLORIOUS INCARNATION

When Christ was born, God became a man. He was   John 1:1-14
not part man and part God; he was completely human
and completely divine. After Christ came, people
could know God fully because he became visible and
tangible in Christ.

The Good News is that Jesus Christ came as a   Romans 1:2-5
human, was part of the Jewish royal line through
David, died and was raised from the dead, and
opened the door for God's grace and kindness to be
poured out on us.

As a man, Jesus was subject to human limitations. He   2 Corinthians 8:9
did not give up his eternal power when he became
human, but he did set aside his glory and rights of his
preincarnate state as equal with God. He became
"poor" so that we could become "rich" in salvation and
eternal life.

As a man, Jesus lived a perfect life, and so he is a   1 Timothy 3:16
perfect example of how to live. As God, Jesus gives
us the power to do what is right. It is possible to live a
godly life—through following Christ.

Jesus had to become human so that he could die and   Hebrews 2:14
rise again, in order to destroy the devil's power over
death. Only then could Christ deliver those who had
lived in fear of death.

Christ is eternal, God came into the world as a   1 John 1:1-3
human, and the apostles were eyewitnesses to Jesus'
life. We have not seen Christ, but we can trust the writings of those who did see him.

---

explained, "During the days of Jesus' life on earth, he offered up
prayers and petitions with loud cries and tears to the one who
could save him from death, and he was heard because of his rev-
erent submission. Although he was a son, he learned obedience
from what he suffered" (Hebrews 5:7-8 NIV). Jesus' human life
was not a script that he passively followed. It was a life that he
chose freely (John 10:17-18); it was a continuous process of making the will of God the Father his own. Jesus chose to obey, even
though his obedience led to suffering and death.

But why did Jesus have to become human in the first place?
Why did he have to die? A holy God cannot overlook sin. The sin-
fulness of humanity had to be punished. In the Old Testament,
God required his people to sacrifice animals ("perfect" animals,
healthy and whole) to atone for their sins. The costly sacrifice of
an animal's life impressed upon the sinner the seriousness of his

or her sin before God. When animals' blood was shed, God regarded the people's faith and obedience, cleansed them, and made them *ceremonially* clean. Why blood? There is no greater symbol of life than blood; blood keeps us alive. "For the life of a creature is in the blood" (Leviticus 17:11 NIV).

At the right time, God dealt once and for all with sin and its ultimate consequence, death and eternal separation from God. Instead of sending all humanity to eternal punishment, God took the punishment himself. "For God has done what the law, weakened by the flesh, could not do: by sending his own Son in the likeness of sinful flesh, and to deal with sin . . ." (Romans 8:3 NRSV). Sin had to be punished, but the punishment was taken by God himself. Jesus shed his blood—gave his life—for our sins so that we wouldn't have to experience spiritual death and eternal separation from God. His sacrifice doesn't just make us ceremonially clean; it transforms our lives and hearts and makes us clean on the inside. Now all people are offered the opportunity to accept Christ's sacrifice on their behalf. How amazing that our God would lay aside his glory and power to face humiliation and torture in order to take the punishment we deserve. "Since, therefore, the children share flesh and blood, he himself likewise shared the same things, so that through death he might destroy the one who has the power of death, that is, the devil, and free those who all their lives were held in slavery by the fear of death" (Hebrews 2:14-15 NRSV).

A RIGHT TO SERVE
Often people excuse selfishness, pride, or evil by claiming their rights. They think, "I can cheat on this test; after all, I deserve to pass this class," or "I can spend all this money on myself—I worked hard for it," or "I can get an abortion; I have a right to control my own body." Obedience, submission, and sacrifice are not popular qualities for humans, and society has little respect for those who practice them. But believers should have a different attitude, one that enables us to lay aside our rights in order to serve others. If we say we follow Christ, we must also say that we want to live as he lived. We should develop his attitude of humility as we serve, even when we are not likely to get recognition for our efforts. Jesus was willing to wait until after his death to receive his glory. Most of us want our glory right now (as expressed in 2:3). Are you selfishly clinging to your rights, or are you willing to serve?

Jesus Christ truly humbled himself when he *became obedient* (or subservient) to the Father and obeyed him all the way to death. He did not have to die, as is the common lot of all humanity. He chose death as an act of obedience to God. "Not my will, but yours be done" (Luke 22:42 NIV) was Jesus' prayer in the Garden of Gethsemane before his death. Paul drove this lesson home for the proud Philippians. If the divine Son of God humbled himself in obedience, how could they maintain their arrogance?

2:9 Therefore God also has highly exalted Him and given Him the name which is above every name.NKJV Because Christ willingly set aside his glory to totally obey the Father's will, God *highly exalted him.* God did not leave Christ in the grave but raised him from the dead, brought him back up to heaven, and glorified him (see Acts 2:33; Hebrews 1:3). God gave Jesus "all authority in heaven and on earth" (Matthew 28:18 NIV), gave him authority to judge (John 5:27), made him the Lord of both the dead and the living (Romans 14:9), and "seated him at his right hand in the heavenly realms, far above all rule and authority, power and dominion, and every title that can be given, not only in the present age but also in the one to come. And God placed all things under his feet and appointed him to be head over everything for the church" (Ephesians 1:20-22 NIV).

That Jesus' name *is above every name* refers not to Jesus' title, but instead to his name that signifies his person. In the Bible, names often reveal a person's character. Jesus' name is above any other name because his dignity and honor are above all others. Because Jesus did not grasp at his equality with God (2:6) but willingly obeyed God in order to carry out the plan of salvation, God honored that obedience by giving Jesus this name above all names, a name with great power, as the following verses show.

EXALT HIM!
God has exalted Jesus, and Paul wanted the Holy Spirit to exalt Christ in his body (1:20). God exalted Christ by restoring him to God's own right hand. Exalting Christ means to lift up his honor, power, and glory. We exalt Christ when we praise him in our worship in all of its forms (see Daniel 7:13-14). We exalt Christ when we live according to his teaching and proclaim him to others. We must acknowledge his true nature and shining moral perfection. Do our thoughts, words, and deeds exalt Christ's name?

2:10 That at the name of Jesus every knee should bow, of those in heaven, and of those on earth, and of those under the earth.NKJV In keeping with Jesus' exaltation and power, one day *every knee* will bow before him. *Those in heaven* refers to the angels; *those on earth* means all humanity; *those under the earth* refers to the underworld—possibly to unsaved people who have died or to demons. Those who love Jesus will bow in adoration and worship; those who refused to acknowledge him will bow in submission and fear (see also Ephesians 4:9-10; Revelation 5:13). This will take place at Jesus' second coming when the forces of evil will be completely defeated and God will form a new heaven and a new earth (Revelation 19:20-21; 21:1).

Paul purposely quoted Isaiah 45:23 here and in Romans 14:11. In so doing, he applied those powerful words to Jesus Christ. Isaiah, proclaiming the unique greatness of God, had said that the same God who would not share his glory with another would receive the homage of every living being. Paul equated that position of God with Jesus' preeminent lordship. John 5:22-23 says that all should honor the Son just as they honor the Father. Again Jesus' true deity and oneness with the Father are revealed.

NOW OR LATER
At the Last Judgment, even those who are condemned will recognize Jesus' authority and right to rule. People can choose to regard Jesus as Lord now as a step of willing and loving commitment, or be forced to acknowledge him as Lord when he returns. Christ may return at any moment. Are you prepared to meet him?

2:11 And that every tongue should confess that Jesus Christ is Lord, to the glory of God the Father.^{NKJV} As every knee will bow (2:10), so every tongue will confess the basic truth of Christianity: *Jesus Christ is Lord.* This does not mean that eventually everyone will be saved. Every tongue in heaven, on earth, and under the earth will recognize Jesus as Lord, either because of belief or because of mere acknowledgement of the undisputable fact. No tongue will be silent; no knee will remain unbowed. All of creation will recognize Jesus Christ as Lord. In this life, personal commitment and affirmation of Jesus' lordship are required for salvation (Romans 10:9).

This will all happen *to the glory of God the Father.* Paul described this to the Corinthians:

- *After that the end will come when he will turn the Kingdom over to God the Father, having put down all enemies of every kind. For Christ will be King until he has defeated all his enemies, including the last enemy—death. This too must be defeated and ended. For the rule and authority over all things has been given to Christ by his Father; except, of course,*

Christ does not rule over the Father himself, who gave him this power to rule. When Christ has finally won the battle against all his enemies, then he, the Son of God, will put himself also under his Father's orders, so that God who has given him the victory over everything else will be utterly supreme. (1 Corinthians 15:24-28 TLB)

GLORIFY HIM!
The ultimate goal of God's saving plan, and indeed of creation itself, is that everything will glorify God. "Glory" refers to the splendor, radiance, and magnificence of God. It refers not only to God in his essential nature, but to the praiseworthy effects of what God has accomplished.

We glorify God because his glory is true and real, and we acknowledge his greatness. In so doing, we see our rightful position as his servants. When we glorify him in our singing, our speaking, and our living, we experience some of his transcendence and thus edify and uplift our own spirits. Glorifying God prompts us to moral action and loving service.

SHINE LIKE LIGHTS IN A DARK WORLD / 2:12-18

Believers ought to follow Christ's example not only to bring unity and peace to the church but also so that no one in the outside world would be able to find any fault with them. Philippi was a pagan city; Paul wanted these believers to be unified, morally pure, and filled with good works so that they could bring the light of Christ into their dark world. Is your light shining for Christ?

2:12 Therefore, my beloved, as you have always obeyed, not as in my presence only, but now much more in my absence, work out your own salvation with fear and trembling.NKJV The word *therefore* ties this verse to the previous section. As Jesus obeyed the Father, so believers also ought to obey.

Paul knew the Philippians had been obedient, and he wanted them to continue that careful obedience, especially since he couldn't be there to teach and remind them. We too must be careful about what we believe and how we live, especially when we are on our own. In the absence of a pastor, youth leader, or parent, we must focus our attention and devotion even more on Christ so that we won't be

> With malice toward none, with charity for all, with firmness in the right as God gives us to see the right, let us strive on to finish the work we are in.
> *Abraham Lincoln, "Second Inaugural Address," 1865*

sidetracked when no one is looking or when our obedience goes unrewarded.

Paul loved these believers (1:7-8), and here he called them *my beloved*, a term of affection not often used by Paul. This church was dear to his heart. He didn't want his absence from them to be a detriment to their spiritual growth. So he requested that they continue in their obedience, and he commanded them, *"Work out your own salvation."* In light of the preceding exhortation to unity (2:3-4), Paul was calling the entire church to work together to rid themselves of divisions and discord. The words "your own" are plural. Many times this verse has been applied to individuals working out their own Christian growth; however, Paul intended the people to work together to grow in Christ. Although believers are saved once for all when they accept Jesus Christ as Lord, it is in the grind of everyday life that salvation is "worked out." For the Philippians, that meant dealing together with any strife and discord in the church. Paul wanted the Philippians to put their salvation into practice for the health of the church. By these words, Paul reminded the Philippians that they were ultimately responsible not to him, but to God. And they would work out their salvation, not in their own strength, but with God's help (2:13).

WORKING OUT THE DETAILS
Choices face us daily. God provides the guidelines, but not always detailed instructions. We know what kind of spouse we should find, but not who it is exactly. We know what career tracks may be useful for serving God, but not which is right for us precisely. Where to live, what school to attend, which relationship to develop—we make all these choices under God's guidance. But God does not put the right answer on our computer screen each morning.

With "fear and trembling" then, we move ahead, forging a life that expresses the salvation God has given us in Christ. We obey and follow God as our top priority. With God's Word as our map and God's Spirit as our companion, we "work out" each day the salvation already won for us.

Today, make a strong choice for God.

As they worked out their salvation in the life of their church, the Philippians were to do so *with fear and trembling*. Paul used the same words in his advice to servants regarding their attitudes in obeying their masters (Ephesians 6:5). Service to the Savior, lived out in everyday life, is each believer's responsibility and should be fulfilled as thoroughly and completely as a slave would accomplish a task for his or her master. And it is a serious matter,

not to be taken lightly. In their hands they held the future of their
church. Would they let division and strife tear it apart, or would
they use their new lives and attitudes to repair and strengthen it?
"Fear and trembling" refers not to service toward a harsh Master;
instead, it is proper reverence and awe for the Lord and a proper
fear of failing him. Believers should do their very best for the
Master, who did so much for them. We must remember that we
are judged by our works (Matthew 16:27; 1 Corinthians 3:12-15;
2 Corinthians 5:10; 1 Peter 1:17; Revelation 22:12).

I WILL

To be like Christ, we must train ourselves to think like Christ. To
change our desires to be more like Christ's, we need the power
of the indwelling Spirit (1:19), the influence of faithful Christians, obedience to God's Word (not just exposure to it), and
sacrificial service. Often it is in *doing* God's will that we gain the
desire to do it (see 4:8-9). Do what he wants and trust him to
change your desires.

What do we do when we don't feel like obeying? God has not
left us alone in our struggles to do his will. He wants to come
alongside us and be within us to help. God helps us *want* to
obey him and then gives us the *power* to do what he wants.
The secret to a changed life is to submit to God's control and
let him work. Next time, ask God to help you *want* to do his will
(see Ephesians 6:6).

2:13 **For it is God who works in you both to will and to do for His
good pleasure.**[NKJV] As the Philippians worked out their salvation in
the life of their church, they would not do it on their own. Through
his Holy Spirit, God "energizes" or "enables" his people for the
tasks he wants them to do (1 Corinthians 12:4-7). He would give
the Philippians wisdom and discernment, helping them act on what
needed to be done in order to bring true unity to the church. The
first change in Christians usually comes in the area of desires: The
new believer wants to obey God and to serve others. Paul underscored this truth in this passage where he explained that God works
in us, on our will. This doesn't mean that we are perfect and never
have wrong desires (see Romans 7). It means that we can have
hope because God is working for change in our lives as we yield
control to him. God would work in them, helping them to *will* (or
want) and then *do* (or act upon) what was God's *good pleasure*—in
this case, unity and restored fellowship among the Philippian
believers. God gives the desire and the ability. God works in believers; believers do God's work. Believers are partners with God. He

has chosen to work through us to accomplish his "good pleasure" in the world (see also Ephesians 1:5).

A quick reading of this verse could lead us to think that salvation is by works and that the Christian life depends on what we do. But a closer look reveals an important phrase: God is working "in you." When we give our lives to Christ, the Holy Spirit takes up residence inside us. There he works to change us from the inside out, making us more like Christ (Romans 8:29; 2 Corinthians 5:17).

2:14 Do everything without complaining or arguing.^{NIV} While the Philippians would "work out" their own salvation for the unity of the church, Paul had advice for how they could go about it—they should stop bickering. Paul returned to the basic problem described in 2:1-4, the arrogance that leads to dissension. *Complaining* translates from a word that describes a bad attitude which expresses itself in constant grumbling. The Israelites constantly grumbled in the wilderness, and God judged them for it (see Paul's words in 1 Corinthians 10:1-5, 10; 1 Peter 4:9). The word for *arguing* has a legal connotation and may refer to the Philippian Christians going to civil courts to settle their differences, an action Paul condemned elsewhere (1 Corinthians 6:1-11). Their arguments may have stemmed from the Philippians' pride in their achievements, which Paul denounced in 2:3. It was popular among the Aristotelian philosophers around Philippi to impress others with their accomplishments; the Christians were not to act that way.

Why are complaining and arguing so harmful? First, they are completely opposite of Christ's attitude (2:5-8), which believers are to emulate. Second, they hurt Christ's cause among unbelievers. If all that people know about a church is that its members constantly argue, complain, and gossip, they get a bad impression of Christ and the gospel. Unbelievers then feel justified in criticizing the Christians. Third, probably more churches have split from causes related to arguing and complaining than from heresy.

COMPLAINT DEPARTMENT
What do people complain about? They complain about pastors, programs, how services are conducted, certain people in office, and issues before the church. If the members in your church are always complaining and arguing, the church lacks the unifying power of Jesus Christ. Stop arguing with other Christians or complaining about people and conditions within the church and let the world see Christ.

**2:15 So that you may become blameless and pure, children of God
without fault in a crooked and depraved generation, in which
you shine like stars in the universe.**NIV Paul explained the
importance of the believers' actions—they needed to clean up
their act in order to fulfill their mission of spreading the gospel.
Paul's advice for their "housecleaning" is summed up in two
words.

First, the church ought to be *blameless,* meaning beyond
reproach, incurring no justifiable criticism. This does not mean
sinless perfection; instead, the church was to be beyond the criticism of the unbelieving world. Second, the church ought to be
pure (also translated "innocent"). The Greek word *akeraioi* was
used to describe wine that had not been diluted or metal that had
no weakening alloys. Jesus used the word when he told his disciples to be "innocent as doves" (Matthew 10:16); Paul employed
it when he told the Romans to be "wise about what is good, and
innocent about what is evil" (Romans 16:19 NIV). There ought to
be nothing within the church that would weaken its strength or
contaminate the truth. When a church is filled with disputes,
arguments, bickering, and divisions, it cannot be blameless, for
unbelievers are the first to spot such problems in the church and
to point critical fingers. Nor can such a church be pure, for such
problems will undermine its strength. If the church can be blameless and pure, it will be able to fulfill its mission in the world and
will be conducting itself "in a manner worthy of the gospel of
Christ" (1:27 NIV).

Then the church's members would be *children of God without
fault in a crooked and depraved generation.* Paul was quoting
from words that Moses used to describe the nation of Israel when
it went astray: "They have acted corruptly toward [God]; to their
shame they are no longer his children, but a warped and crooked
generation" (Deuteronomy 32:5 NIV). Moses was describing apos-
tate Israel, but Paul applied the words to the culture surrounding
the Philippian church. Without a doubt, the Philippian believers
lived in a generation filled with dishonesty and perversion (see
the "setting" section in the introduction). But there is great significance to the little word "in." While believers are rescued out of
the present evil age (Galatians 1:4) and are no longer of the
world (John 17:16), they are not taken out of the world (John
17:15). They are "in" the world and have been given a commission to go "into" the world with the Good News (John 17:18).
The church of Philippi needed to fulfill its mission in the world,
and it could best do so by being blameless and pure children of
God right in the middle of the depraved culture.

When a body of believers remains pure and blameless, the contrast with their culture is so stark that it is as if they *shine like stars*. They bring the light of truth into the darkness of depravity, as stars light up the darkness of the night. Indeed, Jesus told those who believe in him: "You are the light of the world. . . . Let your light shine before others, so that they may see your good works and give glory to your Father in heaven" (Matthew 5:14, 16 NRSV; see also Daniel 12:3).

STAR LIGHT, STAR BRIGHT
The name given to the brightest star in the night sky is Sirius, of the constellation Canis Major. The brightest star in the day sky is the sun. Paul drew a lesson from the night sky when he compared Christians to stars and society to the empty blackness of the universe. It is a bleak and barren skyscape at night, except for the light of stars. Christians are to live as lights in a dark world, shining witnesses to God's truth.

Our lives should be characterized by moral purity, patience, and peacefulness, so that we will "shine like stars" in a dark and depraved world. A transformed life is an effective witness to the power of God's Word. Are you shining brightly, or are you clouded by complaining and arguing? Don't let dissensions snuff out your light. Shine out for God. Your role is to shine until Jesus returns and bathes the world in his radiant glory.

2:16 As you hold out the word of life—in order that I may boast on the day of Christ that I did not run or labor for nothing.[NIV] The church was not to sit in pristine purity, merely reflecting light in the darkness. There was work to be done—the light must disperse or illuminate the surrounding darkness. So the Philippian church should *hold out the word of life* by spreading the truth of the gospel beyond the doors of the church. The Greek word translated "hold out" was used in secular culture for offering wine to a guest. The Philippians were to offer the gospel to a dying world, for the gospel alone brings abundant and eternal life. The phrase is also translated "holding fast to the word of life" (NRSV) and could therefore be an encouragement to the Philippians to be grounded in the truth, refusing to compromise. Both meanings work together—as the believers "hold fast" to the truth, they can "hold out" that truth to others.

Christians can develop a "fortress mentality" about surviving in a depraved world. Such a mind-set prefers to withdraw into church or family, away from the evil world, shutting it out. But Paul didn't support a fortress mentality. Instead, he required believers to take the gospel out into the culture. It is a waste of

energy just to leave a light on. Church people must help illuminate the way so that others can find Christ.

When Paul saw the church remaining pure and blameless and
holding the word of life out to their unsaved neighbors, he would
be able to *boast* on their behalf, knowing that his work among
them had not been *for nothing*. Paul had been the first to bring
the gospel to Philippi; the church existed because of his preaching. Paul's boasting was not prideful, as if he had built the church
with his own hands. Instead, his boasting would be like that of a
parent over a child who has done well. He would not be boasting
to other people—he would boast about the Philippians' faithfulness to God himself *on the day of Christ* (that is, when Christ
returns).

**2:17 But even if I am being poured out as a libation over the sacri-
fice and the offering of your faith, I am glad and rejoice with
all of you.**[NRSV] Paul's reference to being *poured out as a libation*
was a kind of allegory for martyrdom. The libation (drink offering) was an important part of the Jew-
ish sacrificial system. It involved wine
being poured out on an altar as a sacrifice to God (see Genesis 35:14; Exodus
29:40-41; Numbers 28:24). Because the
Philippian church had little Jewish background, Paul may have been referring
to the wine poured out to pagan deities
prior to important public events. Paul
regarded his life as a suitable libation to
complete the Philippians' sacrifice, and
he willingly offered it for the sake of
Christ's gospel and for the many who
had believed in Christ because of his
preaching. Paul's words were solemn
and weighed heavily on him. While in
other parts of this letter he seemed to be
optimistic about being released (1:24-
26; 2:24), here he faced the reality that he might be put to death
for the faith. (He used the same language in 2 Timothy 4:6, when
his death was imminent.)

> We shall be as a city upon a hill. The eyes of all people are upon us, so that if we shall deal falsely with our God in this work we have undertaken, and so cause Him to withdraw His present help from us, we shall be made a story and a byword through the world. *John Winthrop, to Puritans aboard The Arbella, traveling to the New World, 1630*

The Philippians' *faith* had been exhibited to Paul in their *sacrifice and . . . offering* (or "sacrificial service") through their fellowship and financial support. In the allegory Paul was
presenting in this verse, the Philippians' faith is the real sacrifice,
and Paul's lifeblood, pictured in the drink offering, is the accom-
panying libation.

Yet even through these somber words a ray of light was shining. If Paul were indeed to die, he would be *glad and rejoice with all of you.* Paul was content, knowing that he had helped the Philippians live for Christ. Paul was able to have joy, even though he faced possible execution. When you are totally committed to serving Christ, sacrificing to build the faith of others brings a joyous reward.

2:18 And in the same way you also must be glad and rejoice with me.^{NRSV} Paul considered it a privilege to die for the faith, and he wanted the Philippians to take the same attitude in the case of his death.

BE GLAD
How do we experience gladness when our world seems to fall in, when God seems silent, when our group is withering, when loved ones disappoint us, when nothing seems to be happening in our lives? Gladness can be restored, but it may come slowly:
- Remember that he who began a good work in you will carry it on to completion (1:6).
- Remember the love of God is poured out in our hearts by the Holy Spirit.
- Remember that joy often comes as a by-product of serving others (as it was for Paul).
- Remember to seek encouragement from fellow believers (2:1, 19-20).

TIMOTHY AND EPAPHRODITUS WILL SOON COME TO YOU / 2:19-30

Paul had nothing but praise for Timothy and Epaphroditus. Both had proven themselves to be faithful in the ministry and sincere in their love for fellow believers. Because he could not go himself, Paul would soon send Timothy. In the meantime he would send Epaphroditus back to them. Paul explained that Epaphroditus had fulfilled the mission for which the Philippian church had sent him and also that he was being sent back to carry this letter and to share news of Paul with them. Paul was careful to give sincere praise where it was earned. Like him, we ought to willingly praise those who help us in our ministry.

2:19 I hope in the Lord Jesus to send Timothy to you soon, so that I may be cheered by news of you.^{NRSV} Paul loved the Philippians dearly. He had brought them the gospel and he was concerned that they continue to grow spiritually. Sending Timothy

would bring news of Paul to Philippi and then would bring good
news of Philippi back to Paul. Several weeks of travel are encom-
passed in Paul's sentence. While Paul awaited his trial, his dear
friend Timothy was certainly an encouragement. Yet Paul was
willing to forego that companionship so as to send Timothy on
this mission for the sake of the Philippian church.

Timothy was with Paul in Rome when Paul wrote this letter,
although Timothy was not imprisoned. He had traveled with
Paul on his second missionary journey when the church at Philippi was begun, so the Philippians knew Timothy well (see
explanation on 1:1). Paul could not visit the Philippians, thus
he hoped to send Timothy on his behalf. Timothy had traveled
to various churches as Paul's representative at other times (see
1 Corinthians 4:17; 16:10; 1 Thessalonians 3:2). Epaphroditus
would leave immediately and deliver Paul's letter (2:25-30);
then Timothy would arrive later after Paul learned the verdict
of his trial (2:23). Paul hoped that in the meantime the Philippians would take to heart his call to unity in their church and
would iron out their difficulties. Timothy would be able to see
their progress and then could return to Rome with news that
would bring Paul good cheer.

THINKING OF JESUS
What are Jesus' interests? We are told to follow them, but how
do we know what they are?
   Think of Jesus as a shepherd (John 10:14); his big interest
then is the lost sheep. We need to care about people lost from
God.
   Think of Jesus as a potter (Isaiah 64:8); then his big interest
is in shaping beautiful containers. We need to care for the transformation of all believers.
   Think of Jesus as a farmer (Matthew 13:3); then his big interest is raising a crop. We need to care about spreading the truth
of the gospel widely so that every life can grow to God's glory.

But Paul made these plans cautiously because he did not
know what the next day might bring. The hope of sending Timothy is expressed to the Philippians as hope *in the Lord Jesus.*
Paul used the phrase "I hope" with respect to his travel plans
because his schedule was controlled by the Lord (compare
Romans 15:24; 1 Corinthians 16:7; 2 Corinthians 13:2; 1 Timothy 3:14; Philemon 22). Paul made particular mention that, in
the precarious situation of his imprisonment, any plans he
would make would be ultimately governed by God's will concerning the outcome of his trial.

2:20 I have no one else like him, who takes a genuine interest in your welfare.^{NIV} Timothy had *a genuine interest* in the Philippians because he had traveled with Paul on his second missionary journey when the church at Philippi had been begun (Acts 16:1-3, 10-12). The phrase *no one else like him* literally means "no one of equal soul." These words of praise for Paul's protégé reveal that Timothy had become a dependable coworker and friend. Timothy was as concerned about the welfare and well-being of the Philippian church as Paul was.

2:21 For everyone looks out for his own interests, not those of Jesus Christ.^{NIV} This sentence could mean that Paul had spoken to others about possibly taking this trip to Philippi on his behalf, but all of them were more concerned for their *own interests* than in doing Christ's work. Or Paul may not have been indicting his fellow Christians; rather, he may have been reflecting on the state of a selfish world where few truly selfless people can be found. More likely, Paul was using hyperbole. He could not have meant that Luke, Titus, and other disciples cared only for themselves. Rather, he meant that Timothy cared so deeply that the concern of others paled by comparison. While many believers might express concern, too often they are too preoccupied with their own activities to act on that concern. Timothy was concerned for the Philippians' welfare, and he was willing to act on the concern by dropping what he was doing in Rome to make the lengthy and tiring trip to Philippi. Once in Philippi, he might have to deal with problems in the church—certainly not an enviable task. Timothy's willingness to go to Philippi reveals a spirit of selfless service. Here was a man who exemplified what it meant to put others' interests ahead of his own (2:4).

TEACHING AND LEARNING
When Paul wrote these words, most vocational training was done by fathers, and sons stayed loyal to the family business. Timothy displayed that same loyalty in his spiritual apprenticeship with Paul.

Paul encouraged younger Christians to learn, to observe, to help, and then to lead. Paul expected older Christians to teach, to model, to mentor, and then to turn over leadership.

The benefits of such a process are new enthusiasm and vision, new methods and energy. Like Paul, be a caring teacher, and like Timothy, an eager learner.

2:22 But Timothy's worth you know, how like a son with a father he has served with me in the work of the gospel.^{NRSV} Timothy had been with Paul during Paul's ministry in Philippi. The Philippian church well knew Timothy's value, sound character, and worthiness. The church knew that Timothy's coming would be equal to that of the arrival of Paul himself, for Timothy had served with Paul *like a son with a father.* Paul and Timothy had developed a special bond; Paul had led Timothy to Christ during his first missionary journey. In the first century, the Greeks valued highly the service a son gave to his father. Yet Paul realized that both he and Timothy were servants of Jesus Christ; thus he wrote that Timothy served *with* him as they worked to spread the gospel across the empire.

2:23 I hope therefore to send him as soon as I see how things go with me.[NRSV] Paul was in prison (awaiting his verdict) for preaching about Christ. He planned to send Timothy to Philippi (2:19) and hoped to do so when he learned of the court's decision.

CARING FOR YOURSELF
Paul still needed Timothy to help him until the outcome of the case was clear. Christians who serve others may assume that A+ spirituality requires that they neglect themselves. But such neglect often creates more problems than it solves, and it only makes other people more fretful and anxious.

Paul was smarter than that. His love for the Philippians was not careless or ascetic. He even based decisions, such as this one to retain Timothy, on his own needs. Christ does not ask us to intentionally destroy ourselves in the name of Christian service. Be wise in caring for yourself as you serve others.

2:24 And I trust in the Lord that I will also come soon.[NRSV] "In the Lord" could also be translated "if the Lord is willing" (see 1 Corinthians 4:19). Thus Paul again (as in 2:19) shows the uncertainty of any plans he might make. Even if Paul were to be released from prison, he would send Timothy to Philippi with the news, and then Paul would come soon after.

2:25 But I think it is necessary to send back to you Epaphroditus, my brother, fellow worker and fellow soldier, who is also your messenger, whom you sent to take care of my needs.[NIV] But Paul thought it was necessary to send Epaphroditus along immediately. Epaphroditus had come from Philippi to Rome, acting as their *messenger* to deliver a financial gift from the Philippians to Paul and to care for Paul on the Philippians' behalf. Epaphroditus may have been an elder in Philippi (2:25-30; 4:18). While in Rome, he had become extremely ill (2:27, 30). After his recovery,

Paul sent him back to Philippi, carrying this thank-you letter. Epaphroditus is mentioned only in Philippians.

> There are moments when everything goes well; don't be frightened, it won't last. *Jules Renard*

The phrase "take care of" is also translated "minister" and carries the idea of spiritual ministry. Epaphroditus had come not just to deliver money, but to minister to Paul's spiritual needs. In Greek, the verb is "send" not "send back"; thus it seems that Epaphroditus had been sent to Rome to remain with Paul indefinitely, ministering to and encouraging the imprisoned apostle. Like Timothy, this man put others' needs ahead of his own (see 2:4). Epaphroditus came to serve Paul. But Paul felt it necessary to send Epaphroditus back to Philippi with this letter to assure the Philippians of his well-being after his severe illness.

But Paul wanted the Philippians to know how highly he regarded Epaphroditus, so he characterized him with three names: (1) *my brother,* which means he was a fellow believer; (2) *fellow worker,* which means he too was working for God's kingdom—in Philippi, in Rome, or both; and (3) *fellow soldier,* which refers to the solidarity among believers who are fighting the same battle—that of bringing the gospel to an unbelieving and increasingly hostile world. Paul was in chains for the gospel; Epaphroditus and the church in Philippi faced persecution that would soon intensify.

2:26 For he has been longing for all of you, and has been distressed because you heard that he was ill.[NRSV] How easy it is for modern readers to miss the intensity of Epaphroditus's distress for his friends in Philippi. Communication happens so quickly in our world, but Epaphroditus couldn't just pick up the phone or mail a letter that would arrive in a few days saying all was well. The Philippians had heard that Epaphroditus had fallen ill, and word of their concern about him had gotten back to Rome (again, weeks elapsed as the news traveled the forty-day journey between the two cities). When he recovered, Epaphroditus wanted the church to know as quickly as possible. So Paul figured the best way to do that would be to send Epaphroditus himself to Philippi.

2:27 He was indeed so ill that he nearly died. But God had mercy on him, and not only on him but on me also, so that I would not have one sorrow after another.[NRSV] The Philippians' concern about Epaphroditus's illness had been well founded, for he had been so sick that he almost died. While the apostles had been given the ability to heal, it was not a permanent gift to be used at

will, otherwise, Paul would surely have healed his friend.
Instead, Paul could do nothing but pray. Epaphroditus recovered
because of God's mercy. What illness Epaphroditus had and how
he regained his health are unknown. To Paul, these details were
less important than the significance of the healing. God had
mercy on both his servants—on Epaphroditus by healing him and
returning him to ministry; on Paul by not adding the sorrow of
bereaving a friend's death on top of other sorrows rendered by
his imprisonment.

Does Paul's concern that he would sorrow over the loss of his
friend show a lack of faith? What happened to his proclamation
in 1:21 that "to die is gain"? The tension in these two feelings
provides guidance to us. We do not naturally desire to die, nor do
we welcome the death of a friend. Christians need to know that it
is necessary to grieve. Too many Christians feel that grief is
wrong, that we're supposed to rejoice when a loved one goes to
be with the Lord. While we can rejoice in their homegoing, we
also grieve our loss.

PRAYING FOR FRIENDS
Most of our prayers have a two-sided motivation. The altruistic
side seeks God's help for our friend's marriage, job, or health.
The self-oriented side seeks relief from our worry or from the
strain of carrying a friend's load.

Paul felt both sides in his prayers for Epaphroditus. He
wanted God to have mercy on his friend, and he wanted to be
spared from grieving. We may pray likewise: that God would
help a friend or loved one and, as an added benefit, help us too.

2:28 **I am the more eager to send him, therefore, in order that
you may rejoice at seeing him again, and that I may be less
anxious.**[NRSV] With Epaphroditus's unexpected return, the
church might think that his mission to minister to Paul had
failed. They might be concerned that Epaphroditus was leaving
Paul alone in Paul's most desperate time of need. Instead, Paul
took full responsibility for Epaphroditus's return to Philippi
and encouraged the believers to *rejoice* that he had come back
to them. As he planned to do with Timothy (2:19), Paul willingly sent away those closest to him if their ministry were
required elsewhere. Epaphroditus had certainly been an encouragement to Paul, as Paul's description of this brother indicates
(2:25). Yet Paul knew that the Philippians needed to see Epaphroditus for themselves. This would ease Epaphroditus' distress (2:26) and Paul's anxiety.

TOTALLY HUMAN PAUL
Why should someone so strong in faith as Paul feel anxious?
And why admit to it publicly? Paul's transparency concerning
his feelings is a lesson in personal honesty to us, who tend to
think that anxiety is a sign of spiritual weakness. Paul refused
to hide behind a spiritual mask. Solid relationships and genuine
prayers require this kind of honesty. Be encouraged to express
your needs honestly and openly.

2:29-30 Welcome him in the Lord with great joy.[NIV] While Epaphroditus had not been able to remain in Rome to encourage Paul as the Philippian church had hoped, Paul wanted the believers to welcome him back and give him great honor for what he had done. Epaphroditus should be welcomed *in the Lord*—that is, as the Lord would welcome him, or with a welcome befitting members of the Lord's body.

A WELCOME CELEBRATION
Some occasions call for restraint, decorum, and sophistication,
but greeting a fellow believer long absent is not one of them.
Paul urges that we show enthusiasm at the point of first
encounter. Is someone you know coming home this week?
Make it a joyous reunion. First-time visitors in church? Show
them real happiness. Missionaries returning from the field? Welcome them with joy!

Honor men like him, because he almost died for the work of Christ, risking his life to make up for the help you could not give me.[NIV] Paul let the Philippians know that Epaphroditus had not failed in his mission, and that he should be given great honor. Epaphroditus had become ill while working for Christ, so ill that his life had been in danger. If he had died, that too would have been for Christ. Epaphroditus had served Christ by helping Paul on behalf of the Philippian church. Paul needed personal encouragement; the church couldn't give it because of their distance from him. But Epaphroditus had taken that responsibility and had risked his life to help the apostle in his time of need. His return to Philippi was in no way an admission of failure; instead, Epaphroditus had done his work so well that he could report back to Philippi and bring Paul's letter of thanks and encouragement along with him.

WHERE HONOR IS DUE
The world honors those who are intelligent, beautiful, rich, and powerful. What kind of people should the church honor? Epaphroditus was called a brother, fellow worker, fellow soldier, and messenger. These are the emblems of honor. Paul indicates that we should honor those who risk their lives for the sake of Christ and the care of others, going where we cannot go ourselves. Our missionaries do that for us today by providing ministry where we are not able to go.

Philippians 3:1–4:1

Paul warned the Philippian believers to stay clear of the false teachers who taught that what people *did* (like being circumcised), rather than the free gift of grace provided through Christ, made them believers. Paul's conversion to Christ (Acts 9) wasn't based on what he had done, but on God's grace. Paul did not depend on his deeds to please God because even the most impressive credentials fall short of God's holy standards. Are you depending on Christian parents or church affiliation, or are you just being good to make you right with God? Credentials, accomplishments, or reputation cannot earn salvation. That comes only through faith in Christ.

3:1 Finally, my brothers and sisters, rejoice in the Lord.^{NRSV} With the word *finally* (literally, "as to what remains"), it would appear that Paul was ending his letter (see Ephesians 6:10 and 2 Thessalonians 3:1, where Paul's "finally" signaled the end of those letters). But to the Greek audience, "finally" *(to loipon)* could also mean "furthermore." In 3:2, Paul would discuss the false teachers. While false teaching had not become a major threat to the Philippian church, it hounded other churches, and Paul was certain that the Philippians would not be spared. He wanted to stop the problem before it could start in Philippi. Rejoicing would be a safeguard against false teachers.

The tone of Paul's letter to the Philippians is joyous—and as he prepared his final words to them, he exhorted them to *rejoice in the Lord.* He would say this again at the real end of his letter (see 4:4). In this short epistle, a form of the word joy occurs twelve times.

What is true joy? Often happiness is mistaken for joy, but the two are very different:

- Inward joy comes from knowing and trusting God. Happiness comes as a result of pleasant circumstances.

- Inward joy is lasting; we can feel joy in spite of our deepest troubles.

I SAY IT AGAIN, REJOICE

Paul used forms of the words *joy* and *rejoice* several times in his letter. He used *chara* (joy) in three ways (verses quoted from NRSV):

(1) Believers and their progress in the faith are a cause for joy; for Paul, particularly those he had led to Christ.

Philippians 2:2	"Make my joy complete: be of the same mind, having the same love, being in full accord and of one mind."
Colossians 2:5	" I rejoice to see your morale and the firmness of your faith."
1 Thessalonians 2:19-20	"For what is our hope or joy or crown of boasting before our Lord Jesus at his coming? Is it not you? Yes, you are our glory and joy!"

(See also Romans 15:32; 16:19; 2 Corinthians 1:24; 7:9, 16; 13:9; Philippians 1:3-5, 25; 4:1; Philemon 1:7)

(2) Many times, Christian joy comes as a result of suffering for Christ. Although it is difficult to grasp this concept, knowing that God is working in our lives produces this joy.

Philippians 2:17-18	"But even if I am being poured out as a libation over the sacrifice and the offering of your faith, I am glad and rejoice with all of you—and in the same way you also must be glad and rejoice with me."
Colossians 1:11-12	"May you be made strong with all the strength that comes from his glorious power, and may you be prepared to endure everything with patience, while joyfully giving thanks to the Father."
Colossians 1:24	"I am now rejoicing in my sufferings for your sake."

(See also Romans 12:12-15; 2 Corinthians 6:4-10; 8:2)

(3) Joy is ultimately a gift of the Holy Spirit, not something we can produce in ourselves. It comes as a result of God's love for us.

Romans 14:17	"For the kingdom of God is not food and drink but righteousness and peace and joy in the Holy Spirit."
Romans 15:13	"May the God of hope fill you with all joy and peace in believing, so that you may abound in hope by the power of the Holy Spirit."
Galatians 5:22	"The fruit of the Spirit is love, joy, peace."
1 Thessalonians 1:6	"In spite of persecution you received the word with joy inspired by the Holy Spirit."

Happiness is temporary because it is based on external circumstances.

Paul was able to rejoice in spite of his suffering because he knew and trusted God. He did not let his circumstances discourage him. When life goes well for people who don't know the joy of the Lord, they feel elated. When hard times come, they may sink into depression. But true joy enables us to transcend the rolling waves of circumstance. Joy comes from a consistent relationship with Jesus Christ—thus believers "rejoice in the Lord." When believers' lives are intertwined with Jesus' life, he helps them walk through adversity without permanently sinking into debilitating lows, and he helps them manage prosperity without moving into deceptive highs. Joy can be interrupted by life's trials and our own sinful tendencies. To remain joyful, we should remind ourselves daily of God's love for us and our ultimate life with him in heaven. The joy of knowing Christ kept Paul levelheaded, no matter how high or low his circumstances (see also 4:12). While Paul was not happy about being in prison, he could rejoice because he knew God was with him.

To write the same things to you is not troublesome to me, and for you it is a safeguard.NRSV The *same things* about which Paul was writing are open to several interpretations:

- Most likely, Paul was referring to his repeated call to rejoice. Paul may have seen the possibility of the Philippians becoming depressed over his state, or over possible persecution of their church, and reminded them to rejoice as a *safeguard* against despondency.

- Paul was referring to his repeated warnings against disunity in the church. To keep reminding them of that would "safeguard" them from breaking into factions when they needed to stand together. He picked up this theme again in 4:1.

- Paul was introducing what he was to write about next—that the Philippians watch out for false teachers (3:18; see also 1:25-30). Repeated warnings about false teachers would indeed be a "safeguard" because false teaching was a threat to the early church.

- The "same things" was referring back to other letters to the Philippians, now lost, or to topics he had discussed with the Philippians during his stay with them years earlier.

In light of Paul's emphasis on joy, it seems most natural to regard joy as the safeguard Paul recommends. It is impossible to maintain a joyful spirit and conduct the practices Paul so vehemently warned against: dissension, grumbling, and attitudes of superiority. If we lose the joy of the Lord, we are susceptible to these attitudes. Joy acts as a barrier against them. It guarantees the safety of our Christian hope.

Paul did not consider it *troublesome* to take the time to reiterate his teaching. Just as a great basketball team periodically drills over the basics of dribbling and shooting, so Christians need to remember and review the basics of their faith. Paul realized the responsibility and importance of safeguarding their faith by reminding them of the essentials.

JOY
A dear Christian teacher, now deceased, lived on a hillside a mile from his college. His home was filled with simple treasures. Once when a brushfire roared up his canyon, firefighters ordered the house abandoned—no time to pack, just flee. As he walked away with his wife, he said quietly, "Jenny, do you have the joy?"

Paul recommends joy as a safeguard against cynicism, depression, weariness, and despair. All the good reasons people have to bicker, to backbite, and to give up are washed aside in a tidal wave of emotional assurance from God's Spirit. We call it joy.

Declare today your "faith, hope, and joy" day. Feel it, show it, let it flow. God has come, Christ is risen—for you!

3:2 **Beware of the dogs, beware of the evil workers, beware of those who mutilate the flesh.**NRSV Even if Paul had intended to end his letter at 3:1, he had some further words for the Philippians. He wanted them to *beware*—a strong word meaning "look out for" or "be warned against." Paul was issuing a severe warning about a particular group of people.

BEWARE
Religious zeal comes in many shapes and forms, some bizarre and some appealing. The New Age movement, for example, offers meditative peacefulness (a good practice) through crystal gazing (which builds dependency on artifacts and diverts attention from the true God). People try many ways to discover God; most of them are dead ends, and some of them hurt.

To live happily, stay far away from alternative forms of religious teaching that are contrary to the Bible. Instead, dig deep into the good news that God has come in Jesus Christ, to love you and to lead you to heaven.

Paul used the word "beware" three times and then described
this hostile group using three different derogatory terms.
(1) *Dogs* were regarded by Jews as despised and unclean creatures; it was common for orthodox Jews to refer to Gentiles as
"dogs"; however, here Paul switched the designation to refer not
to Gentiles but to an extreme faction in the church. (2) He also
called them *evil workers*. The Jews regarded themselves as good
workers, not evil workers, because they kept the law. Paul
labeled them as evil, not because they were immoral, but because
reliance on the law lessened their reliance on God. Their emphasis on works would ruin Paul's teaching of justification by faith
alone, and not by works of the law. (3) Finally, he called them
those who mutilate the flesh. Some Jewish Christians wrongly
believed that it was essential for Gentiles to follow all the Old
Testament Jewish laws, especially submission to the rite of circumcision (which Paul here calls "mutilating" the flesh), in order
to receive salvation. The Greek word for circumcision is *peri-
tome*, but Paul refused to use it here; instead he used *katatome*,
which refers to pagan mutilation of the flesh. While there was
nothing wrong with circumcision itself, Paul maintained that it
was wrong to teach circumcision as a requirement for salvation.
It had become an empty and meaningless rite. Those who taught
this wrong doctrine were called Judaizers; they were a severe
problem for Paul. For instance, the church in Galatia was threatened by this teaching. Paul wrote a terse letter to the Galatians
explaining exactly why the Judaizers were wrong. The Judaizers'
main argument was that Gentiles had to first become Jews before
they could become Christians. Paul exposed the flaw in that argument in his letter to the Galatians by showing that real children of
Abraham are those who have faith, not those who keep the law
(Galatians 3:6-9). Abraham himself was saved by his faith (Genesis 15:6) *before* he was given the rite of circumcision. Thus all
believers in every age and from every nation share Abraham's
blessing.

Paul criticized the Judaizers because they looked at Christianity backwards—thinking that what they *did* (especially circumcision) made them believers rather than the free gift of grace given
by Christ. What believers do is a *result* of faith, not a *prerequisite*
to faith. The Philippian Christians were unfamiliar with Jewish
laws and customs; the Judaizers were an extreme faction of Jewish Christians. Both groups believed in Christ, but their lifestyles
differed considerably. We do not know why the Judaizers traveled so far to teach their mistaken notions to the new Gentile converts. They may have been motivated by (1) a sincere wish to

integrate Judaism with the new Christian faith, (2) a sincere love for their Jewish heritage, or (3) a jealous desire to destroy Paul's authority. Whether or not these Judaizers were sincere, their teaching threatened these new churches and had to be countered. When Paul called them by such derogatory names, he was not rejecting everything Jewish. Paul was a Jew; he worshiped in the temple, attended the religious festivals, and had been circumcised as a baby. But he was concerned that *nothing* get in the way of the simple truth of his message—that salvation, for Jews and Gentiles alike, comes through faith in Jesus Christ alone.

The early church had already confirmed Paul's teaching at the Jerusalem Council eleven years earlier (see Acts 15). However, this didn't stop many of the Judaizers, who were motivated by spiritual pride. Because they had invested so much time and effort in keeping their laws, they couldn't accept the fact that all their efforts couldn't bring them a step closer to salvation. And the age-old hatred of Gentile "dogs" didn't make it any easier for them to accept Gentiles as brothers in the faith. Whether or not they had come to Philippi as yet, Paul knew it was only a matter of time, and he wanted the Philippians to be forewarned.

TRUE FAITH
Can you see faith, touch it, measure it? Not really. Faith is an attitude, a quality, a disposition, a belief. Objects we can measure; faith we experience.

Throughout history, some Christians have tried to make faith visible and measurable ("I've got more than you!"). To do this, some have added rules that provide behavioral markers, separating "real" faith from mere "profession." Many churches, for instance, ban tobacco products, all forms of alcoholic beverages, dancing, and attending movies.

Paul dismisses man-made rules. He knows that faith requires immense responsibility, but he refuses to patronize the "real Christians cannot do such-and-such" crowd.

In fact, true faith frees us from proving ourselves to God or to others. True faith trusts wholly in Jesus Christ. Watch out for today's legalists and Judaizers. No person should add anything to Christ's offer of salvation by faith through God's grace.

3:3 For it is we who are the circumcision, who worship in the Spirit of God and boast in Christ Jesus and have no confidence in the flesh.[NRSV] Circumcision had been a requirement under the old covenant, a physical sign to God's people of their relationship with him (Genesis 17:9-14). Yet it also had spiritual application, for the physical mark was to be a sign of a spiritual relationship with God (Deuteronomy 30:6). Paul explained that *it*

is we [that is, Christians] *who are the circumcision.* In other
words, at one time the physical sign of circumcision had set
God's people, the Jews, apart from the Gentiles. After Jesus
Christ, all people could become part of God's family by believing
in Jesus as Savior. Those who believe are set apart from unbelievers and inherit the promises that had been made to Israel: "But
you are a chosen people, a royal priesthood, a holy nation, a
people belonging to God, that you may declare the praises of him
who called you out of darkness into his wonderful light. Once
you were not a people, but now you are the people of God; once
you had not received mercy, but now you have received mercy"
(1 Peter 2:9-10 NIV; see also Romans 9:24-26).

The Christian church, made up of circumcised Jews and
uncircumcised Gentiles, is the true "circumcision" because circumcision is no longer merely a bodily mark; instead, it has new
spiritual meaning and is symbolized by baptism: "In [Christ] you
were also circumcised, in the putting off of the sinful nature, not
with a circumcision done by the hands of men but with the circumcision done by Christ, having been buried with him in baptism and raised with him through your faith in the power of God,
who raised him from the dead" (Colossians 2:11-12 NIV).

True believers, those who are the true "circumcision," have
three common characteristics that prove their standing before
God:

(1) They *worship in the Spirit of God.* This could also be translated "worship by the Spirit of God." Believers worship by
means of God's Spirit and in God's Spirit. The Holy Spirit, the
third person of the Trinity, is vital to all aspects of our Christian
life. Paul spoke many times about the vital role of the Holy Spirit
in the life of the believer. In Romans 8:9, he explained that no
one can be considered part of the new community who had not
received the Spirit. In Galatians 3:1-5, Paul argued that the presence of the Holy Spirit made circumcision unnecessary. The
Spirit aids us in our prayers (Romans 8:26) and gives gifts to help
us worship (Ephesians 4:11-13); through the Spirit we are given
access to God in prayer (Ephesians 2:18-21). Christian worship is
intensely spiritual. Whatever outward forms may or may not be
used, worship is always inspired by the Holy Spirit. We must
remind ourselves of this and acknowledge the Holy Spirit's role
in worship.

(2) They *boast in Christ Jesus.* The word translated "boast"
could better be translated "exult." This verb is a favorite one of
Paul's, occuring some thirty times in his writings but only twice
elsewhere in the New Testament. Sometimes the word describes

a religious attitude of proud self-confidence (as in Galatians 6:13); at other times, it describes humble submission to Christ (as in Galatians 6:14). In this case, Paul explained that true believers exult, not in their works as if they somehow saved themselves, but in Christ Jesus alone. Only because of Christ's sacrifice on the cross are believers saved. Any believer who understands the incredible significance of Christ's death cannot help but respond with exultation.

(3) They *have no confidence in the flesh.* The Judaizers depended on their obedience to the Jewish law, and especially the covenant of circumcision, to make them acceptable to God. By contrast, true believers did not place their confidence in anything they did or didn't do, but in what God through Jesus Christ had done for them. Paul used the Greek word *sarx* (often translated as "flesh") to refer to both the unregenerate human nature and also to everything apart from God that people might use as a basis for confidence or pride in their own achievements.

THE GIFT
It is easy to place more emphasis on religious effort ("confidence in the flesh") than on internal faith, but God values the attitude of our hearts above all else. Don't judge people's spirituality by their fulfillment of duties or by their level of human activity. And don't think that you will satisfy God by feverishly doing his work. God notices all you do for him and will reward you for it, but only if it comes as a loving response to his free gift of salvation.

3:4 Though I myself have reasons for such confidence. If anyone else thinks he has reasons to put confidence in the flesh, I have more.[NIV] The Judaizers believed that their accomplishments would earn their salvation, thus giving them reason for having *confidence in the flesh* (see 3:3). Paul challenged any false teachers to a credentials "showdown." If anyone could have confidence in worldly achievements, Paul could; in fact, he probably had more than any of those Judaizers who so adamantly opposed Paul's teaching of salvation by faith alone.

At first glance, it looks as though Paul was boasting about his achievements in verses 5-6. But he actually was doing the opposite, showing that human achievements, no matter how impressive, cannot earn salvation and eternal life with God. Paul had impressive credentials: upbringing, nationality, family background, inheritance, orthodoxy, activity, and morality (see 2 Corinthians 11–12; Galatians 1:13-24, for more of Paul's credentials). Following are seven qualifications that unmistakably belong to a full-blooded Jew. Four of these were from heredity or by birth; three were by choice or personal conviction.

HONEST SELF-ASSESSMENT
What is the basis of your confidence? What have you accomplished? Lots of people may rate you highly in school tests or job performance. You may even place yourself, as Paul rated himself, high on the scale of success.

But God has the last word: no other evaluations count. Only Jesus matters, and the rest you can wrap in old newspaper and toss away. God gave salvation as a gift, not to be won by any test. Our success sometimes reflects, but never earns, God's approval. Next time you tally up all your success, ask how Jesus Christ regards it all.

3:5 Circumcised on the eighth day.NRSV The Judaizers focused on circumcision as the way to be right with God. The first item on Paul's list of credentials in which he at one time placed confidence was the fact that he, too, had been circumcised. That he was circumcised *on the eighth day* after birth shows that Paul was a pure Jew (Leviticus 12:3), not a proselyte (someone who converted to Judaism and would have been circumcised after conversion). If anyone would have known about the true value of circumcision, Paul would. But Paul knew that his being circumcised could not give him salvation.

Of the people of Israel.NRSV Next Paul's list included his membership among God's elect race, the chosen people. Paul's parents were both true Jews, and Paul could trace his heritage back to Abraham (see Romans 11:1; 2 Corinthians 11:22).

Of the tribe of Benjamin. As part of the people of Israel, Paul described his membership in one of Israel's twelve tribes—Benjamin—a heritage greatly esteemed among the Jews. Though the tribe of Benjamin was one of the smaller tribes, it had a special place of honor throughout its history. The patriarch of the tribe, Benjamin, was the only one of Joseph's brothers born in the Promised Land. Along with the largest tribe, Judah, the tribe of Benjamin remained loyal to David's line when the monarchy split, forming northern and southern kingdoms. Israel's first king, Saul, after whom Paul was named ("Paul" is the Greek form of "Saul," see Acts 13:9), was from the tribe of Benjamin (1 Samuel 10:20-24). Mordecai, Esther's uncle and the man who helped save the nation, was a Benjamite. In addition, the tribes of Benjamin and Judah were the only two tribes to return to Israel after the Exile (Ezra 4:1). The tribe also had its low points (King Saul was not a spiritual leader, and the tribe experienced other difficulties, as recorded in Judges 19–21 and 2 Samuel 16:5-14). Paul was pointing out that he was an Israelite by birth, a genuine Jew through and through.

A Hebrew born of Hebrews.[NRSV] Paul was a Hebrew son born of Hebrew parents. He spoke the old languages of his race— Hebrew and Aramaic. This was in contrast to the Hellenists, who were Greek-speaking Jews. The ability to speak Hebrew and Aramaic was a mark of loyalty to Israel and commanded special attention (see Acts 22:2 for the effect on the Jewish crowd when Paul began to speak to them in Aramaic).

These were Paul's qualifications by birth and heredity. Next he turned to his qualifications gained by study and zeal for his faith.

Concerning the law, a Pharisee.[NKJV] Paul was also a Pharisee, a member of the most devout, orthodox, and strict Jewish sect. Pharisees scrupulously followed the Old Testament laws as well as their own numerous rules and traditions thought to be the revealed oral law of God (see Acts 5:34; 22:3; 23:6; 26:5). At one time, Paul had believed, like the Judaizers, that salvation came from perfect obedience to the law. The Pharisees behaved as though their own rules were just as important as God's rules for living; as they attempted to keep all the laws, they looked down on others who were less educated and thus less holy. Instead of being leaders and teachers of the people, they had become hypocrites in ivory towers, yet no closer to God.

The Pharisees first appear in history in the second century B.C. and seem to have descended from pious groups who had stood against the pagan evil of Antiochus Epiphanes. The word "Pharisee" means "separated one." Not only were the Pharisees separated from pagan evil, they were also separated from anything that might mean ethical or ceremonial impurity. They had built up a body of oral tradition that was meant to safeguard the ancient laws by adapting them to changing society. Instead, these traditions managed to make the laws unworkable for even themselves. Yet they spent their lives feverishly attempting to keep them.

3:6 As to zeal, a persecutor of the church.[NRSV] How much more zeal could anyone have than to outright persecute the church? No Judaizer could boast of traveling hundreds of miles in order to find Christians, bring them back in chains to Jerusalem, and cast a vote for their deaths (Acts 9:1-2; 22:3-5; 26:9-11). No Judaizer had stood by holding the coats of those who stoned an early Christian leader (Acts 7:59–8:1).

> In Christ all the treasures of wisdom and knowledge are hidden, but to search them out and appropriate them personally requires a lifetime. *Homer Kent*

But why did Paul persecute the church? Agreeing with the leaders of the religious establishment, Paul had thought that Christianity was heretical and blasphemous. Because Jesus did not meet his expectations of what the Messiah would be like, Paul had assumed that Jesus' claims were false—and therefore wicked (Acts 26:9). In addition, he had seen Christianity as a political menace because it threatened to disrupt the fragile harmony between the Jews and the Roman government.

If salvation could be found in single-minded zeal for a cause, Paul certainly had it. Unfortunately, he also had the wrong cause.

As to righteousness under the law, blameless.[NRSV] As a Pharisee, Paul had to follow the Old Testament law in addition to hundreds of rules and traditions that the Pharisees placed upon themselves. Yet regarding the ceremonial righteousness and legal standards in all these hundreds of laws, Paul was *blameless,* without fault. When Paul did something, he did it with every fiber of his being. He took his position as a Pharisee seriously—whether it included detailed law-keeping or zealous persecution of heretics. Paul tried to appear perfect before people, and it seems as though he had accomplished that. If awards were given for "Pharisee of the Month," Paul would have taken home more than his share of the honors.

SUPERIORITY AND SECURITY
We may not identify with Paul's list of credentials. Who cares that he was a Benjamite? But the same spiritual motives contained in Paul's list drive people today. Some people seek *spiritual superiority* in the right family, right church, right doctrine, or even the right slant on doctrine. But once we start putting confidence in human endeavors, we no longer worship in the Spirit or boast in Christ Jesus.

Other people seek *spiritual security,* thinking that if they have the right attitudes and behavior, they will escape the suffering that is the normal experience of most people. Actually, those people desire spiritual rewards now rather than waiting for God's future rewards.

Place your trust in Christ alone, and earthly motives will lose their forcefulness.

Any of the Judaizers would have loved to have had Paul's qualifications. Such a list would have given certain confidence in salvation according to their teachings. But Paul, who seemingly had
it all, listed his advantages and then set them aside as disadvan-
tages with the little word "yet" in the following verse.

**3:7 Yet whatever gains I had, these I have come to regard as loss
because of Christ.**[NRSV] When Paul spoke of his *gains,* he was
referring to his advantages and credentials listed in 3:5-6. After
showing that he could beat the Judaizers at their own game
(being proud of who they were and what they had done), Paul
showed that it was the wrong game. Despite his great qualifications, Paul had *come to regard* (that is, after careful thought, he
had come to consider) them as *loss.* Paul used an accounting metaphor with a gain and loss column. "Gains" is plural, referring to
individual items of importance. "Loss" is singular, indicating that
all the "gains" are no longer worth being listed separately, but
come under a single category—"loss." Paul illustrated the importance of human decision and resolve in thinking positively. All
the qualifications no longer mattered *because of Christ.* Paul had
learned that *nothing* he could do would earn him salvation—all
his hard work and meticulous law-keeping and zeal for the Jewish faith had gained him nothing. Doubtless Paul's meeting with
Christ on the road to Damascus had sealed this change in Paul.
When Paul understood all that Christ had done for him, his
accomplishments became nothing more than garbage by comparison (3:8).

TROPHIES JUST IN CASE
Many Christian leaders have wanted to be called "doctor," pre-
sumably because learned people hold Ph.D. degrees. Honor-
ary doctoral degrees have been highly prized, widely given,
and always used. Every special guest speaker needed such a
degree. Some leaders who didn't yet have one never bothered
correcting people who called them "doctor" by cordial mistake.
    Paul compared all his doctorates to the joy of knowing Jesus
as Lord and then filled his garbage cans with the former. Christ
had done it all and given to Paul what truly mattered: forgiveness, life, love, and all the promises of God.
    If your case is full of trophies, and letters follow your name
like alphabet soup, remember that Jesus alone saves you. If
you have no degrees, remember that Jesus your Lord gives
you all the privileges of heaven.

**3:8 More than that, I regard everything as loss because of the sur-
passing value of knowing Christ Jesus my Lord.**[NRSV] Not only

were Paul's credentials and accomplishments considered "loss because of Christ" (3:7 NRSV), but Paul had an even stronger pronouncement to make, introduced by the words *more than that* (or "what is more"). Paul wrote in the present tense, meaning that even at that point in time these facts were true. Paul regarded *everything* as loss when compared to knowing Christ. When Paul said "everything," he was referring to any type of credential or honor or acclaim that someone might try to use in order to gain favor with God. As Paul wrote this letter, he was in prison for the faith; he had suffered hardship and had been near death, yet he always pressed on for the sake of the gospel. Paul might have been tempted to rely on these accomplishments in earning salvation. Yet he knew that even great suffering for the sake of Christ was also a loss compared with the *surpassing value of knowing Christ Jesus.* The Greek word for "knowing" here speaks of a personal, experiential, and progressive knowledge. The Judaizers might have their rituals and rules, but Paul (and all true believers) had a wonderful personal relationship and fellowship with Christ Jesus himself (Colossians 2:2-3). Such a relationship far surpasses the value of anything else.

Paul did not rest on his laurels; he did not consider that he had "arrived" or that his imprisonment showed any credentials in the faith. Instead, Paul was pressing on, learning more about Christ and experiencing more about living the life of grace.

HOW DO WE "KNOW" CHRIST?
After Paul considered everything he had accomplished in his life, he decided to write it off as "a loss" when compared with the greatness of knowing Christ. We should value our relationship with Christ as more important than anything else. To know Christ should be our ultimate goal. Yet how do we do it?

- Study the life of Christ in the Gospels. See how Christ lived and responded to people (Matthew 11:29).
- Study all the New Testament references to Christ (Colossians 1:15–2:15).
- As you worship and pray, let the Holy Spirit remind you of Christ's words (John 14:26).
- Take up Christ's mission to preach the gospel and learn from his sufferings (Matthew 28:19; Philippians 3:10).

For his sake I have suffered the loss of all things, and I regard them as rubbish, in order that I may gain Christ.NRSV Not only did Paul consider everything else worth much less by comparison to knowing Christ, Paul had actually given up or lost *all things* for the sake of Christ. And doing so wasn't easy—Paul described himself as having *suffered* that loss. Considering how much Paul had been taught to value his credentials and how hard he had worked at his accomplishments (3:5-6), casting everything away would have been difficult. Yet those accomplishments or credentials were no better than *rubbish* (refuse, dung, or waste), for they were human attempts to gain favor with God and thus were worthless. All too often, what most of us treat as important is actually garbage by comparison. A person cannot depend on personal accomplishments *and* Christ for salvation; only Christ will be sufficient. Only the one who willingly loses all things can gain Christ. Jesus had said, "If any want to become my followers, let them deny themselves and take up their cross daily and follow me. For those who want to save their life will lose it, and those who lose their life for my sake will save it" (Luke 9:23-24 NRSV).

TO GAIN CHRIST
Paul denounced everything as valueless rubbish—education, credentials, family background—compared to knowing Christ and his resurrection power. We too have access to this knowledge and this power, but we may have to make major changes in our thinking to enjoy it fully. Are you willing to change your values in order to know Christ, your crowded schedule in order to set aside a few minutes each day for prayer and Bible study, and some of your plans or pleasures? Whatever it is, knowing Christ is worth the sacrifice.

3:9 And be found in Him, not having my own righteousness, which is from the law, but that which is through faith in Christ.NKJV Paul was looking forward to the day of Jesus Christ. When Christ returned or when Paul died, Paul wanted to *be found in* Christ, that is, living in union with Christ. Any believer living in Christ, and Christ in him or her, has been given, by God's mercy and grace, true righteousness (right standing with God). No amount of law-keeping, self-improvement, discipline, or religious effort can make anyone right with God. While those things may give a false sense of righteousness, they would never hold up under God's scrutiny. The Judaizers had such "righteousness," but it was merely their own; they simply were meeting their own standards in keeping the law. But no one can be good enough; no one can be saved by his or her *own righteousness.* Not even Paul, with all his credentials and accomplishments, could have been good enough.

True righteousness comes only *through faith in Christ.* Thus, it is **righteousness from God based on faith.**NRSV Believers are made righteous by their faith in Christ's sacrifice on the cross on their behalf. Righteousness is God's gift to us; it cannot be earned. God secured the gift and then offered it to us. Because of Jesus' death on the cross, God can exchange our sin and short-comings for his complete righteousness. In a way we humans will never understand, "God made him [Christ] who had no sin to be sin for us, so that in him we might become the righteousness of God" (2 Corinthians 5:21 NIV). Believers are offered a gift; all we have to do is accept it. We are considered righteous at the moment we believe, and we gradually work out the fruit of our righteous life on a day-to-day basis as we live in Christ and he lives through us.

FOUND IN HIM
If you could, where would you choose to be "lost for a day"? A jazz lover might select New Orleans, a scuba diver the Great Barrier Reef, a baseball fan Cooperstown, New York. After the "lost" day, you'd be found full of your experiences, even more drawn to music, tropical fish, or sports trivia than before.

Being found in Jesus Christ is, paradoxically, like being lost in him. Being "lost" in that relationship is to be happily abandoned with Christ, whose attraction works like a magnet. Time flies, love grows, your fascination with Jesus grows stronger than ever. Incorporate your life into Jesus Christ. To be found in him, you must live for him now.

3:10 **I want to know Christ and the power of his resurrection and the fellowship of sharing in his sufferings, becoming like him in his death.**NIV The word for *know* here is the same form used in 3:8, referring to personal, experiential knowledge. To know Christ is more than merely to know facts or doctrine about him. Paul wanted to know Christ better and better, for Christ had changed the very foundation of his life. That should be the goal of every believer—to know Christ more fully and personally, and that can be a lifelong process.

Paul wanted to know *the power of his resurrection.* The power of the Holy Spirit that brought Jesus back from the dead is avail-able to all believers to raise them from spiritual death now (Ephesians 1:19-20) and from their physical death in the future (Romans 8:11). Paul wanted to know this power, personally and experientially, for that power assures Christians of their justifica-tion (Romans 4:25; 1 Corinthians 15:17) and of their regenera-tion as they identify with Christ in resurrection (Romans 6:4; Colossians 2:12; 3:1, 10).

Paul also wanted to know *the fellowship of sharing in his suf-*

ferings. Paul was not referring to sharing Christ's death on the cross; that suffering could not be shared because it was Christ's alone. But Paul wanted to participate with Christ, as a believer, in suffering for the gospel (1:29). Even as Paul had already suffered greatly for the gospel and was suffering in prison at the writing of this letter, he still wanted to know, firsthand, what it meant to suffer for Christ. The sufferings of Christ are those afflictions that we suffer as we do Christ's ministry (2 Corinthians 1:5). At the same time, Christ suffers with his people because they are united with him. In Acts 9:4-5, Christ asked Paul why he was persecuting him, implying that Christ suffered with the early Christians when they were persecuted. (See 1:29; the note and chart on Colossians 1:24; 1 Peter 3:13–4:19.) Paul had already tasted suffering, but he was willing to experience more in order to serve Christ, who had suffered so much for him (Colossians 1:24).

Through fellowship in suffering, Paul was *becoming like him in his death.* According to the Greek, this participial phrase explains how we can know Christ—we know him by participating in his death. While all believers are being "conformed to the likeness of [Jesus]" (Romans 8:29 NIV), they are conformed to his death as they "die" to sin and to the old nature: "Count yourselves dead to sin but alive to God in Christ Jesus" (Romans 6:11 NIV). In a transaction we cannot completely understand, when Jesus died on the cross, we died to our former life. Christ took our punishment on himself, so God looks at us as though we have died to sin and then have been raised, along with Christ, to newness of life. Believers must first die to self before they can live for God. This is described in what Paul wrote to the Galatians: "I have been crucified with Christ and I no longer live, but Christ lives in me. The life I live in the body, I live by faith in the Son of God, who loved me and gave himself for me" (Galatians 2:20 NIV).

When we are united with Christ by trusting in him, we experience the power that raised him from the dead. That same mighty power will help us live morally renewed and regenerated lives. But before we can walk in newness of life, we must also die to sin. Just as Christ's resurrection gives us his power to live for him, his crucifixion marks the death of our old sinful nature. We can't know the victory of the Resurrection without personally applying the Crucifixion.

3:11 If by any means, I may attain to the resurrection from the dead.NKJV When Paul wrote, *if . . . I may attain to the resurrection,* he was *not* implying uncertainty or doubt that he would be resurrected. Rather, this was a way of humbly stating that he trusted in God for his complete salvation—from regeneration to resurrection. Paul did not doubt the fact that he would be raised, but how he would attain the resurrection was within God's plan and power and not his own. Just as Christ was exalted after his resurrection, so we will one day share Christ's glory (Revelation 22:1-7). Paul knew that he might die soon, but he had faith that he would be raised to life again.

The resurrection *from the dead* probably refers to the resurrection of Christians at the time of Christ's return (1 Corinthians 15:22-24; 1 Thessalonians 4:14-15; Revelation 20:5-6). The Greek preposition *ek* ("out of") suggests a resurrection apart from other dead people. Paul's wanting to attain this resurrection is in line with what Jesus said of the resurrection in Luke 20:35-36.

Paul was describing another track of spirituality—not the categorical one where confession of faith makes salvation a transaction from death into life, but a progressive one where, confident all along of God's care and blessing, Paul runs toward salvation as if he is in a marathon. He wanted to attain the finish line without quitting. Paul was not making a point about eternal security in his wording; rather, he was announcing his dramatic and full commitment to persevere in the footrace of spirituality, never giving up until the finish line, where Jesus stands ready with a crown.

FORGET THE PAST AND REACH TO THE GOAL / 3:12–4:1

Paul changed from accounting language to athletic language, saying that his goal was to know Christ, to be like Christ, and to be all Christ had in mind for him. This goal absorbed all Paul's energy. This provides a helpful example. We should not let anything take our eyes off our goal—knowing Christ. With the single-mindedness of an athlete in training, we must lay aside everything harmful and forsake anything that may distract us from being effective Christians. What is holding you back?

3:12 **Not that I have already obtained all this, or have already been made perfect, but I press on to take hold of that for which Christ Jesus took hold of me.**^{NIV} *Obtain* can mean to take hold of, to receive, to make one's own, to apprehend in the moral or spiritual sense. So Paul may have been saying that he had not fully grasped all the meaning of Christ in his life. There is more to receive by pressing on. The power of Christ in Paul's life aroused him to want to know Christ better, and this would take a lifetime.

TRAINING FOR THE CHRISTIAN LIFE

Just as a great amount of training is needed for athletic activities, so we must train diligently for the Christian life. Such training takes time, dedication, energy, continued practice, and vision. We must all commit ourselves to the Christian life, but we must first know the rules as prescribed in God's Word (2 Timothy 2:5).

Reference	Metaphors	Training	Our Goal As Believers
1 Corinthians 9:24-27	Race	Go into strict training in order to get the prize.	We train ourselves to run the race of life. So we keep our eyes on Christ—the goal—and don't get sidetracked or slowed down. When we do this, we will win a reward in Christ's kingdom.
Philippians 3:13-14	Race	Focus all your energies toward winning the race.	Living the Christian life demands all of our energy. We can forget the past and strain for the goal because we know that Christ promises eternity with him at the race's end.
1 Timothy 4:7-10	Exercise	Spiritual exercise will help you grow in faith and character.	As we must repeat exercises to tone our bodies, so we must steadily repeat spiritual exercises to be spiritually fit—like Bible study, self-discipline, and Christian service. When we do this, we will be better Christians, living in accordance with God's will. Such a life will attract others to Christ and pay dividends in this present life and the next.
2 Timothy 4:7-8	Fight/Race	Fight the good fight and persevere to the end.	The Christian life is a fight against evil forces from without (Philippians 3:18) and temptation from within. If we stay true to God through it all, he promises an end, a rest, and a crown.

Paul saw the Christian life as a process. While believers are considered righteous when they accept salvation, their entire lives are marked by growth toward Christlikeness. Complete perfection will not be obtained until Christ's second coming, when he will take his people with him. While Paul may have seemed like a nearly perfect Christian to his Philippian friends, he emphasized that he had not obtained perfect knowledge of Christ, the power of his resurrection, the fellowship of his suffering, and conformity to his death (3:10). All of these were part of the process of sanctification—of getting to know Christ better and better as he lived the Christian life. And even Paul, despite all his sufferings and victories for Christ, still had much to learn. He had not yet *been made perfect.* He knew that only upon Christ's return would all believers be made perfect in knowledge and experience, but he was willing to *press on to take hold of* the goal—living and working for Christ—because of what Christ had done for him. "Pressing on" is a hunting term meaning to chase or hunt down. Christ Jesus *took hold of* Paul almost thirty years earlier when Paul was converted on the road to Damascus. Christ laid hold of Paul so that Paul could lay hold of the prize—knowing Christ completely.

PERSONAL RELATIONSHIP
True Christian faith is often called a "personal relationship" with Jesus Christ, and no verse describes it better than this. A relationship requires two persons, each actively searching, seeking, and building a bond between them.

In your spiritual life, God takes the initiative (Christ takes hold of us), then we enter into it (pressing on) to pursue all that our new friendship offers. We are truly relating to each other, together pursuing God's goal for all creation—eternal life free of all pain, all death, all sin. Are you pressing on, taking responsibility for your progress in faith and character? What steps are you taking to know Christ better?

3:13 Beloved, I do not consider that I have made it my own; but this one thing I do: forgetting what lies behind and straining forward to what lies ahead.[NRSV] Paul had not yet attained perfection or complete knowledge of Christ. Unlike the Judaizers, Paul did not consider that he had achieved spiritual maturity; he was not perfect, but he lived in absolute confidence of his ultimate salvation. Christians know they will be saved, yet they must have perfection as their goal (Matthew 5:48) while not pretending that sin does not exist (1 John 1:8). Like Paul, they should not dwell on the past. The past should not be used as a barrier to the future, as an excuse for dropping out, or for avoiding proper spiritual conduct in their relationship with God. Believers should be devoted to God whatever their present circumstances (Luke 9:62; 17:31-32) and should strain forward to what lies ahead. Paul would forget his past with all its credentials and accomplishments (and sins) and, like a runner in a race with his whole body reaching for the finish line, would press on toward the goal (3:14).

LET IT GO
We have all done things for which we are ashamed, and we live in the tension of what we have been and what we want to be. Because our hope is in Christ, however, we can let go of past guilt and look forward to what God will help us become. Don't dwell on your past. Instead, grow in the knowledge of God by concentrating on your relationship with him *now*. Realize that you are forgiven, and then move on to a life of faith and obedience. Look forward to a fuller and more meaningful life because of your hope in Christ.

3:14 I press on toward the goal for the prize of the heavenly call of God in Christ Jesus.NRSV As a runner straining every effort toward the finish line, Paul pressed on *toward the goal*. In Greek athletic games, the winner's prize was a garland or palm branch. While Paul didn't identify *the prize,* it seems from his writing above that the prize refers to gaining full knowledge of Jesus Christ (see also 1 Corinthians 9:24; 2 Timothy 4:7-8). Paul aimed to win the prize, but all who finish the race win it as well. The full knowledge of Christ is the final prize for which believers gladly lay aside all else.

Scholars have presented several views for the meaning of the *heavenly call,* also translated "called me heavenward" (NIV) or the "upward call" (NASB). The Greek words *ano kleseos* literally mean "high or upward calling."

- Some scholars regard it as the rapture of the church, the call to God's eternal presence. The NIV "called me heavenward" could support this view. However, *kleseos* is not normally used for the rapture of the church.

- Other scholars have seen it to mean the call to be saved. First Thessalonians 2:12 says, "Live lives worthy of God, who calls you into his kingdom and glory" (NIV). God's call on the apostle occurred on the road to Damascus. Paul answered that call and had been in the race ever since. Every believer, not just Paul, receives this call of God to salvation (1 Corinthians 1:26; 7:20; Ephesians 1:18; 2 Thessalonians 1:11; 2 Timothy 1:9). God summons the person out of a life of sinful rebellion upward into a life of fellowship with himself based on what Christ Jesus has done.

- Still other scholars connect it to the high purpose or high vocation of Paul as apostle. Hebrews 3:1 says, "Therefore, holy brothers, who share in the heavenly calling, fix your thoughts on Jesus, the apostle and high priest whom we confess" (NIV). This view, as well as the previous one, equates the nature of the prize with the substance of the calling, making "of the calling" equal to "the prize."

- Yet because of Paul's use of the metaphor of athletic games, it seems more natural to understand the "call" as the calling of athletes up to the winner's stand. Thus, the heavenly call is the summons to win the victor's prize of salvation.

LONG-DISTANCE RUNNING
Like a dedicated athlete, Paul wanted to run the race and gain full knowledge of Christ. The first-time marathon runner has periodic thoughts about quitting, especially during the last six miles. By then, the novelty of the experience has faded to the dull regularity of the pace; early adrenaline has given way to soreness and fatigue. Others around him or her are limping along, and some have dropped out entirely.
   But dedicated runners must keep going. Somewhere out there is a finish line. Ask yourself these questions:
- What kind of race are you running for Christ?
- What prize do you seek?
- What kind of opposition do you face in your struggle to live as a Christian?
- How can Christ help you stay on track and reach the goal?
- What spiritual workout or training this week will help you run your Christian marathon?
- In what way can you renew your commitment to press on toward the goal of being like Christ?

3:15 All of us who are mature should take such a view of things.NIV After Paul described his spiritual goals, he explained to the Philippians that all mature believers should *take such a view.* That is, they too ought to be pressing on toward the goal. Mature believers would understand that they could not, in their own humanity, gain perfection and acceptance by God (as opposed to the teachings of the Judaizers). Yet because of their love for Christ, they willingly pressed on to follow his example in order to become more like him in life, all the while knowing that they were promised to know him fully upon their death (or his return).

And if on some point you think differently, that too God will make clear to you.NIV This verse betrays some of the problems that faced the Philippian church. Spiritual pride had found its

way into some of the believers; apparently a few felt that they
had reached a holier status than their fellow believers, causing
them to look down on those whom they thought less "mature."
Yet Paul made clear that those who were truly mature were those
who realized their dependence on God. They pressed on, not to
make themselves good enough or to gain credentials by their
accomplishments; rather, they pressed on to know their Savior
better. Whatever problem of pride threatened to divide the Philippian church, Paul stopped it. This was the final word on the matter; Paul invoked the illumination of God himself to clarify the
truth of his words to those who thought differently. Those who
were mature were to be committed to what Paul had said. And to
anyone who thought differently about minor points, God would
clarify the truth. God would lead them to the truth if they would
keep their minds open.

A PERFECT SCORE?
Sometimes trying to live a perfect Christian life can be so difficult that it leaves us drained and discouraged. We may feel so
far from perfect that we can never please God with our lives.
Paul used "perfect" (3:12) to mean mature or complete, not
flawless in every detail. Those who are mature should press on
in the Holy Spirit's power, knowing that Christ will reveal and fill
in any discrepancy between what we are and what we should
be. Christ's provision is no excuse for lagging devotion, but it
provides relief and assurance for those who feel driven.

3:16 Only let us live up to what we have already attained.^{NIV} Christian maturity involves acting on the guidance that we have
already received. *Live up (stochein)* is a military term meaning
"to keep in line" or "to keep step." Paul knew the believers were
in different stages, but everyone needed to be faithful to what
they understood. The Christian community needed to march forward together. Paul did not want the believers in Philippi to fail
to live up to what they already had been taught. As they pressed
on toward the goal, they should not use their lack of complete
knowledge as an excuse for taking lightly what they knew or for
getting sidetracked. They should continue to learn and grow,
while at the same time govern their lives by the light they had
already received. Believers must live up to what they already
know before they can expect to learn more.

**3:17 Brothers and sisters, join in imitating me, and observe those
who live according to the example you have in us.**^{NRSV} Paul
used these two key words for discipleship: "imitate" and "exam-

ple." "Imitate" means not only to become like but also to obey.
"Example" means a model or blueprint to use as a pattern for
your life. Paul challenged the Philippians to pursue Christlikeness by *imitating* Paul's own example and the examples of others
whose lives were based on his (those "mature" believers in 3:15).
This was not egotism on Paul's part, for Paul always focused on
Jesus Christ and urged the believers to also follow the example of
others who followed Christ. They should not follow false teachers or the enemies of the cross (3:18). Instead, as Paul focused his
life on being like Christ, so should they. Paul wrote to the Corinthians, "Follow my example, as I follow the example of Christ"
(1 Corinthians 11:1 NIV). The Gospels may not yet have been in
circulation, so Paul could not tell them to read the Bible to see
what Christ was like. Therefore, he urged them to imitate him as
a practical guide for conduct. That Paul could tell people to follow his example is a testimony to his character. Can you do the
same? What kind of follower would a new Christian become if
he or she imitated you?

LIVING UP OR DROPPING OUT
William James Sidis was a well-known child prodigy who taught
university mathematics at age 16, but his adult years were
spent collecting and memorizing streetcar schedules. He died
alone in a ragged apartment, destitute and broken. His rare talents only briefly helped anyone.
   As Christians, we must be responsible to use what we have
been given. We must guard against dropping out—quitting—
and squandering talents. We must not worry about all that we
don't know. We've got plenty to do using what we have.

3:18 **For many live as enemies of the cross of Christ; I have often
told you of them, and now I tell you even with tears.**NRSV The
reason for Paul's admonition to follow his example was to turn
the believers away from following the bad examples of the false
teachers, the Judaizers, and any others who claimed to be believers but refused to live up to Christ's model of servanthood and
self-sacrifice. All of these people satisfied their own desires
before even thinking about the needs of others. All of them
focused on their own attainments, thus making them *enemies of
the cross of Christ*. Believers cannot count on personal achievement and at the same time accept Christ's sacrifice on the cross.
Either Christ's sacrifice was all-sufficient and we can do nothing
more, or Christ's sacrifice wasn't enough and we have to keep on
trying to obey God's laws in order to be made acceptable to him.

Such attempts to nullify Christ's sacrifice saddened Paul greatly. Paul had warned the Philippians about false teachings, and he continued to do so with tears.

The "enemies of the cross" were probably Judaizers—those Jewish Christians who were overly zealous for their law. But some scholars think Paul was referring to another false teaching that had surfaced, called "antinomianism." Those who subscribed to this teaching believed that once their souls had been redeemed by Christ, what they did in their bodies no longer mattered. Thus they threw aside morality and decency, believing that nothing done in the body could stain their already-redeemed souls. Paul may have been combating such teaching in Philippi; however, because there is no mention of two heresies in chapter 4, Paul was most likely targeting the Judaizers.

3:19 Their destiny is destruction.NIV Four characteristics were true of these "enemies of the cross" (3:18). If Judaizers were in view, Paul was explaining that because they refused to accept Christ's sacrifice on their behalf, they could not be saved. Their only alternative was *destruction*—eternal separation from God. "You who are trying to be justified by law have been alienated from Christ; you have fallen away from grace" (Galatians 5:4 NIV). Any false teachers, whether or not they believed they'd been saved, would find their destiny to be different than they had hoped.

(2) Their god is their stomach,NIV meaning they worshiped those temporal elements that satisfy only physical desires. Focusing on the Judaizers, Paul may have been pointing out their absorption with the various food laws. Attempting to keep the laws of distinction between clean and unclean food occupied all their time, causing them to focus only on their stomachs. If Paul were attacking antinomianism, he was pointing out their gluttony and unrestrained fulfilling of physical desires (Romans 16:18; 1 Corinthians 6:13; Jude 11).

(3) Their glory is in their shame.NIV Several meanings are possible for this phrase. Paul may have meant that these false teachers were heaping praise on themselves instead of on God. They gloried in themselves, when they should have been ashamed so that they could turn to God for salvation. If the Judaizers and their teaching about circumcision was again in mind, Paul may have been referring to them glorying in the fact of their being circumcised. Instead of bringing honor, circumcision would bring shame because they were trusting in it for salvation. If antinomianism was in view, Paul may have been speaking of sensuality and carnality in general (see Hosea 4:7).

(4) Their mind is on earthly things.^{NIV} Paul was referring to the Judaizers' dependence on credentials, accomplishments, law-keeping, etc., for salvation. If he had been attacking the antinomians, he would stand against their belief that once saved, people could do whatever they desired. Such an attitude will draw people's focus away from Christ to earthly pleasures. Paul wrote to the believers in Colosse, who faced false teaching, "Set your minds on things above, not on earthly things" (Colossians 3:2 NIV).

PRIORITIES
Paul gets tough with mere earthlings here: people who live to appease their appetites, who believe so strongly in their greatness that they become slaves to pride.

What horrible people these must be, so concerned with earthly trivia that even at worship their minds wander to dinner arrangements and weekly appointments. So consumed with work that worship is inconvenient. So busy planning the next party that prayer gets pushed aside once again. Paul wants none of these people in the church.

Are we in danger of being enemies of the Cross? Is too much of our time spent on efforts that will not endure in eternity, seeking earthly pleasures, satisfying our physical desires? We must set our minds on knowing Christ, not on pursuing the things of this world.

3:20 But our citizenship is in heaven.^{NIV} While the false teachers had their minds on earthly matters (3:19), believers ought to be yearning for their home. Paul's speaking of *citizenship* struck a chord with the Philippians. Philippi was a Roman colony; those who lived in Philippi had their citizenship in far-off Rome, although most of the Philippians had never been there. Roman citizenship was highly prized during Paul's time. The Christians in Philippi, as proud as they had been of their Roman citizenship (Acts 16:20-21), should have valued even more highly their citizenship in heaven. They lived on earth as a colony of believers who were citizens of another kingdom. They should have thought of themselves as "resident aliens" living temporarily in a foreign country with their home elsewhere. One day they would experience all the special privileges of their heavenly citizenship because they belonged to Christ.

And it is from there that we are expecting a Savior, the Lord Jesus Christ.^{NRSV} Jesus returned to heaven in a cloud after his resurrection. "This same Jesus . . . will come back in the same way you have seen him go into heaven" (Acts 1:11 NIV). Thus believers are expecting the Savior to return from heaven to earth

THREE STAGES OF PERFECTION
All phases of perfection are grounded in faith in Christ and what he has done, not what we can do for him. We cannot perfect ourselves; only God can work in and through us to "carry it on to completion until the day of Christ Jesus" (1:6 NIV).

1. Perfect Relationship	We are perfect because of our eternal union with the infinitely perfect Christ. When we become his children, we are declared "not guilty" and thus righteous because of what Christ, God's beloved son, has done for us. This perfection is absolute and unchangeable, and it is this perfect relationship that guarantees that we will one day be "completely perfect." See Colossians 2:8-10; Hebrews 10:8-14.
2. Perfect Progress	We can grow and mature spiritually as we continue to trust Christ, learn more about him, draw closer to him, and obey him. Our progress is changeable (in contrast to our relationship) because it depends on our daily walk—at times in life we mature more than at other times. But we are growing toward perfection if we "press on" (3:12). These good works do not perfect us; rather, as God perfects us, we do good works for him. See 3:1-15.
3. Completely Perfect	When Christ returns to take us into his eternal kingdom, we will be glorified and made completely perfect. See 3:20-21

at his second coming. Paul had absolutely no doubt about Christ's return—although neither he nor anyone else knew or knows when that will happen. But believers are expecting and awaiting his return, when he will "appear a second time, not to deal with sin, but to save those who are eagerly waiting for him" (Hebrews 9:28 NRSV).

CITIZENS OF HEAVEN
Citizens of a Roman colony were expected to promote the interests of Rome and maintain the dignity of the city. In the same way, citizens of heaven ought to promote heaven's interests on earth and lead lives worthy of heavenly citizenship. Too many Christians have failed to transfer their citizenship to heaven. They still seek earthly pleasures and treasures instead of heavenly ones. Paul told the Colossians to set their hearts on the things above, where Christ is (Colossians 3:1-4). Where are your loyalties placed?

Paul very rarely used the word *Savior* for Jesus Christ in his letters. This may have been because of the frequent secular use of the word to apply to the Caesars. Yet Paul probably used the term here in order to purposely set the Lord Jesus Christ up against the Caesars. While on earth, believers were citizens of their country (the Philippians were citizens of Rome itself and thus under Caesar's rule), yet absolute loyalty was to the one and only true Savior, the Lord Jesus Christ, who rules in heaven, where all believers hold their ultimate citizenship.

Paul also used the word to describe Christ's coming on behalf of those facing persecution and hardship. He would come as Savior, vindicating his people and delivering them from their oppressors.

3:21 Who, by the power that enables him to bring everything under his control, will transform our lowly bodies so that they will be like his glorious body.[NIV] When Christ returns, he will *bring everything under his control.* There will be no more sin, no more evil rulers, no more persecution of believers. Christ will be King of kings and Lord of lords, ruler over all (Revelation 19:11-16; 21:22-27; see also Psalm 8:6; 1 Corinthians 15:24-28; Hebrews 2:8-9). It also means that Christ will place all our prized possessions "under his control." It is far better for us to relinquish them now than to have them taken from us later. With that same power, he will transform all believers' earthly bodies into new bodies. The phrase *lowly bodies* refers not to the human body as being inherently evil; rather, Paul was speaking of the present state of humiliation and weakness caused by sin, making the body vulnerable to disease, temptation, and death. In contrast, the bodies we will receive when Christ returns will be *glorious,* like Christ's resurrected body. Our identities will not change, but our

THE GREATEST HOPE
Most people living today with cancer know that their time is limited. Their minds say, "I control my body," but they know a voracious disease is eating it away. For them, the glorious body Paul describes offers a wonderful hope.

Other diseases—MS, Alzheimers, AIDS—wear away until a healthy person weakens and dies. For all afflicted, this verse points to hope.

The aged, blind, and mentally impaired may live without another day of full health. For them, Paul promised Jesus' power to control and transform in its fullness when he returns. No believer need give in to despair. Each of us must trust Christ to renew our bodies when we live with him in eternity.

bodies will be *like* Jesus' glorified body. This won't be an external resemblance, but we will share his nature and life (3:10). We
will be made alive to God (Romans 6:10-11), brothers and sisters
of the firstborn Son, Jesus (Romans 8:29). While the transformation of our souls takes a lifetime of "pressing on," the transformation of our bodies will be instantaneous at Christ's return. God
will perform this wonderful transformation by the same power
that brings everything in creation under Christ's control.

For a more detailed discussion of our new bodies, see 1 Corinthians 15:35-55 and 2 Corinthians 5:1-10.

**4:1 Therefore, my brothers and sisters, whom I love and long for,
my joy and crown, stand firm in the Lord in this way, my
beloved.**^{NRSV} Because of these amazing and certain promises,
therefore the believers in Philippi ought to *stand firm in the Lord*
against false teaching or divisiveness from within and persecution from without. "Stand firm" was used at the beginning of
Paul's first exhortations (1:27; see also Mark 13:13; Hebrews
3:6). Paul underscored once again his love for this congregation
in calling them *brothers and sisters, my joy and crown,* and *my
beloved,* and repeating how he loved and longed for them (see
1:7-8). This congregation was dear to his heart. His words to
them were of vital importance, for he cared about their very
souls. How he longed to see them again; but during this time of
his imprisonment, the yearning words of his letter, carried to
them by a mutual friend, would have to suffice. That Paul would
refer to the Philippians as his "crown" could mean that they
would be his "reward," a wreath of victory, and a seal of his apostleship (1 Corinthians 9:2), proof that his labor had not been in
vain (2:16).

TAKE A STAND
Standing firm in the Lord means steadfastly resisting the negative influences of temptation, false teaching, or persecution. To
stand firm requires perseverance when we are challenged or
opposed. Don't lose heart or give up. God promises to give us
strength of character. With the Holy Spirit's help and with the
help of fellow believers, we can stand firm in the Lord.

Philippians 4:2-23

In 4:1, Paul had urged the Philippian believers to "stand firm" in the Lord. In order to stand firm against false teaching, divisiveness, and persecution, the believers needed to (1) live in harmony with one another, (2) rejoice on all occasions because of their faith in Christ, (3) develop the quality of gentleness in their dealings inside and outside the church, and (4) allow the peace of God to guard their hearts and minds. When believers develop these attitudes in their lives, they can stand firm for God.

4:2 I plead with Euodia and I plead with Syntyche to agree with each other in the Lord.NIV Paul not only warned the Philippian church of doctrinal errors (3:1–4:1), he also addressed some relational problems. Two women, *Euodia* (Euodias in some translations) and *Syntyche* had been workers for Christ in the church, perhaps deacons. Their broken relationship was no small matter: Many had become believers through their efforts (see 4:3), but their quarrel was causing dissension in the church (hence Paul's plea for unity in 2:1-4). We do not know the reason for the disagreement, but Paul pled with them to set aside their differences and *agree with each other in the Lord*. The Greek phrase *to auto phronein* is also translated, "to have the same mind." This same phrase is in 2:2, and Paul may have had these two women in mind when he wrote chapter 2. Apparently the cause of their quarrel was known to Paul, and if one of them had been in error, Paul would certainly have corrected it. It seems that the quarrel was more than merely personal, yet no sin or error was involved; thus Paul did not feel that he needed to handle it. He expected them to work it out themselves and "agree . . . in the Lord." This could mean that they would have to agree to disagree about the matter and set aside their quarrel and personal interests in order to focus with the "same mind" on the good of the church. Or it could mean that they were to completely resolve the matter by coming to some sort of agreement. In any case, the unity of the church was to be their highest concern.

DEAL WITH IT
In any group of people—from churches to bowling leagues—offenses will occur and pride will get hurt. The difference between churches and other groups is that pride should not control a situation. Christians should be eager to forgive, forget, and go on.

Many Christians lack the humility or the motivation to deal with hurts and slights in the proper way. Grudges go on for years, gossip makes mountains of anthills, and hard feelings become like pillars—just part of the architecture.

No one in the church should be expected to agree with everyone else on every issue facing the group, except one, the most important: Jesus is Lord. Around that wonderful common keynote, the harmonies of a thousand different voices sing.

If you hold a grudge against someone in the church, settle it today. Find common ground in Jesus. Make reconciliation and get your Christian service back to full strength.

4:3 Yes, and I ask you, loyal yokefellow.[NIV] The identity of this *loyal yokefellow* remains a mystery. The reference may have been obvious to the Philippian believers, but it is now hidden from us. It is also possible that "loyal yokefellow" in the Greek is a play on a proper name. Paul may have been referring to someone named Syzygus, using a pun on the man's name to ask him to live up to it and work "beside" Paul (as two oxen in a yoke pull the plow together) in helping reconcile Euodia and Syntyche. (Paul used a similar play on words in his letter to Philemon where he played off of the meaning of Onesimus's name, "useful," as he described how "useful" Onesimus had been to him. See Philemon 11.)

If no play on words was intended, scholars have suggested several possibilities for the identity of this "yokefellow": Epaphroditus (the bearer of this letter), Timothy, Silas, Luke (because of his close relationship with the church), an elder in the church at Philippi, or a comrade of Paul in prison (thus the "yokefellow" reference, although this seems unlikely because he could do nothing more than Paul at their distance from Philippi).

Whoever this "yokefellow" was, Paul knew that he could count on this man to help these women work out their disagreement so they could once again fellowship with one another and be good examples in the church.

> Be of humble mind, laying aside all haughtiness, and pride, and foolishness, and angry feelings . . . being especially mindful of the words of the Lord Jesus which He spake, teaching us meekness and long-suffering. *Clement of Rome*

IN THE MIDDLE
Most people would do anything to avoid stepping into the
middle of a personal squabble. Yet some disputes and mis-
understandings require a sympathetic third party, a good lis-
tener, an honest evaluator.

Minister or layman, this person must hear both sides and
attempt to find a solution best for both parties. Part of Christian
service is negotiation, conflict resolution, and peacemaking.
Those who do it well serve a vital need.

If you're facing a conflict you can't resolve, don't let the tension build into an explosion. Don't withdraw or resort to cruel
power plays. Don't stand idly by and wait for the dispute to
resolve itself. Seek the help of those known for peacemaking.

**Help these women who have contended at my side in the
cause of the gospel, along with Clement and the rest of my fellow workers, whose names are in the book of life.**[NIV] Euodia
and Syntyche had worked beside Paul in the spread of the gospel.
In many of the churches Paul visited, men were the key players,
but women played a key role in founding the churches of Macedonia (see Acts 16:14, 40; 17:4, 12). *Contended* is also translated
"labored," and means to struggle against opposition, to strive, to
work earnestly. These women had gotten involved beyond the
comfort level for the sake of spreading the Good News. Sometimes those who work hard to tell others about Christ find it easy
to argue with fellow workers. At Philippi, women were the first
to hear the gospel, and Lydia was the first convert. Those who
were among the first to understand the gospel would be asked to
teach. Thus Euodia and Syntyche were to take an active part in
teaching. Their quarrel was highly visible and threatened to disrupt the unity of the church. This intermediary was asked to help.
The Philippians were to help reconcile these two women. Scripture is clear that Christians should carefully and tactfully help to
resolve relational problems:

- "My friends, if anyone is detected in a transgression, you who
  have received the Spirit should restore such a one in a spirit of
  gentleness" (Galatians 6:1 NRSV).

- "But exhort one another every day, as long as it is called
  'today,' so that none of you may be hardened by the deceitful-
  ness of sin" (Hebrews 3:13 NRSV).

- "Anyone, then, who knows the right thing to do and fails to do
  it, commits sin" (James 4:17 NRSV).

The mention of the women's help in *the cause of the gospel* reminded Paul of *Clement* and other *fellow workers* who had also labored along with Paul.

Some scholars have thought that this Clement might be the very same Clement of Rome who had been a convert and disciple of both Peter and Paul. After the two apostles were martyred in Rome, he became a bishop of the church there. While not much is known about Clement, his writings give insight. He wrote to the church in Corinth trying to help them with problems, much as Paul had done. Tradition says he was martyred about A.D. 100. Other scholars, however, who say that any attempt to make the bishop the same Clement is pure conjecture because Clement was a common Roman name.

While the names of the rest of the fellow workers are not listed, we can be sure that each person's name is *in the book of life*. The names of all believers are registered in "God's book." In the Old Testament this referred to a register of God's covenant people (see Exodus 32:32-33; Psalm 69:28; 139:16). The "book" symbolizes God's knowledge of who belongs to him. Ancient cities had roll books that contained the names of all who had a right to citizenship. Believers are on God's register, and he will admit all on the roll into heaven (3:20). All believers are guaranteed a listing in the Book of Life and will be introduced to the hosts of heaven as belonging to Christ (see Luke 10:17-20; 12:8-9; Hebrews 12:22-23; Revelation 3:5; 20:11-15). No believer will be forgotten, for the names are listed for eternity.

BOOK OF LIFE
Some churches believe this book to be an actual ledger, a "Rolodex" of the saints. Other churches regard the reference as symbolic of God's knowing each believer as an individual. Whatever the nature of the book, it suggests that good deeds done on earth in the name of Jesus are not forgotten. Prizes and trophies may not fill your house, but quiet deeds of mercy have their reward in heaven. God has made a note of it.

4:4 Rejoice in the Lord always. Again I will say, rejoice![NKJV] After writing to a few members of the church in 4:2-3 to correct disunity, Paul returned to writing to the church at large: *Rejoice . . . rejoice!* It seems strange that a man in prison would be telling a church to keep on rejoicing. But Paul's attitude teaches us an important lesson: Our inner attitudes do not have to reflect our outward circumstances. Paul was full of joy because he knew that no matter what happened to him, Jesus Christ was with him. Paul faced false teachers, severe people problems, and threat of death,

yet several times in this letter, he urged the Philippians to be joyful, probably because they needed to hear this (see the chart on
page 82). It's easy to get discouraged about unpleasant circumstances or to take unimportant events too seriously. While believers often will encounter situations in which they cannot be happy,
they can *always* rejoice and delight *in the Lord*. Paul did not call
believers to an empty, put-on show of happiness, for Christians
should not be insensitive to the sorrow of others; he called for
genuine joy, which is possible only "in the Lord." It is only
through a believer's relationship with God that he or she finds joy
in pain, suffering, persecution, and sorrow.

4:5 Let your gentleness be known to everyone.[NRSV] Paul encouraged
the Philippians to be joyful, but joy isn't always visible to others.
Yet acts toward others are readily seen. So Paul encouraged the
Philippians to let their *gentleness* be seen by *everyone*—especially
those outside the church. The Greek word for gentleness, *epieikes*
(also translated "moderation"), is a difficult word to translate in
order to capture the full meaning. Words such as forbearance,
leniency, magnanimity come close but don't quite have it. *Epieikes*
refers to a spirit that is reasonable, fair-minded, and charitable. It
describes someone willing to yield his or her own rights to show
consideration and gentleness to others. We may find it easy to be
gentle with some people, but Paul commanded gentleness toward
everyone. Paul used the same word in 2 Corinthians 10:1, where he
spoke of the "meekness and gentleness of Christ" (NIV). Jesus
never sacrificed truth in order to be gentle, but he always had a gentle spirit that often disarmed those set against him.

APPROPRIATE FORCE
Like all virtues, gentleness must be applied relative to each situation. If your child is attacked by a maniac with a knife, forcefully disarming the maniac without going berserk yourself may
be the essence of gentleness. Using that same amount of force
to shake hands after church would not be considered gentle at
all.

Gentleness, then, requires the use of appropriate force to
achieve God's will in a situation, with a preference for under-
playing the force or leniency. Where normally you might use
intimidation or power, try straightforward, honest conversation.
Where you might swing a mighty club, hold back and seek a
reasonable response.

A gentle person (not merely a weak-willed or passive one)
tells people that God controls the world and we need not worry.
We can take a hit without retaliating, and be forceful without cru-
elty or vengefulness.

The Lord is near.NRSV Believers are motivated to joy and gentleness by remembering that their Lord is near. This "nearness" refers not to his presence in their hearts, but rather to the "nearness" of the Second Coming. The promise of the Lord's second coming encourages careful conduct by his followers. The apostle James wrote, "You too, be patient and stand firm, because the Lord's coming is near. Don't grumble against each other, brothers, or you will be judged. The Judge is standing at the door!" (James 5:8-9 NIV). Harsh and inconsiderate treatment of others would be taking into one's own hands judgment that belongs only to Christ (1 Corinthians 4:5). Paul always had an eager awareness of and watchfulness for the second coming of his Lord. It was never far from Paul's thoughts and motivated everything he did. It should be so for all believers.

4:6 Do not worry about anything.NRSV Attitudes of joy and gentleness, combined with constant awareness of Christ's return, should dispel any worry. For the Philippians, these were certainly encouraging words as they faced foes and needed to stand firm in the faith (see 1:27-28; 3:1; 4:1). Believers should not set aside life's responsibilities so as not to worry about them; Paul was focusing on believers' attitudes in daily life and as they faced opposition and persecution. (See Jesus' words to Martha in Luke 10:41.) Christians are to be responsible for their needs and their families and to care about and be concerned for others, but they are *not* to worry, fret, or have undue concern. In Matthew 6:25-34, Jesus said not to worry about your life, what you eat or drink, your body, adding time to your life, or what will happen tomorrow. Despite what was happening around them, the Philippians did not need to worry about anything because God held them securely.

> Like anybody, I would like to live a long life. Longevity has its place. But I'm not concerned about that now. I just want to do God's will. And He's allowed me to go up to the mountain. I've looked over, and I've seen the promised land. I may not get there with you, but . . . I'm happy tonight. I'm not worried about anything. I'm not fearing any man. *Martin Luther King, Jr., from an address given the night before he died*

Worrying is bad because it is a subtle form of distrust in God. When believers worry, they are saying that they don't trust that God will provide and they doubt that he cares or that he can handle their situation. It leads to a helpless, hopeless feeling that causes them to be paralyzed. But Paul offered prayer as an antidote to worry.

But in everything, by prayer and petition, with thanksgiving, present your requests to God.^{NIV} Prayer combats worry by allowing us catharsis. We can offload our stress onto God. Paul said to take all the energy that is used in worrying and put it into prayer. This includes praying about *everything*. No request is too small, difficult, or inconsequential to God. Paul encouraged the believers to pray in everything—good times and bad—giving petitions and thanksgivings to God. It may seem impossible not to worry about anything, but Paul explained that this can happen if believers truly give their worries to God. Worry and prayer cannot coexist.

The word for *prayer* is a general term meaning worshipful conversation with God, while *petition* refers to a prayer with a sense of need (the Greek word was also used for requests between people). These two words often appear together in Paul's writings. *Thanksgiving* focuses on the attitude of one's heart in approaching God. Prayer combats worry by creating in us a thankful heart. Believers should come to God in prayer, thankful for the opportunity to even approach him, for his tremendous blessings already bestowed, and for the certainty that he will answer his children. When believers focus on God's great love for them and the many prayers he has already answered, they will have no room for worry about whether he will continue to answer. *Requests* refers to directly asking God's help regarding specific needs. Prayer combats worry by building trust.

Paul was speaking to believers when he wrote these words. Prayer, an audience with God himself, is an awesome privilege available to those who have accepted Christ Jesus as Lord. Does God want us to talk to him? Yes. Paul admonished the Thessalonians to "pray continually" (1 Thessalonians 5:17 NIV). Communication with God through prayer allows us to know him better and to know his will and guidance for our lives. Can we talk to God about anything? Yes. While he already knows about our needs and feelings, our sharing these with him builds our relationship. It allows us to rely on God as we sort through decisions or need encouragement in the middle of trials. It allows us to give God alone the praise when his answers come. Presenting our needs to him does not guarantee that God will say yes to every prayer. Jesus prayed that the cup might be taken from him, but it wasn't; Paul prayed that the thorn in the flesh might be removed, but God chose to work through Paul despite his problem. In prayer we are to present our requests to God, but we must focus on God's will, not ours. When we communicate with God, we don't demand what we want; rather, we discuss with him what *he* wants for us.

If we align our prayers to his will, he will listen; and we can be certain that if he listens, he will give us a definite answer.

STOP AND PRAY
Imagine never worrying about anything! That seems like an impossibility—everyone has worries on the job, at home, or at school. But Paul's advice is to turn our worries into prayers. Do you want to worry less? Then pray more! Whenever you start to worry, stop and pray.

4:7 And the peace of God, which surpasses all understanding, will guard your hearts and minds through Christ Jesus.NKJV
If the Philippians would take to heart Paul's words in 4:4-6, then they will turn from anxiety to prayer and be filled with *the peace of God*. This peace is different from the world's peace. It is peace that Jesus promised his disciples and all those who would follow him: "Peace I leave with you; my peace I give you. I do not give to you as the world gives. Do not let your hearts be troubled and do not be afraid" (John 14:27 NIV). True peace is not found in positive thinking, in absence of conflict, or in good feelings; it comes from knowing that God is in control. Believers are given peace *with* God when they believe (Romans 5:1), and they have the inner quiet of the peace *of* God as they daily walk with him.

God's peace *surpasses all understanding*. We simply cannot comprehend such peace. It is not a natural reaction in calamity, sorrow, or pain. Such peace cannot be self-generated; it comes from God alone; it is his gift to us in a difficult world. As with so much of God's dealings with humanity, we cannot understand it, but we can accept and experience God's peace because of his great love for us.

Why does God give his people peace? Because it will *guard* their hearts and minds. The Greek word for "guard" is a military term that means to surround and protect a garrison or city. The Philippians, living in a garrison town, were familiar with the Roman guards who maintained watch, guarding the city from any outside attack. God's peace is like soldiers surrounding believers' hearts and minds (that is, emotions and thoughts), securing them against threatening and harmful outside forces. Peter used the same word when he wrote that "through faith [believers] are shielded by God's power until the coming of the salvation that is ready to be revealed in the last time" (1 Peter 1:5 NIV).

PEACE
Some realities cannot be fully conveyed by dictionary defini-
tion—the peace of God, for instance. We could read books
about it, but somehow never totally understand it. Paul knew
the shortcomings of words to describe God's peace, so he just
admitted that it transcends our human knowledge.

How do you find this peace? First, it is found only in Jesus
Christ. Trust him as your Savior and Lord. Second, God's
peace is attained only by practice. Trust Jesus daily in the small
worries of your life so that you're ready to trust him when big
problems strike. Tell him your needs and anxieties. Third, you
can have peace only through prayer and meditation on God's
promises. Have you discovered God's Word? Have you prayed
through the promises? There is no better time to start than
today. And there is no smarter way to invest the first moments
of your morning.

When we trust God, he gives us peace in a traffic jam, peace
in a phone call, peace in a relationship, and peace when death
draws near.

4:8 Finally, beloved.^{NRSV} Paul again called these Philippian believers
beloved (see 1:12; 2:12; 3:13; 4:1), indicating his love for them.

With the word *finally,* Paul may have been indicating that he
was about to conclude this section of his letter. Or he may have
been using the word in the sense of "it follows then" that if one is
to have this inner peace from God and maintain a life free of
worry, then certain steps must be taken, notably in his or her
thoughts. The following list ends with the words **think about
such things.**^{NIV} Paul knew that a person's thoughts determine
who that person is, his or her attitudes, and how he or she acts
toward others. What do you spend time thinking about? With
what do you fill your mind?

Lists of vices and virtues were common in the Stoic religions
of Paul's day. Paul used lists in other letters (see for example
Romans 1:29-31 and Galatians 5:19-23). This list describes what
should pervade believers' thoughts.

Whatever is true.^{NRSV} First, believers should think about what is
true (alethe). The word "true" has many meanings. Truth
includes facts and statements that are (1) in accordance with reality (not lies, rumors, or embellishments); (2) sincere (not deceit-
ful or with evil motives); and (3) loyal, faithful, proper, reliable,
and genuine. Truth is a characteristic of God (Romans 3:4).

Whatever is noble.^{NIV} Believers should think about what is *noble*
(or "honorable" NRSV; the Greek word is *semnos*). These matters

are worthy of respect, dignified, and exalted in character or excellence. (See also 1 Timothy 3:8, 11; Titus 2:2.)

Whatever is right.^{NIV} Thoughts and plans that are *right* (or "just" NRSV; the Greek word is *dikaios*) meet God's standards of rightness. They are in keeping with the truth; they are righteous.

Whatever is pure.^{NRSV} *Pure (hagnos)* means free from contamination or blemish; these thoughts are unmixed and unmodified; they are wholesome. Paul probably was speaking of moral purity, often very difficult to maintain in thoughts.

Whatever is lovely.^{NIV} The Greek word for *lovely (prosphiles)* is used only here in the New Testament. Paul was referring to thoughts of great moral and spiritual beauty, not of evil. The NRSV translates the word as "pleasing." However, because the sinful human nature can perversely find evil to be "pleasing," the word "lovely" or "beautiful" is preferable.

Whatever is commendable.^{NRSV} The Greek word *euphemos* is also translated "admirable" in NIV. It refers to things that speak well of the thinker—thoughts that recommend, give confidence in, afford approval or praise, reveal positive and constructive thinking. A believer's thoughts, if heard by others, should be commendable, not condemnatory.

If there is any virtue.^{NKJV} *Virtue* was prominent in Greek rhetoric and Roman philosophy, but is found only once in Paul's letters and three times in Peter's (1 Peter 2:9; 2 Peter 1:3, 5). Evidently Paul brought "virtue" up here to counter the false teachers by using a term with which his audience would be familiar. This small word incorporates all moral excellence (hence the NIV translation of this word as "excellent"). In this way Paul summed up what could have been a lengthy list of the qualities that should describe a believer's thought life.

GARBAGE IN, GARBAGE OUT
What we put into our minds determines what comes out in our words and actions. Paul tells us to program our minds with thoughts that are true, noble, right, pure, lovely, commendable, virtuous, and praiseworthy. Do you have problems with impure thoughts and daydreams? Examine what you are putting into your mind through television, books, music, conversations, movies, and magazines. Replace harmful input with wholesome material. Above all, read God's Word and pray. Ask God to help you focus your mind on what is good and pure. It takes practice, but it can be done.

And if there is anything praiseworthy.^{NKJV} This phrase may be restated as "anything that deserves the thinker's praise" or "anything that God deems praiseworthy." For believers, who are developing a mind like Christ's, these two should be one and the same.

4:9 Keep on doing the things that you have learned and received and heard and seen in me, and the God of peace will be with you.^{NRSV} Paul did not sit in prison telling everyone what to do; he had lived out and was continuing to live out his words, so he could urge the believers to follow his example (see also 3:17). If they did not understand how to guide their lives as Paul had suggested in 4:4-8, then they could see it in action in someone they knew well—Paul himself. All they had to do was remember what they had *learned* from him (from his teaching and training) and *received* (in the form of tradition and biblical standards of behavior). The Scriptures were not compiled into a Bible until later, so the standards of belief and behavior were embodied in the teachings and example of those in authority—especially the apostles, but also other leaders in the churches. The Philippians should also remember what they had *heard* with their own ears and *seen* with their own eyes of Paul's conduct and life. Paul could speak confidently; people could follow his example because he was following Christ's example (1 Corinthians 11:1).

If the believers would *keep on doing* or practicing the virtues that Paul cited above, they would experience *the God of peace*. God is the source of peace for all believers. Paul thought so much of this attribute of God that he often used the name "God of peace" as a benediction to his epistles (see, for example, Romans 15:33; 16:20; 2 Corinthians 13:11). This passage is closely linked to 4:7, "the peace of God." Many people today seek to have the peace of God without having to deal with God, who is the author of true peace. But that can't be done. To know peace, we must know God.

HOW EASY, HOW HARD
It's not enough to hear or read the Word of God, or even to know it well. We must also put it into practice. It is easy to listen to a sermon and forget what the preacher said. It is easy to read the Bible and not think about how to live differently. It is easy to debate what a passage means and not live out that meaning. Exposure to God's Word is not enough. It must lead to obedience.

PAUL IS GRATEFUL FOR THEIR GIFT / 4:10-20

Although Paul had already thanked the Philippians for their partnership with him in spreading the gospel (1:5), in this section he
specifically thanked them for their monetary gift. Paul never
asked any of the churches to support him, yet the believers in
Philippi had sincerely wanted to give, so Paul accepted. As he
thanked them, Paul also encouraged them to remember that
whether they had abundance or little, they could be content
because of God's sufficiency. When we stop trusting in ourselves
and start trusting instead in God's limitless resources, we are
truly set free to serve him.

4:10 **I rejoice in the Lord greatly that now at last you have revived
your concern for me; indeed, you were concerned for me, but
had no opportunity to show it.**[NRSV] Next, Paul turned his attention to one of the main reasons for writing this letter—to thank
the Philippian church for their gift to him. Epaphroditus had been
sent to Rome from Philippi with a generous financial gift for
Paul, and it had come during a time of need. Paul's words *at last
you have revived* sound harsh, but that harshness is absent in
Greek. The second phrase explains that the church had constantly
been concerned for Paul, but had *had no opportunity to show it.*
Whatever the reason for that lack of opportunity, Paul rejoiced
not only at the gift and God's wondrous provision for his needs
but also for the church who cared so much about him, had not forgotten him, and had at last been able to show their concern for
him with the arrival of Epaphroditus.

REVIVING CONCERN
Paul was glad that the Philippians had revived their interest in
supporting him. If your interest in a missionary has waned and
you'd like to revive it, here are some suggestions:
- Ask her about her work. Don't wait for the quarterly letter to
  arrive. Take the initiative.
- Send a birthday card. Everyone in the family should sign it,
  and before it gets mailed, pray together for your missionary.
- Send a gift. It doesn't need to be big. Tell him it's just a little
  extra from a friend.

Though Paul never asked for money for himself, he accepted
the Philippians' gift because they gave it willingly and because
he was in need. In 1 Corinthians 9:11-18, Paul wrote that he
didn't accept gifts from the Corinthian church because he didn't
want to be accused of preaching only to get money. But Paul

maintained that it was a church's responsibility to support God's ministers (1 Corinthians 9:14).

4:11 Not that I am referring to being in need; for I have learned to be content with whatever I have.^{NRSV} At this point, Paul took pains to make sure that his words were not misunderstood. The fact that the Philippians had not sent help sooner did not mean that Paul had been disappointed in them or that he had been put in desperate straits at that time. Instead, he had learned an important

> Wealth is a good servant, a very bad mistress.
> *Francis Bacon*

secret to the Christian life—that he could be content with whatever he had, despite his outward circumstances. Paul had to *learn* this because contentment is not a natural human response. The word *content* in Greek means "self-sufficient" and independent of others. Paul used this term to indicate his independence, if need be, of everything *but* Christ, since Christ was the sole source of Paul's life (1:21; 4:13). This contrasted with the Stoic philosophy that used the word "content" to describe a person who impassively accepted whatever came. A Stoic view fostered self-sufficiency to the point that all the resources for coping with life came from within humans themselves. Paul explained that his sufficiency was in Christ alone, who provides strength to cope with all circumstances.

HIS POINT OF VIEW
Paul was content because he could see life from God's point of view. He focused on what he was supposed to *do*, not what he felt he should *have*. Paul had his priorities straight, and he was grateful for everything God had given him. Paul had detached himself from the nonessentials so that he could concentrate on the eternal. Often the desire for more or better possessions is really a longing to fill an empty place in one's life. To what are you drawn when you feel empty inside? How can you find true contentment? The answer lies in your perspective, your priorities, and your source of power.

How do we get to that lofty goal of contentment? It is important for believers to realize that biblical "contentment" is not fatalism or acquiescence to one's lot in life. Such thinking would smother God's ongoing guidance. Rather, contentment involves one's perspective on life. Believers know that "we fix our eyes not on what is seen, but on what is unseen. For what is seen is temporary, but what is unseen is eternal" (2 Corinthians 4:18 NIV).

To have real contentment:

- Remember that everything belongs to God. What we have is a gift from him.

- Be thankful for what we have, not coveting what others have.

- Ask for wisdom to use wisely what we do have.

- Pray for grace to let go of the desire for what we don't have.

- Trust in God to meet our needs.

For more on contentment, see 1 Timothy 6:6-10.

CONTENTMENT
Poverty is a tragedy, but everyone needs to be penniless at some point during young adulthood. People who have nothing begin to see wonders in simple pleasure, to savor simple food, and to enjoy simple diversions. Poverty brings the "rat race" to a halt and teaches the value of relationships. Prayer becomes more important and voice mail less so.
   Francis of Assisi, the great thirteenth-century monk, taught his followers never to own anything in order to be content in Christ alone. We are less severe today about our possessions. But contentment means that we *need* none of them and that we regard them all as God's gift, never God's substitute.

4:12 I know what it is to have little, and I know what it is to have plenty.^{NRSV} The following verses give a bit of Paul's personal testimony. Paul knew what it was like to have very little—to "be abased" (NKJV). The Greek word is the same root word used to describe Jesus humbling himself in 2:8. The picture is of Paul voluntarily accepting a low status, even a life of poverty, for his Master's sake (see also 1 Corinthians 4:11-13; 2 Corinthians 6:4-10). Although he taught that the churches should support their leaders, Paul himself did not demand salaries from the churches that he had planted. This kept him above criticism (see 2 Corinthians 11:7). Thus with travel and food costs, Paul probably had very little to live on.

In the Greek, the opposite of having little is having *plenty*. Literally, the meaning of the Greek word *perisseuein* is "to overflow." This might refer to Paul's pre-Christian days as a fairly wealthy and influential Pharisee.

Whether Paul had plenty or little, he could keep life on an even keel because of contentment. What an important lesson for all believers to learn! No wonder Paul called it a "secret" (below).

In any and all circumstances I have learned the secret of being well-fed and of going hungry, of having plenty and of

being in need.^{NRSV} The Greek words for *learned the secret* are used only here in the New Testament. It was an expression used in the pagan mystery cults to describe initiations of new members. Initiations were rarely easy, and Paul used the word to describe his initiation by his experiences into living a victorious Christian life. Paul's initiation was filled with joys as well as difficulties, *being well-fed and . . . going hungry*—having plenty sometimes and being needy at other times (see discussion on 1:1). (For a more complete testimony of Paul's life as an apostle of Jesus Christ, read 2 Corinthians 11:21-33.)

ALWAYS WANTING MORE
Are you content in any circumstances you face? Paul knew how to be content whether he had plenty or whether he was in need. The secret meant drawing on Christ's power for strength. Do you have great needs? Are you discontented because you don't have what you want? Learn to rely on God's promises and Christ's power to help you be content. If you always want more, ask God to remove that desire and teach you contentment in every circumstance. He will supply all your needs, but in a way that he knows is best for you.

4:13 I can do all things through him who strengthens me.^{NRSV} Paul's contentment was not gained through stoic self-discipline. Instead, it was through Christ alone, literally "the one empowering me" (see 1 Timothy 1:12). In the most reliable manuscripts, Christ's name is not in this verse, but he was surely who Paul had in mind. Paul had already given up all his accomplishments and credentials as he followed Christ (3:7-8); he also realized that he could not live the Christian life on his own. Paul, like every believer, had to depend on Jesus Christ. In context, the *all things* refers to the list in 4:11-12. In every possible circumstance, Paul could truly be content because he did not let outward circumstances determine his attitude. Christ was giving him the strength to continue with his ministry and the work of spreading the gospel whether he had plenty or was in need. Paul had complete confidence that, no matter what the circumstance, Christ would give him the strength to meet it. Thanks to his enabler, Paul had a "can do" attitude.

This verse can be divided into two halves. The first half is, "I can do all things" ("everything"). To stop there and pull the words out of context would imply the idea of self-reliance, cocky self-assuredness. That's the kind of message we often hear from motivational speakers: "You can do anything you want if you put your mind to it." But that's not what the verse says. The last half reveals the source of our strength: Christ. God wants us to accomplish much for him in this world, but only through Christ. Instead of trusting our own strength and abilities, we must rely on Christ and his power.

Paul's confident words can be spoken by every Christian. The power we receive in union with Christ is sufficient to do his will and to face the challenges that arise from our commitment to doing it. God does not grant us superhuman ability nor every resource to accomplish anything we can imagine without regard to his interests. As we contend for the faith, we will face troubles, pressures, and trials. But we do not need to worry about being given more than we can handle; Christ will supply resources sufficient to complete what he asks us to do.

WHAT DOES HE WANT?
Does this verse promise that Christians can do anything they want? No. What God promises is that we can do everything he wants us to do. At times we may wonder if God is expecting too much. How can we possibly heal that relationship, break that sinful habit, tell that neighbor about Christ, or give our tithes to the church? But God promises to give us the strength to do what he asks. What does God want you to do? Step out in faith and do it, trusting him for the strength.

4:14 Yet it was good of you to share in my troubles.^{NIV} The Philippians shared in Paul's financial support while he was in prison, thus communicating their sympathy with him. The sense of this phrase, lost in the English translation, is a closeness between the apostle and the Philippian believers. That they had shared in his troubles refers to having fellowship in them, identifying with the apostle on behalf of his work for the gospel.

IN AND THROUGH
The world expects strong people to win athletic contests, intellectually brilliant people to win scholastic competitions, and powerful people to win tests of will. We don't expect much from the weak and humble. But God's ways are not the ways of the world—his values turn the world's values upside down. God loves to use the small, weak, and insignificant people to accomplish his purposes. Paul wrote the Corinthians that he delighted in his weaknesses because God would be glorified through them—when Paul was weak, then he would be strong (2 Corinthians 12:10). Whenever you feel small and insignificant, remember that God wants to reveal his strength in and through you.

**4:15 You Philippians indeed know that in the early days of the gos-
pel, when I left Macedonia, no church shared with me in the
matter of giving and receiving, except you alone.**^{NRSV} The *early
days* refers to Paul's initial visit to Philippi when the Christian
church began (recorded in Acts 16; see also Philippians 1:5). The
"sharing" the Philippians had done with Paul refers to their partnership with him, revealed in the practical expression of financial support (see 4:10). Only the Philippian church had been ready to give
to Paul's ministry—to send financial gifts from their church to Paul
while he was ministering in other churches. Although Paul ministered in other cities and planted other churches, only the Philippians had shared in *giving and receiving* with Paul. From Paul the
church received spiritual blessings; from the church, Paul received
material blessings. (The same usage of "giving and receiving" is
found in Romans 15:27 and 1 Corinthians 9:11.)

The phrase *when I left Macedonia* could be read, "when I set
out from Macedonia." This could mean that at the time of Paul's
departure from Macedonia, after his first visit to Philippi, no
other churches shared financial gifts with him. It seems that other
churches did support Paul's ministry later (see 2 Corinthians
11:8), but that the Philippians had been especially attentive and
generous, sending gifts not only while Paul was in Thessalonica
(4:16), but later when he was in Corinth (2 Corinthians 11:9).
However, Paul refused to accept gifts from the Corinthian church
because he felt that asking for support in Corinth might be misunderstood. There were many false teachers who were hoping to
make a good profit from preaching (2 Corinthians 2:17), and Paul
wanted to separate himself completely from them. The Philippians might have "known" this because no one arrived to bring
Paul any financial support during his visit with them.

SHARING
What makes money so magnetic and giving it away so stress-
ful? Money measures our energy; it represents our day-to-day
security. Giving money away puts our work and our future at
risk.
    Not every charity deserves your attention, and you're wise to
scrutinize missionary appeals as well. But once you've determined that a project honors the Lord, don't hold back—give
generously and joyfully. Like the Philippians, you'll be establishing an eternal partnership.

**4:16 For even when I was in Thessalonica, you sent me help for my
needs more than once.**^{NRSV} During his second missionary journey,

after Paul left Philippi, his next stop was Thessalonica (see Acts 17:1). The word *even* highlights Paul's gratitude for the Philippians' show of support so soon after he had left them. While Paul was *in Thessalonica,* the Philippians had sent help for his financial needs. The phrase *more than once* means simply that—with no exact number of times. There is also the possibility that this sentence could mean that when Paul was at Thessalonica, and more than once while he was in other places (such as Corinth, see 4:15), the Philippians had sent help. Paul's stay in Thessalonica (recorded in Acts 17:1-9) seems to have been quite short so that more than one visit from Philippi would have been unlikely.

4:17 Not that I am looking for a gift, but I am looking for what may be credited to your account.NIV Paul made it clear that his thankfulness for the Philippians' generosity was not a veiled request for more. In fact, he considered that they had made "full payment" as it were (4:18) and need not send anything else.

Instead, Paul focused on what their good works on his behalf were benefiting them in heaven. The NKJV translates this phrase, "the fruit that abounds to your account" and the NRSV says "the profit that accumulates to your account." The financial language showed the Philippians that their gifts to Paul were investments that paid dividends or accumulated interest (or "profit") that would be *credited* to their heavenly *account.* When we give to those in need, we benefit as well as the receiver, as we grow in the grace of giving (2 Corinthians 8:1, 6-7; 9:14). Paul appreciated the Philippians' spirit of love and devotion more than their gifts. God would remember their gifts to Paul. The writer to the Hebrews explained, "God is not unjust; he will not forget your work and the love you have shown him as you have helped his people and continue to help them" (Hebrews 6:10 NIV). God would reward the Philippian believers for their kind and generous support of his apostle.

4:18 I have received full payment and even more; I am amply supplied, now that I have received from Epaphroditus the gifts you sent.NIV Paul thanked the Philippians for their generous gift by describing it as *full payment and even more.* In the Greek, the word "received" was used for drawing up a receipt in a business transaction. This was Paul's acknowledgement that he had received the Philippians' most recent gift and that Epaphroditus had faithfully fulfilled his mission (see 2:25). Paul told the Philippians that this was payment in full. No more money would be required; their generous gift was more than enough. Surely the Philippian church rejoiced that they had been able to meet Paul's needs.

TRUE GIVING
Giving gifts involves a strange reciprocity. In giving, we create
bonds of friendship that return a strong benefit to us. In giving
to God's work, we generate value in heaven. Some churches
have exploited the latter point where giving is pictured almost
as a down payment on heavenly real estate. In such a system,
the "gift" becomes no gift at all. Paul did not want giving to be
so tainted with self-interest that the giver had personal benefit
as a primary goal.

True giving diminishes the lure and power of money in our
lives. We need not clutch at wealth, but rightly share it with
people we love and strangers we are coming to love. Regular
giving tells God that he is first and that nothing we possess is
more important than him.

**They are a fragrant offering, an acceptable sacrifice, pleasing
to God.**ᴺᴵⱽ Paul described the Philippians' gift as a *fragrant offering*. Paul was referring to the burnt offering, a voluntary offering
given for payment of sins and showing a person's devotion to
God (Genesis 8:20-21; Exodus 29:18; Leviticus 1:9, 13; Ezekiel
20:41). Although the Greek and Roman Christians were not Jews
and had not offered sacrifices according to the Old Testament
laws, they were well acquainted with the pagan sacrificial rituals
(see 2 Corinthians 2:14-16). Paul referred to Christ as a fragrant
offering to God (Ephesians 5:2).

Acceptable sacrifice meant that their very gifts were acts of
worship, and God was the true recipient. The Philippians' gift
had not only helped Paul and added to their heavenly "account"
(4:17), it was, perhaps most importantly, an act of worship, *pleasing to God*. They had given in faith, not so much to Paul as to
God. That should be the ultimate goal of every act of love, care,
concern, and charity—to help, but also to please God (see
2 Corinthians 5:9; Hebrews 13:16).

**4:19 And my God shall supply all your need according to His
riches in glory by Christ Jesus.**ᴺᴷᴶⱽ As the Philippians had met
Paul's needs, so God would meet theirs. The Philippian church
was not wealthy. In fact, when Paul spoke of the Philippians' generosity [referred to as "the Macedonian churches"] in giving to
the impoverished church in Jerusalem, he said:

■ *We want you to know about the grace that God has given the
Macedonian churches. Out of the most severe trial, their overflowing joy and their extreme poverty welled up in rich generosity. For I testify that they gave as much as they were able, and*

> *even beyond their ability. Entirely on their own, they urgently*
> *pleaded with us for the privilege of sharing in this service to*
> *the saints. (2 Corinthians 8:1-4* NIV*)*

There is no human need that God is unable to meet—in fact,
he meets the needs far better than anything on this earth. Paul
was assured by Christ that Christ's grace was sufficient for every
need (2 Corinthians 12:9). Yet he often sends "vertical" help
through people helping one another on the "horizontal" level.
God had met Paul's need through the
generosity of the Philippian church.
God would more than repay that generosity by supplying the need of the Philippian church. Not only would God

> Cast all your cares on
> God; that anchor holds.
> *Alfred, Lord Tennyson*

supply all their needs, but he would do it *according to His riches
in glory by Christ Jesus* (or "his glorious riches"). Believers cannot begin to comprehend God's riches in glory—his riches are
limitless, infinite. If it is from that storehouse that believers'
needs are met, then the Philippian believers could rest assured
that God would indeed meet every need, no matter how large,
desperate, or hopeless it seemed.

This could happen *by Christ Jesus.* That is, because of believers' relationship with Christ, they have access to God and can
"come boldly to the throne of grace [and] obtain mercy and find
grace to help in time of need" (Hebrews 4:16 NKJV).

GOD WILL SUPPLY
We can trust that God will always meet our needs. Whatever
we need on earth, God will always supply, even if it is the courage to face death. We must remember, however, the difference
between wants and needs. Most people want to feel good and
avoid discomfort or pain. We may not get all that we want, but
God will provide what we need. By trusting in Christ, our
attitudes and appetites can change from wanting everything to
accepting his provision and power to live for him.

**4:20 Now to our God and Father be glory forever and ever.
Amen.**NKJV God the Father was both Paul's God and the Philippians' God—and he is also our God. God who supplied Paul's
needs and met the Philippians' needs is the same yesterday, today,
and forever, and he promises to meet our needs. To *our God*
belongs all *glory forever.* Paul broke into a doxology of praise as
he remembered God's great love and provision. God alone
deserves all glory from his creation. *Amen,* so be it.

PAUL'S FINAL GREETINGS / 4:21-23

Paul closed his letter by sending greetings from Rome and the
Christians there to the believers in Philippi. The gospel had
spread to all strata of society, linking people who had no other
bond but Christ. The Roman Christians and the Philippian Christians were brothers and sisters because of their unity in Christ.
Believers today are also linked to others across cultural, economic, and social barriers. All believers are brothers and sisters
in Christ.

**4:21 Greet every saint in Christ Jesus. The friends who are with
me greet you.**NRSV Paul sent his personal greetings to every
believer in the Philippian church; he probably knew each by
name. In addition, the *friends* with Paul in Rome (his coworkers,
such as Timothy) also sent their greetings to the Philippians. In
his letters, Paul often would send greetings from one church to
another.

**4:22 All the saints send you greetings, especially those who belong
to Caesar's household.**NIV Paul expanded his message to include
a greeting from *all the saints*—that is, all the believers in the
Roman church, some of whom are probably listed in Romans
16:1-15.

The mention of *those who belong to Caesar's household* offers
an interesting sidelight. There were many Christians in Rome;
some were even in Caesar's household. This probably did not
refer to Emperor Nero's family or members of his court, but
rather to Christians in civil service (perhaps some soldiers—especially those who guarded Paul!) or on the imperial staff as slaves
or servants. Because Philippi was a Roman colony, there may
have been a link between some on the imperial staff in Rome and
those in some civil capacity in Philippi. Paul rejoiced because the
gospel had infiltrated even into the emperor's household.

**4:23 The grace of the Lord Jesus Christ be with your spirit.
Amen.**NIV This letter to the Philippians begins and ends with
grace (see 1:2). Paul had experienced God's undeserved favor,
and he never tired of praying that others would also experience
that grace.

In many ways the Philippian church was a model congregation. It was made up of many different kinds of people who were
learning to work together. Paul recognized, however, that problems could arise, so in this thank-you letter, he prepared the Philippians for potential difficulties they might encounter. Though a
prisoner in Rome, Paul had learned the true secret of joy and

peace—imitating Christ and serving others. By focusing our minds on Christ we will learn unity, humility, joy, and peace. We will also be motivated to live for him. We can live confidently for God because we have *the grace of the Lord Jesus Christ.*

COLOSSIANS

INTRODUCTION TO COLOSSIANS

The human brain is amazing. God has created us with the ability to think, react, reason, consider, meditate, learn, imagine, understand, philosophize, know, perceive, evaluate, theorize, reflect, predict, and communicate. Enamored with the incredible power of our minds, however, we can become complacent in our wisdom, proud of our mental abilities, and reliant on ourselves.

To be complimented as "smart," "a genius," or "very intelligent" feels great. Beyond this, to have special knowledge feels even better. We like to be seen as experts and sought out, as though we have a secret formula or inside information.

The philosophical system of Gnosticism emphasized the mind and taught that salvation could be obtained through knowledge *(gnosis)* instead of faith. This "knowledge" was esoteric and could only be acquired by those who had been initiated into the mysteries of the Gnostic system, not by study or the normal process of learning. With a strong appeal to human pride (who wouldn't want to be on the "inside," the recipient and owner of secrets and mysteries?), Gnosticism distorted Christian theology and twisted biblical truths in order to support its concepts. Perhaps the most foundational of these false teachings was that matter is inherently evil and only the spiritual or nonmaterial is good. This led to denying the doctrines of Creation and the Incarnation ("How could God take on an 'evil' body?"), elevating the role of angels, and reducing Christianity to just one of many religions (Gnostism sought to combine the "best" of all religions).

A kind of proto-Gnosticism was gaining popularity in Colosse; it was a combination of Gnostic concepts and Judaism. Full-fledged Gnosticism did not appear until the second century. In any event, Paul wrote to refute the error and to get the believers back on track. To do so, Paul highlighted the preeminence of Christ and the importance of godly living.

As you read Paul's letter to the Colossian believers, use your God-given mind to evaluate your own belief system. Is it based on God's Word and centered on Christ? Or do you rely on human philosophy and your ability to think?

AUTHOR

Paul (See the introduction to this volume.)

Colossians begins: "Paul, an apostle of Christ Jesus by the will of God, and Timothy our brother, To the holy and faithful brothers in Christ at Colosse: Grace and peace to you from God our Father" (1:1-2 NIV), thus identifying both the sender and receiver of this letter. This opening line also mentions Timothy, but in the rest of the epistle Paul often uses the first person ("I"—1:24-25, 29; "me"—4:7; etc.). As with Philippians, Paul's authorship was affirmed by the early church fathers and has not been seriously disputed through the centuries.

One of the strongest arguments for Paul as the author of Colossians is this letter's relation to Philemon. Both letters, sent to the same city, probably by the same messenger, contain many of the same names: Paul, Timothy, Onesimus, Archippus, Epaphras, Mark, Aristarchus, Demas, and Luke.

The similarity of Colossians to Ephesians has caused some to propose that Colossians may have been written by someone else (copying Ephesians and using Paul's name on Colossians or vice versa). But similarities should be expected when two letters are written at the same time but sent to different churches in different locations.

Consider the following comparison of Colossians and Ephesians. Some similarities include:

- Both were to be read aloud in the churches (Colossians 4:16). Ephesians may be the letter from Laodicea (4:16).

- The letters are very similar in style.

- Both letters were delivered by the same messenger—Tychicus (Ephesians 6:21-22; Colossians 4:7-8).

- The letters contain some of the same expressions: "your faith in Jesus Christ and your love for all the saints" (Ephesians 1:15 and Colossians 1:4 NIV); "in whom we have redemption, the forgiveness of sins" (Ephesians 1:7 and Colossians 1:14 NIV).

- The letters have similar features: the prayers (Ephesians 1:15-23 and Colossians 1:9-14); references to unity in the body of Christ (Ephesians 4:1-16 and Colossians 3:12-17); instructions for households (Ephesians 5:22–6:9 and Colossians 3:18–4:1).

Differences include:

- Ephesians is substantially longer than Colossians (six chapters to four).

- The central theme of Ephesians is the church (body) of Christ, while the theme of Colossians is Christ as head of the church.

- Ephesians has no hint of the controversy (proto-Gnostic heresy) that is dominant in Colossians.

SETTING

Written from a Roman prison in approximately A.D. 60. (See the introduction to Philippians.)

Colossians was written in the same year as Ephesians and Philemon. According to the reference in 4:3 to being in chains, in 4:10 to fellow prisoner Aristarchus, and in 4:18 to his chains, clearly Paul was in prison when he wrote this letter. Evidently Epaphras, who was visiting Paul or was imprisoned with him (Philemon 23), told him of the problems in Colosse (1:7).

AUDIENCE

The believers in Colosse

Colosse lay about one hundred miles east of Ephesus, in the Lycus River valley in Phrygia, a district of Asia Minor (Turkey) that had been incorporated into the Roman province of Asia in the second century B.C. Located on the great east-west trade route linking the Aegean Sea and the Euphrates River, Colosse thrived as a center of commerce. At one point the city also may have been a military base. Colosse was known for the distinctive, glossy, deep purple wool from the sheep that grazed in the surrounding hills. By the time of Paul's missionary journeys, the trade route had changed, placing Colosse off the beaten path. Thus Colosse had been surpassed in power and importance by Laodicea and Hierapolis (see 4:13), neighboring towns in the Lycus Valley. Colosse was further reduced by an earthquake at about the same time this letter was written.

The population of Colosse was diverse, including native Phrygians, Greek settlers, and Jews descended from Jewish families who had fled to the area during the persecutions of Antiochus the Great (223-187 B.C.).

Although Paul had traveled through Phrygia on his second and third missionary journeys (Acts 16:6; 18:23) and had lived for three years in Ephesus (Acts 19:1–20:1), it seems that he had never visited

Colosse (see 1:9; 2:1-5). Yet Paul considered Colosse, as well as Laodicea and Hierapolis, to be in his area of responsibility, probably because the churches in these cities had been indirectly founded by him during his powerful ministry in Ephesus (see Acts 19:10, 26). Quite possibly both Epaphras and Philemon had been converted to Christ during that time (see Philemon 19, 23).

The church may have been started by Epaphras who had been sent by Paul to preach to the Colossians (1:7). Epaphras probably began the work in Laodicea and Hierapolis as well (see 4:12-13).

The church in Colosse was comprised mainly of Gentiles (including Apphia—Philemon 2). Archippus may have been the church's pastor (4:17). Philemon and his slave Onesimus lived there. In fact, the church met in Philemon's home (Philemon 2). Another group met in Nympha's house (4:15).

OCCASION FOR WRITING

Word had come to Paul of false teaching in Colosse.

Although Paul was a Roman prisoner, his prison was a rented house (Acts 28:16, 30-31). He was allowed to entertain many visitors and to preach and teach. One of Paul's visitors was Epaphras (although he may have been a prisoner as well—Philemon 23). Epaphras reported on the situation in Colosse, including word of false teaching that was threatening the church (1:8; 4:12). Paul wrote quickly to warn the believers of the dangers of this heresy.

Paul also wanted to send a letter to Philemon, along with his runaway slave, Onesimus. He was able to send both letters with Tychicus (4:7-9).

PURPOSE

To encourage the believers in Colosse and to combat errors in the church

Paul had learned from Epaphras that the church at Colosse was threatened by false teaching, partly pagan and partly Jewish (2:8, 16, 18, 20). In fact, it seems to have been a mixture of Jewish and pagan religions.

The Jewish element asserted that true believers had to observe certain days, deny themselves certain foods, and follow certain rituals. The pagan element emphasized self-denial, the worship of angels, and a mystical "wisdom." This probably was an early form of Gnosticism, a complex belief system that would become very prevalent in the second century. Gnosticism emphasized the supremacy of knowledge and that salvation came through knowledge, not by faith. This knowledge was attained through astrology and magic and was available only to those who had been initiated into the Gnostic system. Another Gnostic belief, that all matter is inherently evil and only the spiritual and nonmaterial is of itself good, led to the idea that God could not have created the world and would have no contact with it. Therefore, they taught that God, in Christ, never could have become a human person. If matter is evil, how could God ever be united with a human body? Thus they denied either the humanity or the divinity of Christ (in their view, he couldn't have been both).

The heretical poison in Colosse was a deadly Judaic-Gnostic combination. So Paul wrote to warn the Colossian Christians of these errors of doctrine and practice:

- He warned against ritualism that had strict rules about permissible food and drink, religious festivals (2:16-17), and circumcision (2:11; 3:11).

- He warned against asceticism—the idea that the body is evil and that through self-torture or self-denial a person can attain exalted spirituality (1:22; 2:20-23).

- He warned against relying on human philosophy, knowledge, and tradition (2:4, 8).

- He warned against trying to obtain secret knowledge (2:18; see also 2:2-3).

- He warned against the worship of angels (2:18-19).

- He warned against making Christ any less than the divine Son of God, Lord of the universe, and Head of the church (1:13-20; 2:2-3, 9-10, 17).

Paul recognized that the most dangerous element of this heresy was the deprecation of Christ, so he focused much of his attention on Christ's supremacy. In fact, Colossians is the most Christ-centered book in the Bible.

Today we don't hear much about Gnosticism, but this heresy's false doctrines still abound: secret knowledge, mysticism, human philosophy, and syncretism. In fact, Jesus is seen as just one of many great historical religious leaders, not the unique Son of God and the only way to heaven (John 14:6).

Don't be deceived. These ideas may be popular, but they are wrong. Keep Christ, God's only Son and your Savior, at the center of your life. Follow only him, the God-man, your crucified and risen Lord.

MESSAGE

Christ's Divinity, Christ As Head of the Church, Union with
Christ, Man-Made Religion

Christ's Divinity (1:15-20; 2:2, 9-12). Jesus Christ is God in the
flesh, Lord of all creation, and Lord of the new creation. He is the
expressed reflection of the invisible God. He is eternal, preexistent, omnipotent, and equal with the Father. He is supreme and
complete. In fact, "He is the image of the invisible God" (1:15
NIV), and "in Christ all the fullness of the Deity lives in bodily
form" (2:9 NIV). Jesus is God!

Importance for Today. Because Christ is divine and the Lord of
all creation, our lives must be centered around him. We must
honor him as our God and our Lord; we must not accept any sub-
stitutes, tolerate any additions, or entertain any thoughts of a
diminished role. This means regarding our relationship with him
as most vital and making his interests our top priority.

Is Christ the number one priority, the Commander in chief, the
Lord of your life? Do you honor and worship him as God?

Christ As Head of the Church (1:15-20; 3:15-17, 23-24).
Because Christ is God, he is the head of the church. Christ is the
founder, leader, and highest authority on earth. As such, he
expects his followers to listen to him carefully and obey him completely. Christ requires first place in all of their thoughts and
activities.

Importance for Today. To acknowledge Christ Jesus as our
head, our Lord, we must welcome his leadership in all we do or
think. No Christian individual, group, or church should regard
any loyalty (to family, friends, country, employer, church, or
denomination) more important than loyalty to Christ. Many
voices vie for our attention and loyalty. We can feel pressure
from peers and even from loved ones to think or act contrary to
God's Word. But only Christ should have our total allegiance. We
should obey him regardless of what anyone else thinks or says.
He is our head.

In what ways are your loyalties divided? What can you do to
better acknowledge Christ as your leader?

Union with Christ (1:13, 21-23; 2:6-15, 20; 3:1-4, 11, 15-17).
Because believers' sins have been forgiven and they have been
reconciled to God, they are united with Christ. That union can
never be broken. Being united with Christ means being identified
with his death, burial (2:20), and resurrection (3:1).

Importance for Today. Because we have been united with

Christ, we can have assurance of our salvation. Because we have been united with Christ, we should focus on "things above, not on earthly things" (3:2 NIV). And we should live as those who have been raised with Christ, ridding ourselves of all sinful habits related to life before Christ (3:8-11) and committing ourselves to good works (3:12-17).

Man-Made Religion (2:8, 16-23). False teachers were promoting a heresy that stressed keeping rituals and rules (legalism). They also taught that spiritual growth was attained by discipline of the body (asceticism) and visions (mysticism). Emphasizing human knowledge, they missed God's wisdom; focusing on human philosophy, they didn't understand God; attempting to combine a variety of religious viewpoints, they lost sight of Christ.

Importance for Today. We must not hold on to our own theories and ideas and try to blend them into Christianity. Nor should we allow our hunger for a more fulfilling Christian experience to cause us to trust in a teacher, group, or system of thought more than in Christ and in God's Word.

Don't be swayed or moved away from Christ by smooth-talking teachers, and don't be confused by attractive arguments and sophisticated philosophies. Keep your focus on Christ, and live by God's Word.

VITAL STATISTICS

Purpose: To combat errors in the church and to show that believers have everything they need in Christ

Author: Paul

To whom written: The church at Colosse, a city in Asia Minor, and believers everywhere

Date written: About A.D. 60, during Paul's imprisonment in Rome

Setting: Paul had never visited Colosse—evidently the church had been founded by Epaphras and other converts from Paul's missionary travels. The church, however, had been infiltrated by religious relativism, with some believers attempting to combine elements of Gnostic paganism and secular philosophy with Christian doctrine. Paul confronts these false teachings and affirms the sufficiency of Christ.

Key verses: "For in Christ all the fullness of the Deity lives in bodily form, and you have been given fullness in Christ, who is the head over every power and authority" (2:9-10 NIV).

Key people: Paul, Timothy, Tychicus, Onesimus, Aristarchus, Mark, Epaphras

Key places: Colosse, Laodicea (4:15-16)

Special features: Christ is presented as having absolute supremacy and sole sufficiency. Colossians has similarities to Ephesians, probably because it was written at about the same time, but Colossians has a different emphasis.

OUTLINE OF COLOSSIANS

1. What Christ has done (1:1–2:23)

2. What Christians should do (3:1–4:18)

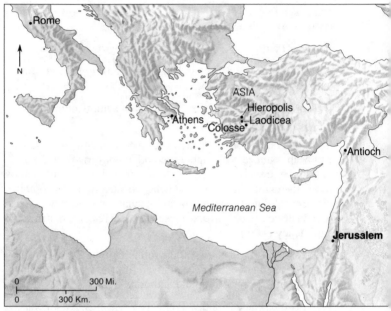

LOCATION OF COLOSSE
Paul had no doubt been through Laodicea on his third missionary
journey, as it lay on the main route to Ephesus, but he had never been to
Colosse. Though a large city with a significant population, Colosse was
smaller and less important than the nearby cities of Laodicea and
Hierapolis.

Colossians 1:1-23

Paul wrote Colossians, along with Philippians, Ephesians, and
Philemon, from prison in Rome. He was allowed to write letters
and to have visitors (Acts 28:16, 30-31). The letter to the Ephesians was sent at the same time as this letter to the Colossians,
carried by the same messenger, Tychicus (see Ephesians 6:21).

1:1 Paul, an apostle of Jesus Christ by the will of God.^{NKJV} As at
the beginning of all of his letters, Paul identified himself by
name. Unlike most personal letters of today, ancient letters often
began with the writer's name instead of adding it at the end. This
was true in Paul's letters to friends (such as 1 and 2 Timothy, and
Titus), letters to church congregations that he knew well (such as
Ephesians and Philippians), and letters to church congregations
whom he had never met (such as Romans and this letter to the
Colossians). Paul's letter to his friends in Philippi was less formal
than others, and he identified himself merely as a servant of
Christ Jesus (Philippians 1:1). But because Paul did not know the
Colossian believers and because he needed to write to them about
some specific doctrinal issues, he identified himself as an *apostle
of Jesus Christ*. Later in this letter he would reinforce that Jesus
is the head of the body, the ultimate authority of the church
(1:18). By contrast, an apostle had authority to teach, lead, and
guide congregations of believers.

Paul was an "apostle" *(apostolos)* meaning "one who is sent."
Because Paul was not one of the original twelve disciples (who
were called apostles after Jesus' resurrection), some doubted his
credentials; yet Jesus had appeared to Paul personally and had
commissioned him (Acts 9:1-6; 26:12-18). Paul did have the
right to claim authority as an apostle.

God had chosen Paul for special work: "He is an instrument
whom I have chosen to bring my name before Gentiles and kings
and before the people of Israel" (Acts 9:15 NRSV). Paul did not
seek this apostleship; instead, he was chosen by God when he
was converted on the road to Damascus. He wrote that he was an

apostle *by the will of God*. Paul's apostleship was not a matter of his own personal aspirations.

And Timothy our brother. Timothy had grown up in Lystra, a city in the province of Galatia. Paul and Barnabas had visited Lystra on Paul's first missionary journey (see Acts 14:8-21). Most likely, Paul had met the young Timothy and his mother, Eunice, and grandmother Lois (see 2 Timothy 1:5) during that visit, perhaps even staying in their home.

On Paul's second missionary journey, he and Silas returned to several cities that Paul had already visited, including Lystra, "where there was a disciple named Timothy, the son of a Jewish woman who was a believer. . . . He was well spoken of by the believers in Lystra and Iconium. Paul wanted Timothy to accompany him" (Acts 16:1-3 NRSV). Timothy probably came to believe in Christ through Paul, for Paul later calls him his true son in the faith (1 Timothy 1:2). Timothy became Paul's assistant and emissary—traveling with him and sometimes for him. Timothy was not imprisoned with Paul, but he stayed in Rome to encourage Paul and to help with ministry needs. Thus, Paul's letter to the church in Colosse includes greetings from Timothy, a *brother* in the faith. Paul and Timothy had traveled together through Phrygia, where Colosse was located (see the map in the introduction). Although neither had visited the church in Colosse, they had, during their earlier travels, met individual Colossians such as Epaphras, Philemon, Archippus, and Apphia who, after their conversion, had returned with the gospel to their native city.

Paul mentions Timothy in other New Testament letters as well: 1 and 2 Corinthians, Philippians, 1 and 2 Thessalonians, and Philemon. Paul also wrote two letters to Timothy (1 and 2 Timothy).

1:2 To the saints and faithful brothers and sisters in Christ in Colossae.[NRSV] The word *saints* was a common term designating believers. It referred to their status because of their relationship with Christ and their separation from the world, not to any attainment of holiness. The word *and* does not signify another group; rather, Paul is saying, "To the saints, that is, the faithful." Paul called the believers in Colosse *faithful* although the contents of the letter could indicate that they were not being very faithful at all. However, Paul often praised the recipients of his letters for what they should be, despite the deficiencies they might have exhibited at the time.

The believers were *in Christ*. Their new identity as Christians made them part of Christ's family; they had found meaning for life in Christ; they had become citizens of heaven (see Philippians 3:20). But they were also *in Colossae* (preferred spelling is "Colosse"). While they had joined a new spiritual kingdom that was separate from the world, they were expected to live out their faith and share the gospel in the physical city of Colosse.

The word order in Greek is "to the in Colosse saints in Christ." The sense of "in Christ" is positional, not mystical. Just as the believers were in the city of Colosse, they were also in Christ. They were placed in both realities to serve as citizens of heaven on site in Colosse. Their position in Christ should not render them so spiritual as to be out of touch with their peers.

TWO PLACES AT ONCE
"You can't be in two places at once" sounds a warning about letting one's schedule become too busy. Yet Paul suggested that Christians at Colosse do just that. They must live both "in Colosse" and "in Christ."

The first refers to a geographic location—a place to farm, raise a family, and conduct business. The second refers to a spiritual location, to be placed in Christ's care and control. This relationship "in Christ" signals the transfer believers took when they came to God for mercy and forgiveness—they migrated from death to life, darkness to light, and the kingdom of this world to the kingdom of God.

How can we be two places at once? As Christians, we must serve God responsibly wherever we live. The Bible calls us stewards and caretakers of this world for God. Christians are also called to grow closer to the Savior, to practice and enjoy our new life as children of God and citizens of heaven. We must have both feet in two worlds.

The city of Colosse was one hundred miles east of Ephesus on the Lycus River, and over one thousand miles from Rome, where Paul was writing this letter. Colosse had early been a stopover along the main road from the east on the way to Ephesus. However, under the Roman Empire, the preferred route was through Laodicea, so Colosse declined in importance although it was still a large and busy city. As a trading center it was a crossroads for ideas and religions. Colosse had become the home of many Jews who had fled there when they were forced out of Jerusalem under the persecutions of Antiochus III and IV, almost two hundred years before Christ. The church in Colosse had been founded by Epaphras (1:7), one of Paul's converts. Although Paul had not yet visited this church, he wanted to write this letter to refute heretical teachings about Christ that were confusing many of the Christians there.

Grace and peace to you from God our Father.NIV Letters in Paul's day frequently began by identifying the writer and the readers, followed by a greeting of peace. Paul usually would add Christian elements to his greetings, reminding his readers of his call by God to spread the gospel, emphasizing that the authority for his words came from God, and giving thanks for God's blessings. *Grace* means God's unmerited favor; *peace* refers to the peace that Christ made between us and God through his death on the cross. In these two words of greeting Paul combined expressions from Jewish and Gentile customs. Jews wished each other "peace" *(eirene* or the Hebrew *shalom); Gentiles* wished each other "grace" *(charis).* Each of these common expressions gained considerable value in Christian use. Christ offers grace in the form of life's great blessings and the ability to handle difficulties; he offers peace that is an inner calm no matter what the outward circumstances.

Only *God our Father* can grant such wonderful gifts. Paul wanted his readers to experience God's grace and peace in their daily living.

PAUL'S PRAYER FOR THE COLOSSIAN BELIEVERS / 1:3-14

Paul made it a habit to pray for the churches—some he had visited, some he had not. He knew that the churches had to withstand difficulties from without and within. Paul wasn't able to go to the churches, and his letters would take weeks to arrive, but he could pray—regularly and persistently—for the strength and growth of the believers. Never underestimate the power of intercessory prayer. Who prays regularly for you? For whom do you regularly pray?

1:3 In our prayers for you we always thank God, the Father of our Lord Jesus Christ.NRSV One characteristic of Paul was his constant prayers for the churches—those he knew well and those he did not. The word *always* could modify thankfulness (as here) or it could modify prayers, referring to Paul always praying for the churches (and specifically the Colossian church) during his regular prayer times (see also 1:9). Some scholars believe that Paul prayed three times each day—morning, noon, and evening. We can picture Paul and Timothy (and others who might have joined with them) regularly kneeling in fervent prayer on behalf of specific congregations and even individual believers who sought to grow in their faith, sometimes in hostile environments. In those prayers, the believers thanked God—Paul explained what they gave thanks for in the following verses.

Paul made his greeting strongly Christian by calling God *the Father of our Lord Jesus Christ*. Right at the start, the readers learned not only of Paul's faith in "God our Father" (1:2) but also about his focus that God is Father of the Lord Jesus Christ. The triple name expresses Jesus' divinity, humanity, and messianic office. He is divine Lord, he is the man Jesus, and he is the Christ (the Messiah).

1:4 **For we have heard of your faith in Christ Jesus and of the love that you have for all the saints.**^{NRSV} Paul had not been to Colosse; he had *heard* of their faith from Epaphras, the probable founder of the Colossian church (1:7). The *faith* was not just any general faith; rather, the Colossians had faith *in Christ Jesus*. These believers had accepted Christ as Savior, and they were living out their faith through their *love . . . for all the saints* ("saints" refers to Christians; see note on 1:2). Their love was not some abstract, self-absorbed, intellectual "love" for God. Instead, it was real love acted out toward real people. "Faith" refers to the vertical component of the Christian life—our trust and reliance on Christ. "Love" refers to the horizontal—our relationships with other believers.

"All the saints" could refer just to the Colossian congregation, but more likely it meant believers in the nearby churches in Laodicea and Hierapolis, as well as believers everywhere.

LOVING ALL THE SAINTS
In any church, you can find a younger couple with a child who cries loudly during the prayer or sermon, or an older couple whose crying takes the form of complaints about how the church lawn is cut or the pulpit flowers arranged. Our reactions to them drive us screaming for the nearest Sunday morning brunch.

For more aggravation, attend a church committee meeting, especially the finance committee, or take up a crusade to make worship services even slightly more relevant. You'll meet adults who could take lessons in getting along from the baboons at your city zoo.

Is it unreasonable for Jesus to ask us to love such people? It can't be done—except that God puts us together and changes hearts. He calls us brothers and sisters. That should make a difference to any church—a difference that sets it apart from all other groups, clubs, and organizations. Jesus wants us to show unconditional and inclusive love for all the congregation.

FAITH, HOPE, AND LOVE

In our days of complex formulas, this simple program for Christian living still holds true. (Verses quoted from NIV. Italics ours.)

Romans 5:1-5	"We have gained access by *faith*. . . . We rejoice in the *hope* of the glory of God. . . . God has poured out his *love* into our hearts."
1 Corinthians 13:13	"And now these three remain: *faith, hope and love*. But the greatest of these is love."
Galatians 5:5-6	"By *faith* we eagerly await through the Spirit the righteousness for which we *hope*. . . . The only thing that counts is faith expressing itself through *love*."
Ephesians 1:15-18	"Ever since I heard about your *faith* . . . and your *love* . . . I have not stopped giving thanks. . . . I pray also that the eyes of your heart may be enlightened in order that you may know the *hope* to which he has called you."
Ephesians 4:2-5	". . . bearing with one another in *love*. . . . You were called to one *hope* . . . one *faith*."
1 Thessalonians 1:3	"We continually remember before our God and Father your work produced by *faith,* your labor prompted by *love,* and your endurance inspired by *hope* in our Lord Jesus Christ."
1 Thessalonians 5:8	"Let us be self-controlled, putting on *faith* and *love* as a breastplate, and the *hope* of salvation as a helmet."
Hebrews 6:10-12	"God is not unjust; he will not forget your work and the *love* you have shown him. . . . We want each of you to show this same diligence to the very end, in order to make your *hope* sure. . . . Imitate those who through *faith* and patience inherit what has been promised."
Hebrews 10:22-24	"Let us draw near to God with a sincere heart in full assurance of *faith*. . . . Let us hold unswervingly to the *hope* we profess. . . . Let us consider how we may spur one another on toward *love* and good deeds."
1 Peter 1:3-8	"Praise be to the God and Father of our Lord Jesus Christ! . . . He has given us new birth into a living *hope* . . . who through *faith* are shielded by God's power until the coming of the salvation. . . . Though you have not seen him, you *love* him."
1 Peter 1:21-22	"Your *faith* and *hope* are in God. . . . Have sincere *love* for your brothers, *love* one another deeply, from the heart."

Only faith in Christ can draw people together in a loving "community"—people who don't know one another, and sometimes people who otherwise might not get along at all. Faith proves its genuineness in its love for others. In an earlier letter to the Galatian believers, Paul had written, "The only thing that counts is faith expressing itself through love" (Galatians 5:6 NIV).

1:5-6 **The faith and love that spring from the hope that is stored up for you in heaven.**NIV Paul knew that the Colossians' faith in Christ Jesus and love for others had a definite source. These were not human-generated emotions; instead, they *spring from the hope that is stored up . . . in heaven*. Why have faith in Jesus Christ if there is no hope for a glorious future? Why love others if it doesn't matter in the end? Why not, instead, find a "faith" that says you can do whatever you want? If we have no hope in heaven, "if being a Christian is of value to us only now in this life, we are the most miserable of creatures" (1 Corinthians 15:19 TLB). Paul, writing from the perspective of a persecuted believer, realized that he would have no reason to face persecution for the sake of his faith if that faith did not anticipate a great hope.

But "hope" makes all the difference. This is not tentative, as when people say, "I hope she'll be at the party." It is confident expectation. As such, it is an inward attitude and an objective reality. Our hope is "stored" in heaven, where Christ returned to be with the Father. That hope will be fulfilled in the future: Paul wrote to Titus that believers must live godly lives "while we wait for the blessed hope—the glorious appearing of our great God and Savior, Jesus Christ" (Titus 2:13 NIV). To Timothy he wrote, "Now there is in store for me the crown of righteousness" (2 Timothy 4:8 NIV). Yet it is also a present reality, a "living hope" (1 Peter 1:3 NIV). We look forward to a hope that is awaiting us; yet we also have that hope within us, enabling us to live our Christian lives with unhindered faith and love. All believers are promised a glorious eternity in heaven with God. We are confident that what we hope for is stored (or "laid up") there, and that we will one day receive it. That confidence, in turn, gives us stronger faith in God and a deeper love for others.

This trilogy of Christian virtues—faith, hope, and love—is used often enough in the New Testament to reveal that it was a major theme for Christianity (see the chart). But it is not some kind of formula. Instead, each word is vitally important in every Christian's life. Faith, hope, and love are tied together like a three-corded braid; one alone cannot signify the Christian life.

A SURE DESTINATION
When Paul says that our hope is stored up in heaven, he is emphasizing the security of the believer. God is in charge of the storehouse. Because we know that our future destination and salvation are sure (1 Peter 1:3-4), we are free to live for Christ and to love others. When you find yourself doubting or wavering in your faith or love, remember your destination—heaven.

Notice that Paul *omitted* "knowledge" in this introduction of virtues. "Knowledge" was added to the Christian trilogy (faith, hope, and love) by a heresy that was gaining ground in Colosse. (A heresy is a teaching that denies one or more essential biblical doctrines.) Paul wrote this letter to the Colossians to combat this heresy that was similar to *Gnosticism,* which was to come later. This heresy is referred to as proto-Gnosticism, an early form of Gnosticism that was combined with the teachings of Judaism. Gnostics believed that it took special knowledge to be accepted by God; for them, even for those who claimed to be Christians, Christ alone was not the way of salvation (see 1:19-20). Like the Gnostics, those subscribing to the heresy in Colosse would add a fourth item: faith, hope, love, and knowledge. (See the chart "The Colossian Heresy" on page 162 for more information.)

In his introductory comments, therefore, Paul commended the Colossians for their faith, love, and hope—three main emphases of Christianity—but he deliberately omitted the word "knowledge" because of the "special knowledge" aspect of the heresy. It is not *what* we know that brings salvation, but *whom* we know. Knowing Christ is knowing God. In 1:9, Paul did pray that they would be filled with the knowledge of God's will, not some speculative or intellectual knowledge *(gnosis)* of the heretics and their false teaching.

BEARING FRUIT
Wherever Paul went, he preached the gospel—to Gentile audiences, to hostile Jewish leaders, and even to his Roman guards. Whenever people believed in the message that Paul spoke, they were changed. God's Word is not just for our information, it is for our transformation! Becoming a Christian means beginning a whole new relationship with God, not just turning over a new leaf or determining to do right. New believers have a changed purpose, direction, attitude, and behavior. They are no longer seeking to serve themselves, but they are bearing fruit for God. How is the gospel reaching others through your life?

You have heard of this hope before in the word of the truth, the gospel that has come to you.^{NRSV} Christ gave this *hope* that is stored up in heaven to the believers in Colosse when they heard and believed *the word of the truth, the gospel.* Paul brought them the "truth" of the gospel as opposed to the heresy of the false teachers. No matter what interesting teaching or ideas they heard, the believers must hold on to the truth as it was taught to them, rejecting anything that contradicted that truth. They could trust Paul's teaching because they could trust the truth of the gospel.

All over the world this gospel is bearing fruit and growing.^{NIV} Paul spoke of the gospel as an entity unto itself—something alive, growing, spreading, bearing fruit, and spreading some more. Paul was not exaggerating when he wrote the words, *all over the world.* He did not mean that every location on earth had been evangelized, but that the gospel was making headway across racial, national, and geographical barriers throughout the Roman Empire. Indeed, nothing could stop it from *bearing fruit and growing.* Like the good seed in Jesus' parable, the gospel "came up, grew and produced a crop, multiplying thirty, sixty, or even a hundred times" (Mark 4:8 NIV).

Before Jesus ascended into heaven, he told his followers, "Go therefore and make disciples of all the nations" (Matthew 28:19 NKJV). The apostles had followed Jesus' command and had spread the gospel beyond the confines of Jerusalem, into Judea and Samaria, but they weren't solely responsible for the gospel's incredible growth. Paul himself had taken the gospel across Macedonia and Achaia, but it had reached Rome before he even got there, and it was in Colosse although he had never visited that city. Many believers took the gospel from where they had heard it back to their homes, where new churches began and flourished. Acts 2:41 gives us the amazing account of three thousand people believing in Christ after Peter's sermon. Many of those people were foreigners who would return to their homelands with this living gospel (Acts 2:9-11). Philip (not the apostle, but one of the members of the church in Jerusalem) spoke in Samaria (Acts 8:4-8), then had the privilege of sharing the gospel with a lone man from Ethiopia who believed and surely returned to share the gospel in his country (Acts 8:26-39).

So it has been bearing fruit among yourselves from the day you heard it and truly comprehended the grace of God.^{NRSV} Not only was the gospel growing and bearing fruit across the known world, it was doing the same right in the city of Colosse.

When Epaphras first brought them the Good News of the gospel (1:7; 4:12-13), the Colossians *truly comprehended the grace of God*. The NIV translates this "understood God's grace in all its truth." Commentators debate whether "truth" refers to the gospel and the full reliability of it, or to grace and our full comprehension of it. It seems most natural to interpret the phrase as the NRSV (above) does.

Here, in short summary, Paul emphasized what makes the Christian gospel so wonderfully helpful to us and so different from every other religion in the world. Through that gospel, God enabled us human beings to understand, with our limited ability, his grace upon us—his unmerited favor to his lowly creation. When we hear that gospel and understand that grace, the truth almost overwhelms us: God has invited us to an eternal banquet that we do not deserve! No wonder the gospel grows and bears fruit all over the world. People who really listen find this invitation irresistible. Of all the world religions, Christianity alone offers salvation without demands for pious works. Followers of Christ set down their load of sin and guilt at the cross and begin a life of pleasing God, who lovingly guides and directs them. Who can resist such an opportunity? Who can say no to such a God? Who would desire something other?

Unfortunately, many do. Satan is very powerful and has led some to believe that they can be saved by being good. Paul knew that for those who hear and understand, the gospel of God's grace is truly Good News. It brings faith, hope, love, security, and a desire to share the incredible news with others.

1:7 You learned it from Epaphras, our dear fellow servant, who is a faithful minister of Christ on our behalf.NIV Paul reminded the Colossians that they had first heard the gospel from one of their own, a native of Colosse (4:12). Epaphras had founded the church at Colosse while Paul was living in Ephesus (Acts 19:10). Epaphras may have been converted in Ephesus and then had returned to Colosse, his hometown.

Paul called Epaphras a *dear fellow servant* and a "fellow prisoner" (Philemon 23). The letter to the Colossians and the personal letter to Philemon were written at about the same time and sent to the same destination (the Colossian church met in Philemon's house). It is unclear from this verse whether Epaphras was actually in prison with Paul, or if Paul's words were metaphors of warfare or "captivity to Christ." It is more likely that Epaphras was with Paul voluntarily and would return to Colosse.

In any case, Epaphras was a *faithful minister of Christ*. Paul's words emphasize Epaphras's trustworthiness. He returned to his hometown to bring the Good News, and he had begun the church. Paul's comment that Epaphras was a minister *on our behalf* was his endorsement of Epaphras's ministry to cities that Paul and the other apostles had not been able to visit. The Colossian believers could trust Epaphras, and they could trust his message. Paul was saying that Epaphras was speaking on behalf of the apostle himself. Epaphras's authority gave them good reason to *not* accept teachings that had come to them later and which were contradictory to Epaphras's teaching.

1:8 And he has made known to us your love in the Spirit. NRSV
Undoubtedly, Epaphras had told Paul all about the church in Colosse. Some concern from Epaphras about the false teaching that had come into Colosse prompted Paul's response through this letter. But Epaphras had also told Paul about the character of the church—they loved one another, they showed love outside the fellowship, and they loved the well-known Paul as a brother in Christ, even though they had never met him. Such love comes from our relationship with Christ and the indwelling of the Holy Spirit because this love is a fruit of the Spirit.

SHORT ON LOVE?
The Bible speaks repeatedly about God's love for us, Christians' love for each other, and love of family and friends. Yet not everyone feels love; not everyone knows how to enjoy it or even find it.

What should you do if your experience really doesn't match the Bible's description of love? What if you're too lonely, abused, or introverted to reach out to find friends?

First, understand that coming to Christ does not bring instant change to your life situation or personality type. God fills the real you with his Spirit; not some ideal you. God redeems *you*—the lonely, introverted, loveless you. You may not always feel like loving others.

Second, know that God brings the real you into a new set of relationships. This can be difficult as well as wonderful. The difficulty occurs when some believers don't meet our expectations or don't respond as we feel they should. They may be grumpy, tired, or "stressed-out" and not in the mood to be friendly. The wonderful part is God's constant work in the Spirit to make these relationships deep and selfless.

Third, realize that whatever your personality, God calls you to a new life of service. Suddenly you realize that a genuinely loving church depends on you. If you want friends, be friendly. Take the initiative, be consistent, and trust God's Spirit completely to replenish your love-bank. Then you will know what love in the Spirit can be.

Because of their Spirit-empowered love for one another, Christians can have an impact far beyond their neighborhoods and communities. Christian love comes from the Holy Spirit (see Galatians 5:22). The Bible speaks of it as an action and attitude, not just an emotion. Love is a by-product of our new life in Christ (see Romans 5:5; 15:30; 1 Corinthians 13). Christians have no excuse for not loving because Christian love is a decision to *act* in the best interests of others. See 1:4-5 for more on the source of this love.

1:9 For this reason, since the day we heard about you, we have not stopped praying for you.NIV In 1:3, Paul had already mentioned that he was praying for these believers (as he did for all the churches; see for example Romans 1:8-9 and Philippians 1:3-6, 9-11). Here Paul explained that the encouraging report from Epaphras about the Colossians' love in the Spirit had prompted Paul (perhaps Timothy is included in the *we*) to pray constantly for these believers. Paul didn't know about a church in Colosse until he had heard from Epaphras, and Paul rejoiced to be able to pray for another growing church. That Paul had *not stopped* praying since he first heard about the Colossian church refers to his vigilant habit of praying for all the churches.

> The church is to be stocked with good teaching as a palace is filled with treasures.
> *N. T. Wright*

Asking that you may be filled with the knowledge of God's will in all spiritual wisdom and understanding.NRSV Paul did not stop at saying that he prayed constantly for the Colossian believers; he went on to explain exactly what he prayed for them. He asked God that they be filled with *knowledge*—but not the secret knowledge advocated by the heresy. This was the knowledge *of God's will* available to all who believe.

This knowledge of God's will comes from *wisdom and understanding*. These are not merely abstract concepts; instead, Paul was referring to the true wisdom and understanding made available by God's Holy Spirit. In a similar prayer for the Ephesians (Ephesians 1:17-18), Paul asked God to give them a spirit of wisdom and revelation to understand all the spiritual blessings that they had been given in Christ. The Colossians also needed to be *filled* with this type of spiritual wisdom and knowledge, leaving no room for any other type of false "knowledge" advocated by gnostic heretics. Only by being filled with spiritual wisdom and understanding could believers apply that knowledge to their daily lives. Knowledge must be tempered by spiritual understanding if the Colossians were to make wise decisions and correct judgments. Then they could

- lead lives worthy of the Lord (1:10)

- fully please the Lord (1:10)

- bear fruit in every good work (1:10)

- grow in the knowledge of God (1:10)

- endure everything with patience (1:11)

- joyfully give thanks to the Father (1:11-12)

God measures true wisdom and understanding by our practical obedience. Wisdom and understanding refer to discretion and discernment. When believers possess those, they will be able to discern the truth from false teaching.

1:10 **So that you may lead lives worthy of the Lord, fully pleasing to him, as you bear fruit in every good work and as you grow in the knowledge of God.**^{NRSV} True knowledge of God's will is inseparable from living in harmony with it. True knowledge leads

---

PLEASING GOD
How do we please God? (Verses quoted from NIV, italics ours.)

- Genesis 8:21, "The Lord smelled the *pleasing* aroma" of the sacrifice. In the Old Testament, God's pleasure in the aroma of a sacrifice meant that he accepted the sacrifice for sin. Thus, pleasing God means making the acceptable sacrifice to him.

- Psalm 19:14, "May the words of my mouth and the meditation of my heart be *pleasing* in your sight." Our love for God should guide what we think and what we say (see also Psalm 104:34).

- John 5:30, "I seek not to *please* myself but him who sent me." Jesus taught us not to try to please ourselves but to please God (see also John 8:29).

- Romans 12:1, "Offer your bodies as living sacrifices, holy and *pleasing* to God." God wants us to turn over our lives to him daily, renouncing our own desires and trusting him to guide us (see also Romans 14:8-18).

- Ephesians 5:10, "Find out what *pleases* the Lord." We must live in contrast to those who live immorally.

- Philippians 4:18, "The gifts you sent . . . are a fragrant offering, an acceptable sacrifice, *pleasing* to God." Our offerings of money please God.

- Hebrews 11:6, "Without faith it is impossible to *please* God." God rewards, with his presence, those who trust him fully.

(See also Colossians 3:20; 1 Timothy 2:3; 5:4; 1 John 3:22.)

to obedience; complete obedience cannot occur without the knowledge of God's will given by the Holy Spirit.

The Colossians' lifestyles should be *worthy* of their high calling as God's children. Their behavior should match their status as God's holy people. They ought to be following God closely—their lives being transformed to Christlikeness. A Christian must be active in order to grow spiritually and to live worthy of the Lord. When a Christian is inactive, stagnation and even regression set in. Paul did not hesitate to urge the Colossians to extra effort. We must not use the grace of Christ as an excuse for inaction.

Is it possible for Christians to be *fully pleasing* to God? Apparently so, for Paul prayed exactly that for the Colossian believers. Perfection will not be achieved in this life, yet believers press on toward the goal of God's high calling (Philippians 3:12-14). In the meantime, believers can be fully pleasing to God by virtue of their relationship with him and their attempts to "live in order to please" him in all areas of life (1 Thessalonians 4:1 NIV).

Paul prayed that the believers in Colosse would *bear fruit in every good work*. As the gospel is bearing fruit and growing (1:6), so believers in that gospel ought also to "bear fruit" and *grow in the knowledge of God*. As believers bear fruit (this could refer to the fruit of the Spirit described in Galatians 5:22-23, or to growth in the Colossian church by adding members), they will grow in their knowledge of God. Knowing God is progressive. Just as we don't fully know a person upon meeting him or her, so we don't fully know God the minute we are saved. Instead, we grow to know him better and better as we seek to serve him and bear fruit in our lives and in our ministry.

FRUIT BEARERS
The false teachers valued the accumulation of knowledge, but Paul pointed out that knowledge in itself is empty. To be worth anything, it must lead to a changed life and right living. Paul's prayer for the Colossians has two dimensions: (1) that they might be filled with the knowledge of God's will through all spiritual wisdom and understanding, and (2) that they would bear fruit in every good work, growing in the knowledge of God. Knowledge is not merely to be accumulated; it should give us direction for living and acting. Paul wanted the Colossians to be wise, but he also wanted them to *use* their knowledge for Christian service. Knowledge of God is not a secret that only a few can discover; it is open to everyone. God wants us to learn more about him and also to put belief into practice by helping others.

1:11-12 May you be made strong with all the strength that comes from his glorious power.NRSV The Colossians' growth in the knowledge of God and the resultant fruit would help to strengthen them. Paul continued his prayer for the believers, asking God that they be *made strong with all the strength* that comes from his glorious power. One can hardly pray a more wonderful prayer. To be made strong with God's power is to be given incredible strength—it was God's glorious power that created the universe and that brought Jesus back to life. One can hardly imagine more power. In fact, Paul's words here show the inadequacy of describing God's power—it is beyond our words or our human minds to comprehend. Yet that power is available to believers and to the church so they can fulfill their mission in the world. Paul wanted the Colossian believers to be strengthened with God's power so they would not be pulled away from their faith and their witness to the world.

So that you may have great endurance and patience.NIV *Endurance (hupomone)* is the ability to continue toward a goal regardless of the obstacles. *Patience (makrothumia)* is the ability to stand firm against opposition without giving up. "Endurance" is often used in relation to difficult circumstances; "patience" is often used in describing one's dealings with difficult people. Both would be needed by the believers in Colosse, and both come from the empowerment of God's glorious strength. Paul reminded the Colossians that even when they were surrounded by persecution and false teaching, they had the strength to continue toward the goal of their faith and to stand firm against the opposition.

HOW TO PRAY FOR OTHER CHRISTIANS
How many people in your life could be touched if you prayed this way?
- Be thankful for their faith and changed lives (1:3-4).
- Ask God to help them know what he wants them to do (1:9).
- Ask God to give them deep spiritual understanding (1:9).
- Ask God to help them live for him (1:10).
- Ask God to give them more knowledge of himself (1:10).
- Ask God to give them strength to endure (1:11).
- Ask God to fill them with joy, strength, and thankfulness (1:11).

While joyfully giving thanks to the Father, who has enabled you to share in the inheritance of the saints in the light.NRSV Scholars have had difficulty with the placement of the word *joyfully*. Some place it with endurance and patience, meaning that Paul was praying that the Colossians could have endurance and patience, but do so with joy. It is God's power alone that makes it even possible to be joyful during difficult times. Other scholars place the word "joyfully" as modifying *giving thanks*. Either way, it makes little difference to Paul's meaning. It is God's power that helps believers endure and be patient even as they are filled with joy that overflows in thanksgiving.

Thanks is given to God *the Father.* Why? Because through Jesus Christ, he made it possible for the believers to *share in the inheritance of the saints.* They are *enabled* only because God, by his grace, enabled them (see 1:13-14). By using the word "inheritance," Paul was alluding to the inheritance of the Promised Land, first promised to Abram for his faithfulness to God (Genesis 13:14-17). God's people, the Old Testament saints, inherited a portion of a bountiful land (Numbers 26:52-56; 34:2, 13). God's people in the New Testament are the very sons of God, and as such they have the right to inherit Christ and a glorious eternity in *the light.* The promise of land is broadened to include the whole creation (Romans 4:14; 8:17-25). The NIV adds the words "kingdom of" on the basis of 1:13, which mentions the "kingdom of the Son," but the words "kingdom of" are not in the Greek. Paul was most likely setting up the contrast between the state of "light" that the believers have been transferred to from their previous state of "darkness" as described in 1:13. Paul wrote to the Corinthians, "For God, who said, 'Let light shine out of darkness,' made his light shine in our hearts to give us the light of the knowledge of the glory of God in the face of Christ" (2 Corinthians 4:6 NIV).

PRAYING FOR STRANGERS
Sometimes we wonder how to pray for missionaries and other leaders whom we have never met. Paul had never met the Colossians, but he faithfully prayed for them. His prayers teach us how to pray for others, whether we know them or not. We can request that they (1) understand God's will, (2) gain spiritual wisdom, (3) please and honor God, (4) bear good fruit, (5) grow in the knowledge of God, (6) be filled with God's strength, (7) have great endurance and patience, (8) stay full of Christ's joy, and (9) give thanks always. All believers have these same basic needs. When you don't know how to pray for someone, emulate Paul's prayer for the Colossians.

1:13 For he has rescued us from the dominion of darkness and brought us into the kingdom of the Son he loves.[NIV] This verse continues the thought from 1:12; Paul still had in mind the analogy of Israel inheriting the Promised Land. The book of Exodus tells the story of how God *rescued* (or delivered) his people from Egypt (typifying Satan's dominion of darkness) and took them to the Promised Land (typifying the kingdom of his Son). (See Exodus 6:6; 12:27; 14:30.) Jesus referred to the dominion of darkness at his arrest in the Garden of Gethsemane (Luke 22:53), describing the forces of evil that he had to combat in his final hours. In Scripture, *darkness* is a metaphor for evil; it is the dominion of those who are without God. True believers, however, have been transferred from darkness to light, from slavery to freedom, from guilt to forgiveness, and from the power of Satan to the power of God:

- "I . . . am sending you [Paul] to [the Gentiles] to open their eyes and turn them from darkness to light, and from the power of Satan to God, so that they may receive forgiveness of sins and a place among those who are sanctified by faith in me" (Acts 26:17-18 NIV).

- "For you were once darkness, but now you are light in the Lord" (Ephesians 5:8 NIV).

- "You are a chosen people . . . that you may declare the praises of him who called you out of darkness into his wonderful light" (1 Peter 2:9 NIV).

- "This is the message we have heard from him and declare to you: God is light; in him there is no darkness at all. If we claim to have fellowship with him yet walk in the darkness, we lie and do not live by the truth. But if we walk in the light, as he is in the light, we have fellowship with one another, and the blood of Jesus, his Son, purifies us from all sin" (1 John 1:5-7 NIV).

We have been rescued from a rebel kingdom to serve the true King. That King, the Son God loves, is described in the following verses (1:15-20).

The words *Son he loves* allude to Jesus' baptism, when God anointed Jesus with the Spirit saying, "You are my Son, whom I love; with you I am well pleased" (Mark 1:11 NIV). By so doing, God announced Jesus as the anointed king of Israel. Matthew 2:15 quotes Hosea 11:1: "When Israel was a child, I loved him, and out of Egypt I called my son" to show that Christ fulfilled the expectation and hope of the Old Testament. The son inherited the kingdom from his Father. Now we are coheirs with him and can share in his kingdom (Romans 8:17).

1:14 In whom we have redemption, the forgiveness of sins.NIV Believers are qualified "to share in the inheritance of the saints in the kingdom of light" because through Jesus Christ, God's beloved Son, we have received *redemption*. The word "redemption" has a rich Old Testament meaning and goes back, once again, to the analogy of Israel's escape from Egypt. The last disaster visited on the Egyptians was the death of the children (Exodus 12:29-30). Every firstborn son of the Egyptians died, but the Israelite children were spared because the Israelites placed the blood of a lamb on their doorframes (Exodus 12:22-23). That's where the story of "redemption" begins in the Bible.

"Redemption" means "to buy back" or "to save from captivity by paying a ransom." One way to buy back a slave was to offer an equivalent or superior slave in exchange. That is the way God chose to buy sinful people back—he offered his Son in exchange for us. Paul was reminding the Colossian believers that they were not saved by knowledge or by good works or by inclusion in some sort of secret religious cult; they were saved by the blood of Jesus Christ. Through him alone had they received redemption, *the forgiveness of sins.*

If we want to be freed from the deadly consequences of our sins, a tremendous price must be paid. But we don't have to pay it. Jesus Christ, our substitute, has already redeemed us by his death on the cross. Our part is to trust him and accept his gift of eternal life. Our sins have been paid for, and the way has been cleared for us to begin a relationship with God.

BEAUTIFUL BENEFITS
Paul lists five benefits God gives all believers through Christ:
1. He made us qualified to share in his inheritance.
2. He rescued us from Satan's dominion of darkness and made us his children.
3. He brought us into his eternal kingdom.
4. He redeemed us—bought our freedom from sin and judgment.
5. He forgave us for all our sins.
Thank God for what you have received in Christ.

PERSON AND WORK OF CHRIST / 1:15-23

In the Colossian church there were several misconceptions about Christ that Paul directly refuted in this section:

■ Believing that matter is evil, false teachers argued that God would not have come to earth as a true human being in bodily form. Paul stated that Christ is the image—the exact likeness—of God and is himself God, and yet he died on the cross as a human being.

- They believed that God did not create the world because he would not have created evil. Paul proclaimed that Jesus Christ, who was also God in the flesh, participated in the creation of the universe.

- They said that Christ was not the unique Son of God but rather one of many intermediaries between God and people. Paul explained that Christ existed before anything else and is the firstborn of those resurrected.

- They refused to see Christ as the source of salvation, insisting that people could find God only through special and secret knowledge. In contrast Paul openly proclaimed the way of salvation to be through Christ alone. Paul continued to bring the argument back to Christ.

1:15 He is the image of the invisible God, the firstborn over all creation.NKJV Many New Testament scholars believe that this section was based on a hymn written before Paul wrote his letter to the Colossians. If this was a hymn, we can assume that it was known to the church at Colosse and to other Christians. Paul would not have quoted something unknown to them. However, Paul was very capable of writing such poetic lines, as demonstrated in passages such as Romans 8:37-39 and 1 Corinthians 13:4-8. These verses are regarded as some of the most important verses in the New Testament establishing the deity of Jesus Christ. Jesus is not only equal to God (Philippians 2:6), he *is* God—the verb is present tense, describing Jesus' position now and forever (John 10:30, 38; 12:45; 14:1-11). As the *image of the invisible God,* Christ is the exact visible representation of God (in Greek, *eikon*). God as spirit is invisible and always will be (1 Timothy 6:16). God's Son is his visible expression. He not only reflects God, but, as God, he reveals God to us (John 1:18; 14:9; Hebrews 1:1-2). Christ's glory expresses divine glory (2 Corinthians 4:4). He is not a copy, but the very embodiment of God's nature. We are given "the light of the knowledge of the glory of God in the face of Jesus Christ" (2 Corinthians 4:6 NRSV). Jesus is "the reflection of God's glory and the exact imprint of God's very being" (Hebrews 1:3 NRSV).

As *the firstborn over all creation,* he has all the priority and authority of the firstborn prince in a king's household (Hebrews 1:2). He came from heaven, not from the dust of the earth (1 Corinthians 15:47), and he is Lord of all (Romans 9:5; 10:12; Revelation 1:5; 17:14). Christ is completely holy (Hebrews 7:26-28; 1 Peter 1:19; 2:22; 1 John 3:5), and he has authority to judge the world (Romans 2:16; 2 Corinthians 5:10; 2 Timothy 4:1). Therefore, Christ is supreme over all creation, including the spirit world. While in

THE COLOSSIAN HERESY
Paul answered the various tenets of the Colossian heresy that threatened the church. This heresy was a "mixed bag," containing elements from several different heresies, some of which contradicted each other (as the chart shows).

The Heresy	Reference	Paul's Answer
Spirit is good; matter is evil.	1:15-20	God created heaven and earth for his glory.
One must follow ceremonies, rituals, and restrictions in order to be saved or perfected.	2:11, 16-23; 3:11	These were only shadows that ended when Christ came. He is all you need to be saved.
One must deny the body and live in strict asceticism.	2:20-23	Asceticism is no help in conquering evil thoughts and desires; instead, it leads to pride.
Angels must be worshiped.	2:18	Angels are not to be worshiped; Christ alone is worthy of worship.
Christ could not be both human and divine.	1:15-20; 2:2-3	Christ is God in the flesh; he is the eternal One, head of the body, first in everything, supreme.
One must obtain "secret knowledge" in order to be saved or perfected—and this was not available to everyone.	2:2, 18	God's secret is Christ, and he has been revealed to all.
One must adhere to human wisdom, tradition, and philosophies.	2:4, 8-10; 3:15-17	By themselves, these can be misleading and shallow because they have human origin; instead, we should remember what Christ taught and follow his words as our ultimate authority.
There is nothing wrong with immorality.	3:1-11	Get rid of sin and evil because you have been chosen by God to live a new life as a representative of the Lord Jesus.

English the word "firstborn" *(prototokos)* conveys the eldest child of human birth, 1:16 clarifies that the meaning of Jesus' title is that he is Creator. In Psalm 89:27, God states, "I will make him the firstborn, the highest of the kings of the earth" (NRSV).

Paul explained in no uncertain terms that the Colossian believers had to focus on the deity of Jesus Christ (that Jesus is God) or their Christian faith would fall prey to false teaching. To put Jesus any lower is to lose the central truth of Christianity.

CHRIST IS SUPREME
Multiculturalism refers to a widespread movement which in many ways is very good and in one way is very bad. The good parts recommend that we be open to different traditions and languages, to have growing interest in people of different color and custom. The bad part implies a leveling of all religious beliefs so that the supreme value becomes respect for all, rather than the truth of one. Such relativism regards all religious points of view as equally valid.

Colosse, no less than Des Moines or Kansas City, was a town of diverse cultural traditions. But Paul firmly taught the supremacy and divinity of only one person, the Lord Jesus Christ. In this letter and the entire Bible, we find no arbitrating this point: Jesus is the God-man; he was Creator and is Redeemer. Christ is Lord of all and superior to all powers, whether good or evil.

Christians should learn from and respect world cultures, urging all people of all colors to find peace with God. That's our missionary calling: to tell all the world the Good News that God loves us and saves us in Christ.

1:16 For in him all things in heaven and on earth were created, things visible and invisible, whether thrones or dominions or rulers or powers—all things have been created through him and for him.^{NRSV} Lest anyone misunderstand that "firstborn" in the previous verse meant that Jesus was merely the first thing God created, Paul went on here to explain that all things were created *in, through,* and *for* Christ. That final little word "for" shows us the goal of all creation—to glorify Christ. The apostle John wrote, "All things were made through Him, and without Him nothing was made that was made" (John 1:3 NKJV). The writer to the Hebrews wrote of Christ, "through whom [God] made the universe. The Son is the radiance of God's glory and the exact representation of his being, sustaining all things by his powerful word" (Hebrews 1:2-3 NIV). Just as all the fullness of Deity is in him (1:19), so in him are all the creative powers that make him the supreme Lord.

Because the false teachers believed that the physical world was evil, they thought that God himself could not have created it. If Christ were God, they reasoned, he would be in charge only of the spiritual world. But Paul explained that all the thrones, dominions, principalities, and powers on heaven and earth, of both the visible and invisible world (physical government and spiritual

forces) are under the authority of Christ himself. There is little to
be gained by trying to identify each of Paul's words here, except
to see the two main categories: (1) those in heaven are invisible;
(2) those on earth are visible. Some scholars have seen in these
words hierarchies of angel princes. Others have seen parallels to
the spiritual enemies of Christians—law, sin, the flesh, and death.
Paul listed these because of people's belief that the world was
inhabited by powers and beings that worked against humanity.
The false teachers may have given undue prominence to these, so
Paul quickly put them under Christ's rule. Christ has no equal
and no rival. Because Christ is the Creator of the world, all powers, whether the spiritual forces the Colossians wished to study or
any material force, were under Christ's final authority.

Paul's words here refuted the false teaching that Christ was
one of many intermediaries and that the angels were to be worshiped. All angelic and celestial powers in heaven and on earth
are subject to Christ. He is the Lord of all.

**1:17 He himself is before all things, and in him all things hold
together.**NRSV Christ is *before all things,* both in time and in rank.
He is not only the Creator of the world, he is also its Sustainer.
By him everything came to be, and by him everything continues
to be. In him, everything is held together, protected, and prevented from disintegrating into chaos (see Acts 17:28). Because
Christ is the Sustainer of all life, nothing in creation is independent from him. *Hold together (sunestaken)* implies being held
together in a coherent or logical way, sustained and upheld, prevented from dissolving into chaos. In him alone and by his word,
we find the unifying principle of all of life (Hebrews 1:2-3). The
Colossians, and all believers, are his servants who must daily
trust him for protection, care, and sustenance.

1:18 And He is the head of the body, the church.NKJV While 1:15-17
unveiled the Son's relationship to the "old creation" (the world),
this verse describes his relationship to the "new creation"—that
is, *the church.* The church (meaning *the body* of believers)
existed because Christ was its beginning, its source, its *head.* Just
as the parts of the body function under the direction of the brain,
so Christians are to work together under the command and authority of Jesus Christ.

The church is composed of many types of people from a variety of backgrounds with a multitude of gifts and abilities. Despite
the differences, all believers have one unifying principle—faith
in Christ. On this essential truth all believers find agreement. All
believers are baptized by one Holy Spirit into one body of believ-

ers, the church. Each person doesn't lose his or her individual identity, but all have oneness in Christ, the head of the body. The image of the body shows the church's unity. Each member is involved with all the others as they go about doing Christ's work on earth (Ephesians 4:15).

He is the beginning, the firstborn from the dead, so that he might come to have first place in everything.^{NRSV} Paul repeated again that Christ is *the beginning (arche),* but he elaborated another aspect of that beginning. Christ is the *firstborn from the dead.* He was the first to die and come back to life. He was "first" both in time and rank; there will be many more who will live forever after physical death (1 Corinthians 15:20). All who trust in Christ will also defeat death and rise again to live eternally with him (1 Corinthians 15:20; 1 Thessalonians 4:14). But he will always be preeminent—that is, holding first place.

There is no contradiction between Paul's words that Jesus "is before all things" (1:17) and that he will *come to have first place in everything.* The explanation is found in Philippians 2:5-11. Christ, although he was preeminent, willingly humbled himself to die on the cross. Because of Christ's death on the cross, he has been exalted and elevated to the status that was rightfully his. "Therefore God exalted him to the highest place," raising Christ to his original position at the Father's right hand, where he will reign forever as Lord and Judge.

BEGINNINGS
Schoolchildren know about beginnings: new teachers, new supplies, and new learning goals. The start of school in the fall is a brand new chance to improve your record. Weddings also signal new beginnings joyously. Most people savor the smell of a new automobile. We need and celebrate newness regularly.

We celebrate life at birthdays and baby showers. Yet each of us will one day wear out and die. In Jesus, the world begins a new era and people find new life. What a magnificent gift: it makes all other beginnings sensible and happy.

God's Good News is life eternal in Jesus. Your life begins anew in him. Let this be your reason to celebrate each day with him.

Jesus' resurrection is the cornerstone of the Christian faith, the reason that the church even exists. Only Christianity has a God who became human, died for his people, and was raised again in power and glory to rule the old creation and the new creation (the church) forever. The Resurrection assures believers that Christ is not a legend; he is alive and ruling his kingdom.

Because Christ is spiritually supreme in the universe, surely we should give him first place in all our thoughts and activities.

1:19 For God was pleased to have all his fullness dwell in him.NIV The little word *for* explains why Christ will have first place in everything. God wanted his *fullness* (meaning "completeness" or "totality") to *dwell* (meaning "live permanently") in Christ. This verse has been translated various ways: (1) that Christ was pleased to have God's fullness dwell in him; (2) that the fullness was pleased to dwell in Christ; and (3) as here, that God was pleased to have the whole Godhead dwell in the Son. The Greek supports all three possibilities, but the main point is not lost. Paul wanted to explain to the Colossians that Christ is God's dwelling place; therefore, Christ is divine, sovereign, and preeminent. Christ perfectly displays all the attributes and activities of God: Spirit, Word, wisdom, glory.

By this statement, Paul was refuting the Greek idea that Jesus could not be human and divine at the same time. Christ is fully human; he is also fully divine. Nor is there more than one God; one God, in all his fullness, resides in Christ. Paul was also refuting the false teaching that God's "fullness" meant all the angelic powers that emanate from God, fill the space between heaven and earth, and act as intermediaries between God and humans. Instead, Paul affirmed that God's "fullness" dwells in Christ alone. Christ has always been God and always will be God. All of God (including his attributes, characteristics, nature, and being) indwells the Son. When we have Christ we have all of God in human form. Any teaching that diminishes any aspect of Christ— either his humanity or his divinity—is false teaching. In him we have everything we need.

1:20 And through him God was pleased to reconcile to himself all things, whether on earth or in heaven, by making peace through the blood of his cross.NRSV Continuing from 1:19, Paul explained that God's fullness dwells in Christ and in that fullness he reconciled all things to himself. This reconciliation was accomplished through him (Christ) and *through the blood of his cross.* "Reconciliation" means reestablishing a relationship, causing the relationship to become friendly and peaceable when it had not been so. Because Christ is Creator and Sustainer of "all things" (1:17), his death on the cross provided reconciliation for *all things.* But what did Paul mean by "all"?

First, consider what this reconciliation means for humanity.

WHO IS CHRIST?
Colossians 1:15-20 lists seven characteristics of Christ:

(1) He is the image of the invisible God.   1:15
(2) He is the firstborn over all creation.   1:15
(3) By him all things were created.   1:16
(4) He is the head of the body, the church.   1:18
(5) He is the beginning, the firstborn from the dead.   1:18
(6) All God's fullness dwells in him.   1:19
(7) Through Christ, God was pleased to reconcile to   1:20
himself all things.

Because of who Christ is

• we ought to worship him with praise and thanks;

• we ought to learn about him, for he is God;

• we ought to obey him, for he is the ultimate authority;

• we ought to love him for what he has done for us.

There can be no peace between sinful humans and a holy God. Because people are born into sin, they cannot become good enough to be acceptable to God. In Old Testament times, God accepted symbolic offerings. Jesus had not yet been sacrificed, so God accepted the life of an animal in place of the life of the sinner. When Jesus came, he substituted his perfect life for our sinful lives, taking the penalty for sin that we deserve. The penalty for sin is death. We are guilty and culpable, but Jesus took the punishment. Thus he redeemed us from the power of sin and reconciled us to God.

Second, does this reconciliation of "all things" mean that everyone will be saved? From other passages, we know that Paul understood salvation to be something accepted or rejected by humans, who are given the choice (for example, see 2 Thessalonians 1:5-10). The *scope* of God's reconciliation is universal—it is offered to all people. But reconciliation is accomplished only for those who accept Christ as Savior: "So if anyone is in Christ, there is a new creation: everything old has passed away; see, everything has become new! All this is from God, who reconciled us to himself through Christ" (2 Corinthians 5:17-18 NRSV).

Third, what does this reconciliation mean for "all things" (besides humans)? Just as all of creation fell when Adam sinned, so all of creation will be reconciled. Sin has caused all creation to fall from the perfect state in which God created it. Thus the world is subject to decay so that it cannot fulfill its intended purpose. One day, all creation will be liberated and transformed. This is described in what Paul wrote to the Romans:

The creation waits in eager expectation for the sons of God to be revealed. For the creation was subjected to frustration, not by its own choice, but by the will of the one who subjected it, in hope that the creation itself will be liberated from its bondage to decay and brought into the glorious freedom of the children of God. (Romans 8:19-21 NIV)

The original sense of perfect order in the world was marred by sin. The created order functions in spite of its flaws, but diseases, deformities, and suffering constantly remind us that all is not right with us or with the world. All creation looks forward to its liberation from the effects of the Fall. God has plans for a new heaven and a new earth (Revelation 21:1).

In addition, Paul's reference to things *on earth or in heaven* was meant to be another blow to the false teachers. Nothing in the universe escapes Christ's reach. There is no neutral ground; everything falls under his power. No alien force of darkness can undermine his work or his church. Satan and demons *will not* be reconciled to God; instead, their end is certain (see Revelation 20:7-10).

A RIGHT RELATIONSHIP
Christ's death provided a way for all people to come to God. It cleared away the sin that keeps us from having a right relationship with our Creator. This does not mean that everyone has been saved, but that the way has been cleared for anyone who will trust Christ to be saved. We can have peace with God and be reconciled to him by accepting Christ, who died in our place. Is there a distance between you and the Creator? Be reconciled to God. Come to him through Christ.

It *pleased* God to do this! Christ willingly shed his blood on the cross so that we could have a relationship with him and live eternally. The Fall did not come as a surprise to God; in his eternal purposes, he allowed sin so that he might come and bring salvation to those who loved and followed him. "You see, at just the right time, when we were still powerless, Christ died for the ungodly. . . . God demonstrates his own love for us in this: While we were still sinners, Christ died for us. . . . We also rejoice in God through our Lord Jesus Christ, through whom we have now received reconciliation" (Romans 5:6, 8, 11 NIV). The only way of reconciliation is the way of the Cross.

1:21-22 **Once you were alienated from God and were enemies in your minds because of your evil behavior. But now he has reconciled you by Christ's physical body through death.**NIV Paul gave the reason why we need reconciliation. The believers in Colosse had, at one time, been *alienated* (separated, estranged) from God and they were his *enemies*. Their thoughts and behaviors had revealed, not apathy or ignorance, but hostility toward God because of sin. They were strangers to God's way of thinking. Wrong thinking leads to sin, which further perverts and destroys thoughts about him. When people are out of harmony with God, their natural condition is to be totally hostile to his standards.

God made peace by Jesus' blood on the cross (1:20). In order to answer the false teaching that Jesus was only a spirit and not a true human being, Paul explained that Jesus' fleshly, physical body actually died. Jesus suffered death fully as a human; thus we can be assured that he died in our place. Since Jesus, as perfect God, faced death, we can be assured that his sacrifice was complete and that he truly removed our sin.

How did Jesus' death remove sin? Jesus became human and lived on earth among people. Although he was without sin, he experienced life and temptation as we do. On the cross, Jesus took the punishment for our sin. At the same time, Jesus is God. Therefore, in Jesus, God identified with our sin, meeting it head-on at the cross, taking the total punishment (death) and breaking its power over humanity. Those who are part of Christ's body, the church (1:18), can also claim victory over sin and are now *reconciled* with God.

The "how" is answered, now for the "why." What is the goal of this reconciliation?

To present you holy in his sight, without blemish and free from accusation.NIV Some scholars have understood *present* to mean "to offer a sacrifice" (as in Hebrews 9:14; 1 Peter 1:19). More likely, it refers to believers being presented pure and faultless, acquitted of all charges (Ephesians 5:27; Jude 24). Christ's act of reconciliation put believers in perfect standing with God. By Christ's death on the cross, God already dealt with sin. His goal is to make believers his holy people, to transform their character so they can live consistent with their faith. The pattern is the perfect life lived by Jesus Christ. In one sense, the Colossian believers were already perfect because they had been made acceptable to God; yet they were still being perfected so that, in the end, they would truly be:

- *Holy*—"As obedient children, do not conform to the evil desires you had when you lived in ignorance. But just as he who called you is holy, so be holy in all you do; for it is written: 'Be holy, because I am holy'" (1 Peter 1:14-16 NIV).

- *Without blemish*—"So that you may become blameless and pure, children of God without fault in a crooked and depraved generation, in which you shine like stars in the universe as you hold out the word of life" (Philippians 2:15-16 NIV).

- *Free from accusation*—"Who will bring any charge against those whom God has chosen? It is God who justifies" (Romans 8:33 NIV).

The process of living the Christian life will end with the resurrection and will result in believers being presented to God as his dear and beloved children. There will be no fear, for God has already reconciled us to himself and made us acceptable *in his sight*.

NO WAY!
No one is good enough to save himself or herself. If we want to live eternally with Christ, we must depend totally on God's grace. This is true whether we have been murderers or honest, hardworking citizens. We have all sinned repeatedly, but *any* sin requires us to come to Jesus Christ for salvation and eternal life. Apart from Christ, there is no way for us to be forgiven.

1:23 Provided that you continue securely established and steadfast in the faith, without shifting from the hope promised by the gospel that you heard, which has been proclaimed to every creature under heaven.[NRSV] The certainty of believers' present and future status with God should not be an excuse for careless living or dabbling in heresy. Paul warned the Colossian believers to *continue securely established and steadfast in the faith*. As they built their lives upon the foundation laid by the gospel, they ought to build carefully through obedience. Then their "building" would stand firm. "Continue securely" means to remain stable, to persevere. The Colossians should not wander off into false teaching that contradicted the gospel they had heard and the hope they had believed for salvation. Paul urged all believers, like those in Colosse, to build carefully, persevering in their faith. (For more encouragement in perseverance, see John 8:31; 15:1-8; Acts 14:21-22; James 1:1-4.) Genuine faith perseveres to the end, focusing on *the hope promised,* which is the very content of the gospel. Hope is both the inward attitude of expectancy and the objective reality of the gospel. Christ is Lord, and he has promised that one day we will be with him.

As Paul closed his introductory section, he made one final stab at the doctrine of the false teachers by proclaiming that the gospel *has been proclaimed to every creature under heaven.* This did not mean that every person had heard the gospel. Rather, Paul was pointing out the scope (as in 1:20) of that gospel—it is available to all people, regardless of class, group, age, race, gender, etc. Spiritual reality was not, as the false teachers claimed, available only to a select group of intellectually elite people. The hope of the gospel is available to the whole world.

I, Paul, became a servant of this gospel.[NRSV] Instead of repeating the word "apostle" (see 1:1), Paul here called himself a *servant.* Paul may have wanted to use the same title that he had used for Epaphras in 1:7, where he called Epaphras a "dear fellow servant." To align himself in this way with Epaphras, Paul was defending and endorsing Epaphras's teaching and ministry in Colosse. He was also defending and endorsing Tychicus, the deliverer of this letter (4:7).

This gospel was what Paul had outlined thus far in this letter. This was the gospel to which Paul had become a servant; this was the only true gospel. This was what the Colossians had heard and believed. There ought to be no excuse for wandering away into false teaching.

GOD'S SOLUTION
The way to be free from sin is to trust Jesus Christ to take it away. We must remain established and steadfast in the truth of the gospel, putting our confidence in Jesus alone to forgive our sins, to make us right with God, and to empower us to live the way he desires. When a judge in a court of law declares the defendant not guilty, the person has been acquitted of all the accusations or charges. Legally, it is as if he or she had never been accused. When God forgives our sins, our record is wiped clean. From his perspective, it is as though we had never sinned. God's solution is available to you. No matter what you have done or what you have been like, God's forgiveness is for you.

Colossians 1:24–2:23

Paul was combating a false teaching in the Colossian church similar to Gnosticism (from the Greek word for knowledge, *gnosis*). This heresy can be called "proto-Gnosticism" because full-fledged Gnosticism did not blossom until the second century. It undermined Christianity in several basic ways: (1) It insisted that important secret knowledge was hidden from most believers; Paul, however, said that Christ provides all the knowledge we need. (2) It taught that the body was evil; Paul countered by affirming that God himself lived in a body—that is, he was embodied in Jesus Christ. (3) It contended that Christ only seemed to be human, but was not; Paul insisted that Jesus is fully human and fully God.

Though Gnosticism did not become fashionable until the second century, even in Paul's day these ideas sounded attractive to many, and exposure to such teachings could easily seduce a church that didn't know Christian doctrine well. Similar teachings still entice many in the church today. We combat heresy by becoming thoroughly acquainted with God's Word through personal study and sound Bible teaching. In this chapter, Paul wanted to help the Colossian believers guard against those who would undermine the simple faith and sufficiency they had found in Christ.

1:24 Now I rejoice in what was suffered for you, and I fill up in my flesh what is still lacking in regard to Christ's afflictions, for the sake of his body, which is the church.^{NIV} The little word *now* communicates more than just providing a transition. Paul could rejoice precisely because of all that he had just written in 1:15-20; and he could rejoice now (at present) in prison. Sitting in his prison in Rome and suffering for his faith, Paul was able to rejoice. Paul had encouraged the Philippians by explaining that suffering was a privilege (Philippians 1:29) and that the early apostles had rejoiced when they were considered worthy to suffer for believing in Christ (Acts 5:41). Paul informed the churches to whom he wrote that his suffering was not a punishment, nor was

CALLED TO SUFFER

Paul never feared suffering, for he knew that God was in control, that his suffering helped others to be more courageous in spreading the gospel, and that one day all suffering would end and he (along with all believers) would be with the Father. The New Testament abounds with warnings about suffering and words of comfort for those who are suffering.

Speaker	Reference	Words about Suffering
Jesus	Matthew 5:10-12	Those who are persecuted are called "blessed."
Jesus	Matthew 20:23	The Son of Man will return and end all suffering.
Jesus	John 15:20	Jesus was persecuted; we will be persecuted.
The Apostles	Acts 5:41	We can rejoice for being considered worthy to suffer for Christ.
Jesus	Acts 9:16	Paul was called to suffer for Jesus' name.
Paul	Romans 8:17	As children and heirs, we will share in Jesus' suffering.
Paul	2 Corinthians 1:3-7	God gives comfort in suffering.
Paul	2 Corinthians 4:7-12	Paul suffered so that others might be saved.
Paul	2 Corinthians 6:4-5, 9-10	Paul suffered yet rejoiced.
Paul	Ephesians 3:13	Our sufferings can glorify God.
Paul	Philippians 1:29	Suffering for Christ's name is a privilege.
Paul	2 Timothy 1:12	We must not be ashamed of suffering; trust Christ.
Paul	2 Timothy 2:10	Paul suffered for the sake of other believers.
Paul	2 Timothy 3:11	God will rescue us from suffering—now or in eternity.
Paul	2 Timothy 4:5	We are called to endure hardship.
Author of Hebrews	Hebrews 10:32-34	We can face suffering because we know we have God's inheritance.
James	James 1:2	We can consider it pure joy to face trials.
Peter	1 Peter 1:6	Our suffering is refining our faith.
Peter	1 Peter 2:21	We suffer because Christ suffered.
Peter	1 Peter 3:13-14	We are blessed for suffering for what is right.
Peter	1 Peter 4:1, 13, 16	We suffer yet rejoice because we suffer for Christ.
Jesus	Revelation 2:10	We must be faithful, even to death; the crown of life awaits us.

it accidental (as though God had somehow lost track of him). Instead, Paul was honored to be suffering, and he rejoiced at what God was doing in the churches and in the believers who were gaining courage and faith by watching Paul's example. Perhaps the false teachers had pointed to Paul's imprisonment as proof that his leadership and his teachings were in question. Paul explained that, instead, his imprisonment *proved* the truth of his words, and he could rejoice in that imprisonment knowing that it was all part of God's plan, *for the sake of his body, which is the church.*

Paul's words, *I fill up in my flesh what is still lacking in regard to Christ's afflictions,* did not mean that Christ's suffering was inadequate to save people. Paul believed that Christ's suffering on the cross alone paid for believers' salvation from sin: "All have sinned . . . and are justified freely by his grace through the redemption that came by Christ Jesus. God presented him as a sacrifice of atonement, through faith in his blood" (Romans 3:23-25 NIV). (See also 1 Corinthians 1:18-31; 2 Corinthians 5:16-21; Galatians 1:4; Colossians 2:13-14.)

While we know what Paul did *not* mean by these words, we must consider several interpretations regarding what he *did* mean. How could Paul say that he filled up what was still lacking? There are three main views:

(1) *Affliction refers to the "Messianic Woes."* Some commentators explain that Paul was referring to a concept of the "Messianic Woes" or "Afflictions of the Messiah" that the Jews believed were a sign and requirement of the Messiah. The Jews believed that before the end time, an anointed ruler would come and God's people would be called upon to suffer (Daniel 12:1). However, God would set a limit to these sufferings. Some believe Paul took this idea and adapted it for Christians. This view held that the Messiah had already come, but he had promised to come again. Paul saw himself as suffering on behalf of the church, thereby filling up what was lacking of that set amount of suffering. Some commentators consider that Paul thought that by his suffering he actually was saving others from suffering. The more suffering Paul endured, the more suffering was fulfilled, and the less others would have to suffer. This view seems unlikely, however, because Paul was tying suffering to the spread of the gospel, not to preparation for the end times.

(2) *Paul's lacking referred to his own deficiency, not Christ's.* Referring to Paul's words in Philippians 3:10 where Paul claimed a desire to "know . . . the fellowship of sharing in his sufferings" (NIV), he may have meant that he wanted to fill up in himself

what was lacking in his understanding of Christ's afflictions. This also seems unlikely in this context, however, because Paul was emphasizing the believers' completeness in Christ (2:10).

(3) *Christ's afflictions refer to the mystical union between Paul and Christ and between Christ and the church.* This view shows the corporate identity of Paul and Christ, as well as between the church and Christ. That union is best expressed in Paul's words that the church is Christ's body. What Paul suffered, Christ suffered, because Paul was a member of Christ's body on earth. What Christ began as suffering with his persecution and rejection on earth, all believers complete in his continuing body on earth. This view seems most likely because it stresses that the cause of the suffering would be the extension of the gospel to all the world. Paul shared the suffering of the Messiah as he brought the Messiah's message to the world.

DO YOU SUFFER WELL?
Most people try to avoid suffering, and people who do suffer would prefer not to. We are not created to enjoy pain. As babies, we cried when hungry; later, we cry at grief or loss or impending death.

Paul was not promoting the idea that pain is good, that suffering is joy, and that hurt should be our high ambition. Pain is almost always bad news.

But in Christ, affliction points to good news. As Jesus suffered on Friday, he rose on Sunday. Christians called to endure hardship for the sake of Christ (and this includes even personal suffering like cancer and car accidents) endure their affliction with the assurance that Sunday comes: restoration and resurrection, eternal life. Because Christ guarantees our resurrection, we can handle anything until then.

But until then, we must take our share of pain for Jesus: work hard for his kingdom, give him our best energy and resources, and take the pain of others on ourselves, as Jesus did.

Jesus had warned his followers to expect affliction: "If they persecuted me, they will persecute you also . . . They will treat you this way because of my name, for they do not know the One who sent me" (John 15:20-21 NIV). This suffering would not be limited to Paul. By identifying themselves with Christ, all believers would face affliction. Not all would face imprisonment, as Paul did, but all would have varying degrees and kinds of suffering simply because they have allied themselves with Christ in a world hostile to Christ. Some affliction is external, some is internal. But suffering comes as an inevitable consequence of believing in Christ and may be unavoidable for those who bring the

Good News of Christ to the world. Suffering, affliction, and persecution, therefore, come naturally as part of the process for building up Christ's church. But this suffering should be cause for rejoicing. Suffering does not mean that Christ is losing ground, but that he is gaining it and that the present age is passing away to eventually herald in the age to come when Christ will reign.

If Christians are not on the firing line, not confronting sin in our culture, or if our standards are too compromised, we won't have any affliction tied to the spread of the gospel. Have we become too comfortable?

1:25 I became its servant according to God's commission that was given to me for you.^{NRSV} In 1:23, Paul had referred to himself as "a servant of this gospel"; here Paul again referred to himself as a *servant,* this time as a servant of the church. The Greek word *diakonos* is used in both verses and translated "servant" (or "minister").

Paul's service came because of *God's commission.* To the Galatians, Paul wrote, "Paul an apostle—sent neither by human commission nor from human authorities, but through Jesus Christ and God the Father" (Galatians 1:1 NRSV). No human had commissioned Paul; no human authority had called him; instead, Jesus Christ himself had spoken to him (Acts 9:4-6). Paul's credentials as an apostle need never be questioned. Although Paul was called after Jesus' resurrection and ascension, he and the other apostles were called by Jesus Christ and God the Father, and they answered to God as their final authority.

Paul explained that this commission was given to him *for you,* that is, for Gentile congregations such as the one in Colosse. When Paul was commissioned by God, the focus of his ministry was made clear. God said of Paul, "This man is my chosen instrument to carry my name before the Gentiles" (Acts 9:15 NIV). Paul was keenly aware of who had commissioned him, to whom he had been commissioned, and what he had been called to do. To the Corinthians, Paul had written, "Yet when I preach the gospel, I cannot boast, for I am compelled to preach. Woe to me if I do not preach the gospel! . . . I am simply discharging the trust committed to me" (1 Corinthians 9:16-17 NIV).

The word translated "commission" (*oikonomia,* from which we get our word "economy") means "management" or "stewardship." As a well-trusted servant would manage his master's estate, so Paul was entrusted with a special task. He was commissioned **to make the word of God fully known.**^{NRSV} Literally translated, this means "to fulfill the word of God." It is the same root word used in 2:24 for "filling up" Christ's afflictions. Paul's ministry among the Gentiles was to fully make known the word of God and to bring the preaching of the word of God to completion. Without Paul's ministry concerning God's plan for Christ and the church, God's Word, the revelation of his will, would be unfinished. The heresy in Colosse focused on mystical knowledge, and only a few could find the "fullness of knowledge" needed for inclusion in their special group. Thus, when Paul wrote of making God's word fully known to all the believers, he was pointing out once again that God's word is for all people. They could have all the wisdom they needed to be saved and to grow in Christ.

1:26 **The mystery which has been hidden from ages and from generations, but now has been revealed to His saints.**NKJV The false teachers in Colosse believed that spiritual perfection was a hidden plan (or "mystery") that only a few privileged people could discover. Their secret plan was meant to be exclusive. Paul wrote that he was making the word of God fully known (1:25), not just a part of it. Making God's word fully known meant revealing *the mystery which has been hidden from ages and from generations.* The Greek word for "mystery" *(musterion)* means "a secret revealed to the initiates." Thus, it could be mysterious to those without and a secret to those within. This mystery was hidden, not because only a few could understand it, but because it was hidden until Christ came. In 1:27, the mystery relates to "riches" because God lavished his riches in a wonderful way. The mystery also relates to God's glory because it shares in his very nature. With Christ's coming and the beginning of Christianity, that mystery is no longer hidden; it *has been revealed* to those who believe, that is, *to His saints.* God's plan was hidden from previous generations, not because God wanted to keep something from his people, but because he was going to reveal it in his perfect timing. Paul was explaining that God's time for action was then and there.

What is that mystery? Paul wrote the answer in Ephesians 3:1-6: "This mystery is that through the gospel the Gentiles are heirs together with Israel, members together of one body, and sharers together in the promise in Christ Jesus" (Ephesians 3:6 NIV). The mystery hidden throughout the ages was that one day Jews and Gentiles would be joined together in one body because of their common belief in Jesus Christ as Savior. The Old Testament revealed that the Gentiles would receive salvation (Isaiah 49:6), but it was never explained that Gentile and Jewish believers would become *equal* in the body of Christ, with no divisions between them. In the Old Testament, Gentiles could convert to Judaism but would always be considered "second-class" Jews, not pure Jews. With the coming of Christ, however, and the new union he created through his church, all believers were joined together in Christ's body, where "there is neither Jew nor Greek [Gentile]" (Galatians 3:28 NKJV). Christ is now in you!

1:27 **To them God has chosen to make known among the Gentiles the glorious riches of this mystery, which is Christ in you, the hope of glory.**^{NIV} To these believers, these New Testament "saints," God chose to make his mystery known among the Gentiles. These words would have been joyful to Paul's Gentile audience, that God *chose* to offer salvation to the Gentiles. They did not need to acquire some secret knowledge in order to find God; God had reached down to them because he wanted to save them.

God's "mystery" is not a puzzle to solve; instead, it is like a treasure chest filled with *glorious riches,* and it is available to anyone who looks for it. Those "riches" are *the hope of glory*—eternity with God the Father. That "hope" is a certainty because of God's provision in Jesus Christ.

SOLVING MYSTERIES
Two questions make up the mystery to which Paul refers:
(1) How could *Yahweh,* the God of the Jews, care about Gentiles now, since the entire Old Testament story is about God giving the Jews victory over the Gentiles? (2) How does *Yahweh,* fearsome and distant, come close to us, since Moses, when he got close, was affected physically for days thereafter?

It's a double mystery of breadth and depth. And here is the clue: it is for you. God has extended his love to all people and has placed his love in your very heart and soul through Christ, who died and rose, and who lives in you. God has come to you in two ways: historically in time and place, and personally in your mind and heart.

Now it's your job to live as though Christ is in you, free of fear and confident of eternal life.

God made the "mystery" available to Jews and Gentiles alike, and the mystery is *Christ in you.* Jews and Gentiles will have that oneness in Christ's body because God had planned from the beginning of time to have Christ live in the heart of each person who believes in him. The indwelling Christ gives believers certainty of their "hope," being in Christ's glorious, eternal kingdom. Believers are in Christ; Christ is in them; therefore, believers can look forward to sharing Christ's glory.

1:28 **It is he whom we proclaim, warning everyone and teaching everyone in all wisdom, so that we may present everyone mature in Christ.**^{NRSV} Paul switched from "I" to *we* so that he could include his coworkers, particularly Epaphras and Tychicus who served the Colossian church, and also so that he could *exclude* the false teachers. Paul and his coworkers were proclaiming the Good News about Jesus Christ, who at present was dwelling in them as well as in the Colossian believers, making all of them one body awaiting a glorious future.

Their proclaiming of Jesus Christ included both *warning* and *teaching*. The word "warning" (also translated "admonishing") connects with repentance and refers to a person's conduct and heart attitude. "Teaching" is connected to faith and doctrine and refers to a person's intellect. Paul needed both, especially when dealing with false teachers. He needed to warn the believers about straying from the faith, straighten out any confusion they might have, and strengthen them with the truth of the gospel. Paul pointed out that this warning and teaching was for *everyone,* not an elite group, and that it was always done *in all wisdom*— with every ounce of wisdom Paul and his fellow teachers possessed.

WARN AND TEACH
Christ's message is for everyone; so everywhere Paul, his coworkers, and the other apostles went, they brought the Good News to all who would listen. An effective presentation of the gospel includes warning and teaching. The warning is that without Christ, people are doomed to eternal separation from God. The teaching is that salvation is available through faith in Christ. As Christ works in you, tell others about him, warning and teaching them in love. Who do you know who needs to hear this message?

The warning and teaching always had one goal in mind: *so that we may present everyone mature in Christ*. This "presentation" would have been when Christ returned, so that every person presently living in union with Christ (every believer) would be complete, full grown, and perfectly instructed in doctrine, faith, and practice. Believers are not to remain like babies in the faith, easily led away by something new (see also 1 Corinthians 3:1-2). Instead, they are to grow up into spiritual maturity so that they cannot be enticed by false teachings. Paul used the word "everyone" twice in this sentence, revealing the availability of this teaching to all believers and the goal of maturity for all believers.

God makes this possible only through a personal relationship
with Christ. This relationship with Christ, empowered by the
indwelling of the Holy Spirit, helps believers grow in faith and
maturity until the day when Christ returns.

GROW UP
The word "mature" is also translated "perfect." Paul wrote here
of the earthly goal of spiritual maturity and completeness, not of
flawless and sinless perfection, which is unattainable in this life.
Paul wanted to see each believer mature spiritually. Like Paul,
we must work wholeheartedly like an athlete, but we should not
strive in our own strength alone. We have the power of God's
Spirit working in us. Learn and grow daily, motivated by love,
and not by fear or pride, knowing that God gives you the ability
to become mature.

**1:29 To this end I labor, struggling with all his energy, which so
powerfully works in me.**[NIV] This verse vividly portrays the
necessity of cooperation and combined effort between believers
and Christ. The will of Christ and the will of the person must
work together. The work of salvation is "all of Christ and none of
me." The daily practice of servanthood is "all of Christ and all of
me." Paul says, *I labor, struggling,* meaning that he was putting
all the effort of his mind and body into the task.

Paul was laboring and struggling for the goal, that he may
"present everyone mature in Christ" (1:28 NRSV). Both words
describe hard physical work, striving, and conflict, as with an athlete in an arena. Paul's commission (1:25) was not an easy one.
His task was not simple. He did not dash around the world
preaching the gospel and then return to a comfortable office. Paul
struggled against false teaching, persecution, and questions about
his qualifications. He bore heartache and concern on behalf of the
churches because he had his goal always before him. Not only
did he want people to accept the gospel, but he also wanted them
to mature in their faith. Thus he wrote letters, prayed constantly,
traveled to many churches, stayed and worked and taught in
some places, sent emissaries on his behalf, wrote more letters
upon the reports of these emissaries in order to deal with specific
situations facing some churches, and sent emissaries back for
reports.

Paul did not struggle with his own strength alone, however.
His goals were always aligned with God's goals. His labor was
empowered, enabled, and energized by God's Spirit *with all his
energy* (see 1:11; 2:12). Paul needed God's supernatural power,

and God supplied it to Paul when he was at work (see 1 Corinthians 15:10).

2:1 For I want you to know how much I am struggling for you, and for those in Laodicea, and for all who have not seen me face to face.^{NRSV} Paul's labor and struggle (1:29) were not limited to those churches he had planted or even to people he knew personally. Paul also worked on behalf of those who had never met him. He struggled for the Colossians in prayer and with the concern that had prompted the writing of this letter. Paul struggled, knowing that the false teaching threatened to keep the Colossian believers from maturing in their faith.

Laodicea was located a few miles northwest of Colosse. Like the church at Colosse, the Laodicean church was probably founded by one of Paul's converts while Paul was staying in Ephesus (Acts 19:10), perhaps even Epaphras, who had founded the Colossian church. The city was a wealthy center of trade and commerce, but later Christ would criticize the believers at Laodicea for their lukewarm commitment (Revelation 3:14-22). The fact that Paul mentioned this city and either wanted this letter to be passed on to the church there or wrote a separate one (4:16), indicates that false teaching may have spread there as well. Paul was counting on ties of love bringing the churches together to encourage each other to stand against this heresy and to remain true to God's plan of salvation in Christ. Our churches should be encouraging, unified communities committed to carrying out Christ's work.

UNITED IN LOVE
Many ways of being "united" sidestep the crucial ingredient of love. Citizenship unites people by birth to a nation, just as skill and mutual interest unite athletes on a team. In neither situation is love a prominent quality. Sometimes even marriages are more a unity of law and habit than of love.

The church—believers united in Jesus Christ—should be a melting pot of love. These people should act for each other selflessly and feel for each other caringly. No one can mandate or manufacture such love. It comes from God and gets replenished and distributed by the Holy Spirit. We can ask for it, and God will hear our prayers.

Pray often for love in your church. Pray that your love will flow to other relationships and become a witness to a different and better way of life.

2:2-3 My purpose is that they may be encouraged in heart and united in love.^{NIV} Paul wanted those he had not been able to visit to know that he was interested in them and was praying diligently for them. They would also be relieved of their anxiety about Epaphras's teachings since Paul endorsed them as true. When writing to churches where he had previously taught, Paul addressed their particular situation in detail. To those he had not yet visited, he wrote more general principles of Christianity; thus, here he simply prayed for the Colossians' encouragement (inner strength) and unity (outer strength). These two characteristics would help them resist false teaching.

So that they may have the full riches of complete understanding, in order that they may know the mystery of God, namely, Christ.^{NIV} This is Paul's goal. The encouragement believers receive when they unite together in love gives them a rich and full understanding of God's mystery—Christ. Paul did not want any believers to stop at knowing the glorious riches of his mystery (1:27), he wanted them to have the *full riches of complete understanding*. In the Old Testament, "full riches" meant not only material prosperity, but spiritual blessing. Isaiah 33:6 says, "a rich store of salvation . . . the fear of the Lord is the key to this treasure" (NIV). There is no understanding of God apart from Christ. There is no complete understanding of God apart from a personal relationship with his Son. Christ is the mystery, yet he is a mystery revealed to those who believe—as is the mystery of "Christ in you, the hope of glory" (1:27), and the mystery that Gentiles and Jews can be united in one body (1:26).

PUBLIC OR CHRISTIAN EDUCATION?
If Christ is the key to understanding, and all knowledge revolves around Christ, should our children be taught by Christian teachers in a Christian school? Many parents face this question.

The Bible requires this: Youngsters need to acquire a Christ-centered worldview. Faithful discipleship has no secular or value-free closets of knowledge. Everybody we know is linked to an interpretive scheme or set of assumptions about how the world holds together. That scheme should have Christ at its center.

If a public school is your choice, you will need to provide Christian education at home and in church. If a Christian school is your choice, you will need to support and supplement your child's education.

Too many teenagers emerge from basic education with no idea how science, math, social studies, or literature relate to their faith. A Christ-centered worldview puts all knowledge in proper perspective.

This complete understanding obtained through personal relationship with Christ himself assures believers of the truth and helps them recognize and avoid heresy. Everything anyone wants to know about God and his purposes in the world is answered in the person of Christ. The mystery is revealed because it is Christ **in whom are hidden all the treasures of wisdom and knowledge.**NKJV True wisdom is found only in Christ; true knowledge is found only in Christ. Knowledge is often described as good judgment, wisdom as application of that good judgment in the form of good actions. The false teachers claimed to have, through their relation with a supposed hierarchy of supernatural beings, a higher knowledge than what ordinary believers possessed. Against this, Paul argued that all wisdom and knowledge were in Christ and that Christ's treasures were accessible to every believer. *Hidden* does not mean concealed, but rather that they were laid up or stored away to be made available to those who desire relationship with Christ.

Certainly these words greatly comforted the Colossian believers who did not have to look any farther for wisdom and knowledge than to their Savior, Jesus Christ. The believers already possessed all wisdom and knowledge, yet they had a long way to go to attain maturity and complete understanding.

DRAWN IN
Christian faith is a growth track into knowledge of the truth, but along the way, how do we guard against lies?

If your track is too narrow, you become thickheaded and insular—no one can teach you a thing. Before long, you can't teach anyone around you, for no one is listening. You are isolated. Love disappears from your life.

If your track is too wide and every idea is an exciting new possibility, you'll waste a lot of time just keeping on track and risk some dangerous detours.

The key is centering on Christ and grounding yourself in his Word. Learn daily about the Savior. Study the Bible. Develop your theological knowledge. Stay humble and curious about the amazing complexity of the world God has made. Ask lots of questions about the assumptions behind ideas new to you. Press toward wisdom. Pray for understanding. God has given us minds for learning—never quit using yours.

2:4 I am saying this so that no one may deceive you with plausible arguments.NRSV The believers in Colosse already knew what they needed to know to be saved; they already knew the One they needed to know to have eternal life. But they needed to grow to maturity in the faith they had received. Paul reaffirmed this to them in 2:1-3 so that they would not be deceived by any arguments from false teachers. At first, lies don't sound like lies. The false teachers did a good job of making their teachings sound plausible and of using persuasive tactics to cause the believers to question their faith. When believers are fully committed to the truth in Jesus, they will not be easily deluded when others offer "treasures of wisdom" not found in Christ.

2:5 For though I am absent in body, yet I am with you in spirit.NRSV Paul wrote to the Colossians to warn them against false teaching. He explained that although he couldn't be with them due to his imprisonment, he was always with them in spirit. His thoughts were with them, and he was with them because they were united through the Holy Spirit.

Rejoicing to see your good order and the steadfastness of your faith in Christ.NKJV Paul's presence in spirit was so real to him that he wrote of actually "seeing" them—their good order and steadfast faith. *Good order* refers to 2:2 where Paul spoke of their unity as a well-organized, orderly body of believers, resulting in high morale. *The steadfastness of your faith* revealed the solid foundation on which the church had been built. These two characteristics caused Paul to rejoice, for they meant that the Colossians had not succumbed to the false teaching. They were a unified body, steadfast in their faith. Paul's prayers, toil, and struggle had not been in vain. Does your church reflect the same kind of unity and solidarity in faith that Paul rejoiced to see?

NEW LIFE IN CHRIST / 2:6-15

Paul rejoiced in the Colossians' unity and steadfast faith because these proved they had not given ground to the heresy. But Paul wanted to insure that they wouldn't give in and believe the lies of the false teachers. So he launched into a full-scale rebuttal of the false teaching.

2:6 As you therefore have received Christ Jesus the Lord, so walk in Him.NKJV The Colossians had not merely received the doctrines of Christ, they had *received Christ* himself. The verb "received" (in Greek, *parelabete*) means more than the moment a person asks Christ into his or her heart. Paul most likely used the word, taken from Judaism, to describe the transmitting and safeguarding of traditions and teachings from one person or generation to another. Thus when Paul reminded the Colossians of when they received Christ Jesus, he was reminding them of their receiving the proclamation and teaching, and their confession of faith, their baptism, and their new status as members of Christ's body.

Because Christ dwells within all believers through the Holy Spirit, they should *walk* (conduct their lives) in union with the indwelling Christ. The word "walk" refers to ethical conduct and behavior appropriate for those who claim Christ. The verb indicates continuous action: "continue to live" (NIV). The past event of receiving Christ should be a present reality in the believers' daily lives.

2:7 Rooted and built up in him, strengthened in the faith as you were taught, and overflowing with thankfulness.NIV Paul used several metaphors in these verses, first telling believers to walk, then to be rooted like a plant, built like a building, and established like a legal document. Each metaphor has a specific and profound point for Christian living.

First, the Colossians were to be *rooted* in Christ. Just as plants draw nourishment from the soil through their roots, so the believers should draw life-giving strength from Christ. The more they would draw strength from Christ, the less they would be fooled by those who falsely claimed to have life's answers. Paul used the perfect tense of the word, describing a present state that had resulted from a past action. A better translation would be "having been rooted." The Colossians were still rooted in Christ because they had received him.

Second, the Colossians were to be *built up*. This word is in the present tense, describing continuous action. Like a plant, they were "rooted" once and for all, but they had to grow continuously (1:28). Or like a building, they had a solid foundation, but had to keep on building with solid materials in order to be strong.

Third, the Colossians were to be *strengthened in the faith*. This can also be translated "established in the faith" (NKJV). "Established" was a legal term, often used for a binding contract. This too is continuous action, an ongoing process. In these words, Paul might

> The first act of the Christian life is to receive Christ, and every moment afterward we must continue receiving him. The act must become an attitude. Breathe in the love and power of Jesus. Take deep breaths. Then we shall be rooted in him in secret, and built up in him in our outward walk and behavior. If we have Christ, we have all God's fullness. . . . What need have we for celestial beings, like those invented by the Gnostics, or for the rite of circumcision, as insisted on by the Jews? We have everything in Jesus.
>
> *F. B. Meyer*

TRUST: YESTERDAY, TODAY, AND TOMORROW!

Living under the lordship of Christ means realizing that each day brings new opportunities to trust Christ and experience his powerful work in us. Have you trusted this day to Christ?

Trusting Christ	=	Living in vital union with Christ day by day (2:2-7)
Accepting Christ as Head or Lord	=	He is in control (1:15-18; 2:19; 3:10, 17)
Experiencing the power of the Holy Spirit	=	God's mighty energy at work in us (1:11, 28, 29)
Inward and outward results	=	• assurance of forgiveness (2:15) • freedom from evil desires (2:11) • joy (2:7) • personal growth (1:28) • opportunities to tell others the gospel (1:4, 28) • thankfulness to God (2:7)
Direction	=	God becoming involved in our decisions (3:1, 16)

have meant any of three things: (1) that they should become more established (stronger) in their personal faith,
(2) that their faith should establish and strengthen them for daily living, or (3) that they should become more established (stronger) in *the* faith, Christianity. The words *as you were taught* indicate that the third option is probably closest to Paul's meaning. Paul wanted the Colossians to be built up and established in order to continue to stand firmly against any false teaching.

The faith in which these Colossian believers were rooted, built up, and established should be a source of abundant thanksgiving. True understanding of what Christ has done on behalf of believers can lead to no other response than gratefulness. This too ought to characterize believers' faith and walk.

2:8 See to it that no one takes you captive through hollow and deceptive philosophy, which depends on human tradition and the basic principles of this world rather than on Christ.[NIV] The Colossians needed to be on their guard. Paul strongly warned about the heresy's effect on those who believed it. They would be taken *captive*. The word used here means "to kidnap" or "to capture and take away." The false teachers used seductive tactics; the believers had to *see to it* that they didn't allow themselves to let down their guard and be captured intellectually.

THE BEGINNING
Receiving Christ as Lord of your life is the beginning of life with Christ. But you must continue to follow his leadership by being rooted, built up, and strengthened in the faith. Christ wants to guide you and help you with your daily problems. You can live for Christ by (1) committing your life and submitting your will to him (Romans 12:1-2); (2) seeking to learn from him, his life, and his teachings (3:16); and (3) recognizing the Holy Spirit's power in you (Acts 1:8; Galatians 5:22).

According to Paul, the heresy amounted to nothing more than *hollow and deceptive philosophy.* The word translated "philosophy" occurs only here in the New Testament, so this may have been a significant feature of this heresy. In Greek, the word "philosophy" means "love of wisdom." Paul was a gifted philosopher, so he was not condemning education or the study of philosophy. Instead, he was condemning false philosophy, the kind that is deceptive because it keeps people from seeing the truth.

Paul was so disparaging toward this heresy because it was based merely on *human tradition.* Traditions are fine but have little value in a search for the truth. The heresy also was based on *the basic principles of this world.* The Greek phrase *stoikeia tou kosmou* has also been translated "elements of the world" (in Galatians 4:3 NKJV). This phrase (also used in Colossians 2:20) has three main interpretations:

(1) Some have interpreted "basic principles" to refer directly to the law of Moses. This interpretation agrees with Paul's view that the law taken by itself leads only to slavery, but the meaning must be much broader to fit the context of the Colossian believers.

(2) Others have interpreted "basic principles" or "elements" to mean the four basic elements of Greek philosophy—earth, air, fire, and water. Later, these elements became associated with the gods and then with the stars and planets. Many pagan religions (and, at times, the Jewish people) worshiped stars and planets because of their supposed effect on human destiny. This interpretation is also unlikely in this context.

(3) A third, and most likely, interpretation is that these "basic principles" are the elementary stages of religious practice, whether in the Jewish religion, or the rites and rituals in any heathen religion. Paul may have been referring to the local gods worshiped by the pagans across the Roman Empire. Every city had its own deity. In Greek, a deity was called a *dai-*

mon (demon). The source of these deities or demons was the same—Satan. Because the heresy did not come from Christ, it had to have been inspired by Satan in order to "kidnap" people away from the truth.

No man-made religion can lead to the truth, for truth can be found only in Christ. In Christ are hidden "all the treasures of wisdom and knowledge" (2:3 NKJV). No one can come to God except through Christ (John 14:6). True philosophy will focus on Jesus Christ—it will not put Christ in any lower position, nor will it focus on human endeavor.

2:9 For in Christ all the fullness of the Deity lives in bodily form.NIV Again Paul asserted Christ's divine nature (see 1:19). *In Christ* designates a local or spatial relationship rather than a mystical relationship. God's saving action happens in the person of Jesus Christ. In 2:9-13, every verse contains the phrase "in Christ" (or "in him") or "with Christ" (or "with him") to show that Christ is the center of God's saving activity. *All the fullness of the Deity* refers to the whole total of deity *(pleroma theotaitos)* or all the divine attributes. God's nature and person are centered in Christ. *Lives in bodily form* means "dwells permanently" or "continues to live" in a human body.

The false teaching said that Christ could not have been both man and God. But Paul clearly stated that this was indeed the case. Paul made two significant points in this sentence: (1) Christ was not another deity along with God; instead, God's fullness was dwelling uniquely and supremely in Christ. (2) Christ was not less than God. He was not merely one in a hierarchy of angels who would act as intermediaries between people and God. Instead, Paul emphasized to these Colossian believers, and to us today, that when we have Christ, we have everything we need for salvation and right living. He is our leader. No man-made religion or philosophy can give what Christ gives—salvation and right relationship with God.

2:10 And you have come to fullness in him.NRSV Not only does all the fullness of the Deity dwell in Christ, but all believers have been given fullness (completeness) in Christ. The Colossians lacked nothing outside of Christ; in him they had everything they needed for salvation and right living. Because they had "received" Christ (2:6) through Paul's doctrine, the Colossians didn't need to seek God in other philosophies.

But what does this "completeness" mean? It means that there is nothing lacking in a believer's relationship with God. God pours his love and power into believers, giving them fullness for this life and readying them for the life to come. Believers need not look anywhere else. Christ is the unique source of knowledge and power for the Christian life. Christ alone holds the answers to the true meaning of life because he *is* life.

FILLING THE GAPS
Look around you. People are searching for something to give their lives a boost. Few people seem content within themselves. A strange and often hard-to-identify inner vacuum gives most people an uneasy sense of incompleteness.

But Christ fills the vacuum. As Jesus' person is fully divine, so we, united by faith to Jesus, find personal fulfillment in him. We are complete in Christ.

Some days may not feel like it, but, in fact, in Jesus the vacuum is gone; the full power and presence of God has taken up residence in your mind and heart. You are a new person, equipped for life and satisfied in God. So . . .
1. Take more risks—God will guide you.
2. Give more generously—God will supply you.
3. Love more freely—God will energize you.
4. Say "can do" more often—God will amaze you.

Who is the head of every ruler and authority.NRSV Christ is not just one of many intermediaries or angels who must be worshiped, as the heresy maintained. Instead, he *is the head of every ruler and authority.* Because Christ is the head and is superior to any angel or archangel, it would be absurd to worship or venerate any angel. Believers are part of Christ's body, the church (1:24), of which Christ is the "head." Even more than that, Christ is "far above all rule and authority, power and dominion, and every title that can be given, not only in the present age but also in the one to come" (Ephesians 1:21 NIV).

Even today, we must not let curiosity over the nature of angels or any other being in the spirit world cause us to respect, revere, or follow such beings. No spirit guide or intermediary can replace or improve upon what Christ does for us in the Holy Spirit.

2:11 **In him you were also circumcised, in the putting off of the sinful nature, not with a circumcision done by the hands of men but with the circumcision done by Christ.**NIV Jewish males were circumcised as a sign of the Jews' covenant with God (Genesis 17:9-14). Circumcision was an expression of Israel's national identity and was a requirement for all Jewish men. Circumcision (cutting off the foreskin of the penis) was a physical reminder to Jews of their national heritage and privilege. It symbolized "cutting off" the old life of sin, purifying one's heart, and dedicating oneself to God (Deuteronomy 10:16; Jeremiah 4:4; Ezekiel 44:7).

However, with the death of Christ, bodily circumcision was no longer necessary to be identified as God's people. Paul explained that all believers *were also circumcised,* but *not with a circumcision done by the hands of men.* Instead, their circumcision involved *the putting off of the sinful nature.* The phrase "putting off" (from the Greek *apekdysei,* meaning "total breaking away from") occurs only here in the New Testament and describes a complete break from the old sinful life. "Sinful nature" translates *somatostas sarkos,* literally "the body of the flesh." This phrase about putting off the body of flesh has two main lines of scholarly interpretation. (1) It could refer to the spiritual work of Christ done on the hearts of believers—the putting off of the old sinful nature (3:9), or (2) it could refer to Christ's putting off his body of flesh at the Crucifixion, where he died on behalf of believers. This second view seems unlikely because there is no reference to "his" (Christ's) body being put off. Besides, such a stripping off of the body would support the very teaching that Paul was combating.

The Colossian believers had become God's children. The sign of their new life was not a cutting of the flesh, but a "cutting off" of the sinful nature. Their commitment to God had been written on their hearts, not on their bodies. Only Christ could perform this circumcision, for only by accepting him as Savior can people be saved. Christ sets people free from their evil desires by a spiritual operation, not a bodily one. He had removed the Colossian believers' old natures and had given them new ones. *The circumcision done by Christ* was not when he was circumcised as an infant, but when he died on the cross.

2:12 When you were buried with him in baptism, you were also raised with him through faith in the power of God, who raised him from the dead.[NRSV] Paul assumed that these Colossian believers had been baptized at conversion and would vividly recall the experience. Paul wrote to the Romans that those who believe in Christ are "baptized into Christ Jesus . . . baptized into his death" (Romans 6:3 NIV). Baptism parallels the death, burial, and resurrection of Christ, and it also portrays the death and burial of the believer's sinful way of life. So how are we buried with Christ in baptism? In the church of Paul's day, many people were baptized by immersion—that is, new Christians were completely "buried" in water. They understood this form of baptism to symbolize being buried with Christ, thus the death and burial of the old way of life. When Christ died, our old nature died with him also. This was a spiritual circumcision (2:11). Baptism also portrays the death of our old nature.

Coming up out of the water symbolized resurrection to new life with Christ. It also symbolized the future bodily resurrection. Believers' faith is in the power of God that raised Christ from the dead, and thus it is faith in the power that will one day raise us from the dead.

This is true freedom! The Colossian believers already possessed it! They didn't need a false heresy filled with powers and authorities and rituals and practices. All they needed was Christ— and they would be complete in him!

DEAD AND BURIED
Remembering that our old sinful life is dead and buried with Christ gives us a powerful motive to resist sin. Not wanting the desires of our past to come back to power again, we can consciously choose to treat our desires as if they were dead. Then we can continue to enjoy our wonderful new life with Christ (see Galatians 3:27 and Colossians 3:1-4).

2:13 And when you were dead in trespasses and the uncircumcision of your flesh, God made you alive together with him, when he forgave us all our trespasses.ᴺᴿˢⱽ The Colossians were Gentiles, so they were uncircumcised, but that was not the cause of their spiritual death. It was their uncircumcised sinful nature that made them dead in their sins (see 2:11-12). In Deuteronomy 10:16, Moses told the people of Israel to circumcise their hearts. He wanted the people to go beyond physical surgery; they needed to submit to God in their hearts as well as in their bodies. Jeremiah echoed that teaching in Jeremiah 4:4. In Romans 2:29, Paul taught, "real circumcision is a matter of the heart" (NRSV). People were physically alive, but spiritually dead. God's power had raised Christ from the dead (2:12); he raised the believers from the dead also, because they had been dead in their sins. The Colossians, as Gentiles, had been dead in sin and outside the scope of God's mercy. What Paul wrote to the Ephesians applies here: "Remember that at that time you were separate from Christ, excluded from citizenship in Israel and foreigners to the covenants of the promise, without hope and without God in the world" (Ephesians 2:12 NIV).

FREE TO LIVE
Before we believed in Christ, our nature was evil. We disobeyed, rebelled, and ignored God (even at our best, we did not love him with all our heart, soul, and mind). The Christian, however, has a new nature. God has crucified the old, rebellious nature (Romans 6:6) and has replaced it with a new, loving nature (3:9, 10). The penalty of sin died with Christ on the cross. God has declared us not guilty, and we need no longer live under sin's power. God does not take us out of the world or make us robots—we will still feel like sinning, and sometimes we will sin. The difference is that before we were saved, we were slaves to our sinful nature; but now we are free to live for Christ (see Galatians 2:20). How are you using your freedom?

To defeat death, God made us alive; to deliver us from sin, he made us alive with Christ. Because God raised Christ, those who belong to Christ are raised as well. God made the Colossian believers *alive together with him.* As opposed to being dead alone in their sin, being alive together with Christ means that believers do not need to live any longer under sin's power. The penalty of sin and its power over believers were miraculously destroyed by Christ on the cross. Through faith in Christ, believers are acquitted, or found not guilty, before God, their judge.

How did this happen? The answer is simple: *He forgave us all our trespasses [sins].* If our sinful nature caused us to be dead, then that sinful nature had to be dealt with before God could make us alive. The word "forgave" is in the past tense, referring to Christ's work on the cross. God's forgiveness opens the way for believers to experience new life in Christ.

PAID IN FULL
We can enjoy our new life in Christ because we have joined him in his death and resurrection. Our evil desires, our bondage to sin, and our love of sin died with him. Now, joining him in his resurrection life, we may have unbroken fellowship with God and freedom from sin. When you feel weighed down by a load of sin, remember that your debt for sin has been paid in full; your sins are swept away and forgotten by God; and you are clean and new.

2:14 **Erasing the record that stood against us with its legal demands.**[NRSV] Paul went on to explain the nature of Christ's forgiveness. In forgiving all our sins (2:13), Christ *erased the record that stood against us.* This record was like a handwritten ledger of our trespasses against the law. Humanity could not pay the debt for these offenses, so God wiped out the record of our sin.

He set this aside, nailing it to the cross.[NRSV] Christ canceled the written record against us by taking the ledger to the cross and nailing it there. In so doing, our debts were canceled; what stood against us can no longer hinder us. Christ set us free by his sacrificial death on the cross. No regulations or human-made rituals can substitute or be added to what Christ has done for us—neither Judaism nor any false teaching can give the salvation that Christ gave. Jesus' death took care of believers' indebtedness to God.

CANCELLED

In 1940, a twenty-one-year-old black man named W. D. Lyons was arrested for a brutal triple murder in Tulsa, Oklahoma. His conviction was based on a coerced confession, and his trial was a farce.

While the truth was never fully determined, the murders were probably committed by organized crime figures, who had framed Lyons because he had a prior criminal record. No court in the country, including the U.S. Supreme Court, had rules sufficient to get at the truth. Lyons was a man caught in a system with no way out.

After twenty-five years in prison, Lyons was released by the governor of Oklahoma using his executive authority. Prison gates opened and Lyons walked free.

Spiritually, we are all left without a defense on a one-way trip into darkness and death. Yet our pardon comes with a promise. God will guide and prosper us in new life in Christ. Not only is our conviction cancelled, but we get power for rebuilding our lives. Make eternal life your wonderful goal and hope.

2:15 And having disarmed the powers and authorities, he made a public spectacle of them, triumphing over them by the cross.[NIV] Not only did Christ's death on the cross pay humanity's debt to God, his death also meant his triumph over the *powers and authorities.*

Who are these "powers and authorities"? Several suggestions have been made, including (1) demonic powers, (2) the gods of the powerful nations, (3) the government of Rome, or even (4) angels (highly regarded by the heretical teachers). Since Paul did not identify who these powers and authorities were, it could be any one of them, or all four. What Christ *disarmed* on the cross was any embodiment of rebellion in the world—whether that be Satan and his demons, false idols of pagan religions (as in

SALVATION THROUGH FAITH

Salvation by faith in Christ sounds too easy for many people. They would rather think that they have done something to save themselves. Their religion becomes one of self-effort that leads either to disappointment or pride, but finally to eternal death. Christ's simple way is the only way, and it alone leads to eternal life.

	Religion by Self-Effort	Salvation by Faith
Goal	Please God by our own good deeds	Trust in Christ and then live to please God
Means	Practice, diligent service, discipline, and obedience, in hope of reward	Confess, submit, and commit yourself to Christ's control
Power	Good, honest effort through self-determination	The Holy Spirit in us helps us do good work for Christ's kingdom
Control	Self-motivation, self-control	Christ in me; I in Christ
Results	Chronic guilt, apathy, depression, failure, constant desire for approval	Joy, thankfulness, love, guidance, service, forgiveness

2:16), evil world governments, or even God's good angels when they become the object of worship (as in the Colossian heresy).

This "disarming" occurred when Jesus died on the cross. The word for "disarmed" is literally "stripped," as in stripping a defeated enemy of armor on the battlefield. The powers and authorities of this evil world stripped Christ of his clothing and popularity, made a public spectacle of him on the cross, and triumphed over him by putting him to death. Ironically, the victory belonged to Christ. Actually he stripped the evil powers of their hold on the world, held them up to public contempt, and triumphed over them by taking his rightful power and position.

Evil no longer has any power over believers because Christ has disarmed it. Paul already had told the Colossians, "For he has rescued us from the dominion of darkness and brought us into the kingdom of the Son he loves" (1:13 NIV). As a triumphant Roman general would lead a procession of captives and booty gained in a great victory, so Christ had turned his captors into captives, displaying them in his victory procession. The Colossians, too, had participated in that victory. We also must not act as helpless slaves to the heresy of false teachers; instead, we should proclaim the truth and victory of our Savior, Jesus Christ.

FREEDOM FROM LEGALISM / 2:16-23

Paul wondered aloud in this section why the Colossian believers would choose to return from freedom to slavery. Why were they living as if they belonged to the world? Why should they submit to these rules? Paul was not speaking of all rules and regulations, but of those that were rooted in rebellion against God, rules that were self-serving rather than God-honoring. Such regulations only served to enslave people. Believers must never set aside freedom in order to follow a series of negative rules and regulations regarding every facet of life. We died with Christ; he has set us free.

2:16 Therefore do not let anyone condemn you in matters of food and drink or of observing festivals, new moons, or sabbaths.NRSV Because Christ had canceled the written code (2:14) and had disarmed evil powers (2:15), believers have been set free from legalistic rules about what they eat or drink or what festivals they observe. Although it is most likely that Paul was referring to Jewish laws about diet and festival observances, pagan food laws and celebrations, or a combination of the two, cannot be excluded as a possibility. Some Greek philosophies promoted fasting in order to prepare for a vision. In any case, Paul's point was that the believers should not give up their freedom for legalism. They must not let anyone *condemn* them by saying that certain actions would exclude them from God's people. If the Colossians submitted to any of the regulations imposed by the false teachers, they would be saying that evil powers still held authority over them. They needed to remember that Christ had set them free.

FOCUS ON FAITH
Paul told the Colossian Christians not to let others criticize their diet or their religious ceremonies. Instead of outward observance, believers should focus on faith in Christ alone. Our worship, traditions, and ceremonies can help bring us close to God, but we should never criticize fellow Christians whose traditions and ceremonies differ from ours. More important than how we worship is that we worship Christ. Don't be discouraged if others judge you. Remember that you are responsible to Christ.

2:17 These are a shadow of the things that were to come; the reality, however, is found in Christ.NIV Paul did not condemn the keeping of some Old Testament dietary laws or observing some of the celebrations. Instead, he condemned doing so in order to somehow earn credit with God. The Old Testament laws, holidays, and feasts were *a shadow of the things that were to come*. In the analogy of the cave in Plato's *Republic,* Plato distinguished between the shadow (outward appearance) and reality (inward spiritual truth). But Paul was using "shadow" in the sense of foreshadowing. The law pointed to the future—to Christ. Anything that is not Christ or found in Christ is, by contrast, a shadow or unreal. At one time these laws were needed as God prepared a nation for himself. These people would be keepers of his laws and ancestors of his Son. The ceremonial and civil regulations of Judaism set God's people apart from the world. Through Christ, however, God was preparing a new people for himself—a worldwide family. What the Old Testament promised, Christ fulfilled. If we have Christ, we have what we need in order to know and please God.

2:18 Do not let anyone who delights in false humility and the worship of angels disqualify you for the prize.NIV By turning the Colossian believers away from the reality back to the shadow, the false teachers served only to *disqualify* the believers. Paul did not mean that the believers would lose their salvation, but that they would lose their *prize* (that is, their rewards; see also 1 Corinthians 3:10-15).

Some versions say that the false teachers were "insisting on self-abasement" (NRSV), meaning that not only did they enjoy their pretense of humility, but they also attempted to impose it on the Colossian believers. The false humility, revealed by self-abasement and self-denial, came from observances of rituals and regulations that had no bearing on salvation. This sort of humility was self-absorbing and self-gratifying, a kind of pretentious piety.

TRUE WORTH
The false teachers were proud of their humility! This false humility brought attention and praise to the teachers rather than to God. True humility means seeing ourselves as we really are—from God's perspective—and then acting accordingly. Today, people practice false humility when they talk negatively about themselves so that others will think they are spiritual. Humility is a Christian virtue, but true Christian humility comes from realizing that our only worth is due to Christ's intervention on our behalf. False humility is self-centered; true humility is God-centered.

In addition, these teachers' false humility said that the people could not approach God directly—he could be approached only through various levels of angels. They taught, therefore, that people had to worship angels in order to eventually reach God. This is unscriptural; the Bible teaches that angels are God's servants and it forbids worshiping them (Exodus 20:3-4; Revelation 19:9-10; 22:8-9). No amount of fascination with angels should overshadow the majesty of Christ.

DISCONNECTED
This picture of the body—all Jesus' followers united in the church—portrays dynamic growth; it is not static, not standing still. Anyone who becomes disconnected from Christ stops growing and loses the ability to discern the truth.

If you're disconnected, you may be getting more confused (or unthinkingly rigid) every day. Consider the consequences: At its extremes, such disconnection causes people to justify killing doctors in the name of saving unborn babies. More typically, the disconnection makes us soft on issues like sexual fidelity, truth telling, and respect for others.

If you're losing momentum and you need to get connected again to Jesus, do it today. Pray with a Christian friend and let God know it's time you got on the move.

Such a person goes into great detail about what he has seen, and his unspiritual mind puffs him up with idle notions.[NIV] The false teachers took great pride in what they had seen in visions—most likely these were part of an initiation rite that climaxed in some sort of vision that supposedly revealed great secrets of the universe. These visions caused division because only an elite few could experience them. This only puffed up the false teachers with all kinds of interpretations and ideas that Paul dismissed as *idle notions* because their minds were not centered on Christ; they were *unspiritual* (see Romans 8:5-10). While the false teachers may have thought that they had a "corner on God," their thoughts and actions betrayed a mere human origin. Their desire for attention from others showed that, in reality, they were obsessed with and controlled by the physical realm. They were putting their confidence in their visions and rule keeping, and not in Christ.

2:19 He has lost connection with the Head, from whom the whole body, supported and held together by its ligaments and sinews, grows as God causes it to grow.[NIV] The fundamental problem with the false teachers was that they were not connected to Christ, the Head of the body of believers. If they had been joined to him, they would not have taught false doctrine or lived immorally. The false teachers had become detached from Christ. Just as a limb that is detached from the body loses life, so these false teachers, detached from the body of Christ and no longer under his headship, had lost the most vital connection. By losing connection with Christ, the natural result was that these teachers would fall into error and find themselves separated from the church.

Spiritual "judges" were not connected with Jesus or with his body. If they truly held fast to him, they would not be worried about human regulations. The *ligaments and sinews,* by connecting all the members of the body to one another, allow the power to grow (which comes from the head) to reach all the body. The Greek medical ideas behind this imagery stressed that the head supplied energy and nourishment to the body by means of the joints and ligaments. Along with the muscles, these were the supply channels to the body. The body of Christ can only grow when the believers are connected to one another under Christ (see also 1 Corinthians 12:12-31; Ephesians 4:15-16). Using a similar analogy, Jesus had told his disciples, "I am the vine, you are the branches. He who abides in Me, and I in him, bears much fruit; for without Me you can do nothing" (John 15:5 NKJV).

TRUST GOD FOR A CHANGE
People should be able to see a difference between the way Christians and non-Christians live. Still, we should not expect instant maturity in new Christians. Christian growth is a lifelong process. Although we have a new nature, we don't automatically think all good thoughts and have all pure attitudes when we become new people in Christ. But if we keep listening to God, we will be changing all the time. As you look over the last year, what positive changes have you seen in your thoughts and attitudes? Change may be slow, but your life will change significantly if you trust God to change you.

2:20-21 Since you died with Christ to the basic principles of this world, why, as though you still belonged to it, do you submit to its rules: "Do not handle! Do not taste! Do not touch!"?NIV
Believers have died with Christ and are no longer under the power of *the basic principles of this world*—the evil spirits and demonic powers that work against Christ (see commentary on 2:8). When Christ died, he "disarmed the powers and authorities" (2:15). Believers have died with Christ; thus, they are no longer under the control of those powers and authorities. Their "death" released them from their previous slavery. Paul wondered, somewhat incredulously, why these Colossian believers would even think about submitting themselves to a conquered power. (The

verb implies not a reprimand for having done something, but a warning against doing it.)

2:22 **All these regulations refer to things that perish with use; they are simply human commands and teachings.**^{NRSV} *These regulations* (referring to the commands not to handle, taste, or touch in 2:21) focused on rule keeping that had nothing to do with God's holy laws. The focus was on how well a person could keep the rules and then congratulate himself or herself for rule keeping. There were two problems with this: (1) These were physical laws, from the world, dealing with things that could be tasted and touched and would therefore eventually *perish with use*. In these words we hear an echo of Christ when he explained to the Pharisees: "It is not what goes into the mouth that defiles a person, but it is what comes out of the mouth that defiles. . . . Do you not see that whatever goes into the mouth enters the stomach, and goes out into the sewer?" (Matthew 15:11, 17 NRSV).

(2) These were *human commands and teachings*. The false teachers were attempting to teach as doctrine their own ideas; they were placing their regulations and rules on level with God's commands; they were trying to make their regulations a condition of God's grace. They were wrong on all counts. Again we hear an echo of Christ speaking to the Pharisees, "You hypocrites! Isaiah prophesied rightly about you when he said: 'In vain do they worship me, teaching human precepts as doctrines'" (Matthew 15:7, 9 NRSV).

CAN'T REACH HIGH ENOUGH
We cannot reach up to God by following rules of self-denial, by observing rituals, or by practicing religion. Paul wasn't teaching that all rules are bad. But no keeping of laws or rules will earn salvation. The good news is that God reaches down to human beings, and he asks for our response. Human-made religions focus on human effort; Christianity focuses on Christ's work. Believers must put aside sinful desires, but doing so is the by-product of our new life in Christ, not the reason for our new life. Depend on the power of Christ's death and resurrection for salvation, not on your own discipline and rule keeping.

2:23 **Such regulations indeed have an appearance of wisdom, with their self-imposed worship, their false humility and their harsh treatment of the body, but they lack any value in restraining sensual indulgence.**^{NIV} To the Colossians, the discipline demanded by the false teachers seemed good. Actually, forms of legalism still attract many people today. Following a long list of religious rules requires strong self-discipline and can make a person appear sagacious and spiritual. But such people are empty shells, giving only *an appearance of wisdom.* True wisdom is found only in Christ, the source of all wisdom. *Self-imposed worship* refers to human-made religion that, by its very nature, cannot focus on Christ (2:18-19). Thus it does not honor God. The *humility* supposedly shown by these rule-keeping ascetics was false humility. In reality, their ability to keep the rules and their *harsh treatment of the body* as they attempted to carry out the regulations caused them to be proud and to place themselves above others. But all this piety and asceticism was worthless. No amount of religious rules can change a person's heart; they have no value in *restraining sensual indulgence.* Only the Holy Spirit can do that. It is important to note that it is not just sensual indulgence (as NIV translates it), but self-indulgence of any kind.

Therefore, all human attempts at religion are worthless. By extension, then, the heresy with all its positive-sounding rules was also worthless.

QUESTIONS TO ASK
We can guard against human-made religions by asking these questions about any religious group:
- Does it stress human-made rules and taboos rather than God's grace?
- Does it foster a critical spirit toward others, or does it exercise discipline discreetly and lovingly?
- Does it stress formulas, secret knowledge, or special visions more than the Word of God?
- Does it elevate self-righteousness, honoring those who keep the rules, rather than elevating Christ?
- Does it neglect Christ's universal church, claiming to be an elite group?
- Does it teach humiliation of the body as a means to spiritual growth rather than focusing on the growth of the whole person?
- Does it disregard the family rather than holding it in high regard as the Bible does?

Colossians 3:1–4:6

Whereas chapter 2 was mostly a criticism of false teachers, this section affirms the Christian's new position in Christ. In chapter 2, Paul exposed the wrong reasons for self-denial. Chapter 3:1-4 functions like Romans 12:1-2. It provides a powerful transition from the theoretical discussion of chapters 1 and 2 to the practical issues of chapters 3 and 4. In chapter 3, Paul explains true Christian behavior—putting on the new self by accepting Christ and regarding the earthly nature as dead. We change our moral and ethical behavior by letting Christ live within us, so that he can shape us into what we should be.

3:1 Since, then, you have been raised with Christ, set your hearts on things above, where Christ is seated at the right hand of God.[NIV] Paul did not want to leave his readers with merely a negative dimension to their faith—for example, "Since you died with Christ to the basic principles of this world" (2:20 NIV)—so he turned their focus to the positive. They had died, but they had also been raised. The Greek words in the phrase *since . . . you have been raised with Christ* express certainty. There was no doubt in Paul's mind of the sincerity of the Colossians' faith. Once dead in their sins, they had been raised from death, just as Christ had been raised from the dead by God's power (3:3-4 will explain this). They had received new life from God through the power of the Holy Spirit. They did not need to struggle and work to attain that life, as the false teachers were trying to tell them; they already had new life! What remained was to work out its implications in daily life. Because they had been raised, they had a clear responsibility to Christ, who had raised them.

In the Bible, the "heart" is the center of one's being. Jesus had told his followers, "Store up for yourselves treasures in heaven. . . . For where your treasure is, there your heart will be also" (Matthew 6:20-21 NIV). Paul explained that their hearts should be *set . . . on things above*. The Greek word for "set" *(zeteo)* means to seek something out with a desire to possess it. Their hearts should be seeking after what is above (in the spiritual, eternal world) in contrast to what is below (in the earthly, transitory world). Paul contrasted the desirable "things" with the basic principles of the universe (2:20) and the human commands and teachings (2:22-23). They were to get their direction from Christ, not from the ascetic principles discussed in 2:8-23.

The other religious teachers stressed "heavenly things" also, but Paul was appealing to the highest power of all, the exalted Christ. The believers must take their focus off the world and turn it to Christ, who *is seated at the right hand of God*. Jesus had told his accusers that "from now on, the Son of Man will be seated at the right hand of the mighty God" (Luke 22:69 NIV). Even David saw the coming Messiah and his position: "The Lord says to my Lord: 'Sit at my right hand until I make your enemies a footstool for your feet'" (Psalm 110:1 NIV). Christ's seat at God's right hand reveals his power, authority, and position as both judge and advocate.

Because the believers had been raised with Christ, they were participating with Christ in the spiritual realm to which he had been exalted. Indeed, Paul wrote to the Ephesians, "God raised us up with Christ and seated us with him in the heavenly realms in Christ Jesus" (Ephesians 2:6 NIV). The Colossian believers already had experienced this exaltation; they needed to set their hearts and treasures there so that they would live out their lives on earth as citizens of heaven.

DUAL CITIZENSHIP
Christians have one calling and two venues, one purpose and two passports. We are to both love God with our heart and soul and love our neighbor as ourselves. And we do that here and now, where we are, with the life God has given us.

Proper strategy for this lifelong calling requires us to set our minds on Christ daily. In practical terms, that means we

- regard money as a means to do God's will, not merely to accumulate or to use for our own pleasure;
- find a spouse who shares our desire to seek Christ and things above;
- not set our hearts on clothes, cars, and entertainment options;
- find a church that is spiritually on the move;
- get the best training we can for our particular area of service, whether medical school or ministry, jazz performance or journalism.

We must do our best for Christ.

3:2 Set your mind on things above, not on things on the earth.NKJV Setting their "hearts on things above" (3:1) meant "striving" to put heaven's priorities into daily practice. Setting

FROM DEATH TO LIFE

The Bible uses many illustrations to teach what happens when we choose to let Jesus be Lord of our lives. Following are some of the most vivid pictures.

1. Because Christ died for us, we have been crucified with him.	Romans 6:2-13; 7:4-6 2 Corinthians 5:14 Galatians 2:20; 5:24; 6:14 Colossians 2:20; 3:3-5 1 Peter 2:24
2. Our old, rebellious nature died with Christ.	Romans 6:6; 7:4-6 Colossians 3:9-10
3. Christ's resurrection guarantees our new life now and eternal life with him later.	Romans 6:4, 11 Colossians 2:12-13; 3:1, 3

This process is depicted in baptism (Colossians 2:12), based on our faith in Christ: (1) the old sinful nature dies (crucified), (2) we are ready to receive a new life (buried), and (3) Christ gives us new life (resurrected).

their *minds on things above* meant "concentrating" on the eternal rather than the temporal, letting their thoughts dwell in the realm of Christ. They were to focus on the Lord Jesus. Thoughts can influence actions, so if the believers would place their thoughts above and not on the earth, their actions would please God. The ascetics stressed the body; Paul stressed commitment of the whole person, not mindless bodily discipline. *Not on things on the earth* refers to the legalistic rituals, the false methods used to achieve holiness, and even to the basic principles of the world described in chapter 2.

But on what "things" were they to set their minds? Paul had explained this in another letter: "Finally, beloved, whatever is true, whatever is honorable, whatever is just, whatever is pure, whatever is pleasing, whatever is commendable, if there is any excellence and if there is anything worthy of praise, think about these things" (Philippians 4:8 NRSV; see also Colossians 3:12).

They were not to live as ascetics in some mystical, visionary realm; rather, Paul was saying that, by setting their hearts and minds above, their lives on this earth would be pleasing to God and would help accomplish Christ's work.

3:3 For you died, and your life is hidden with Christ in God.NKJV
The Greek aorist tense in the phrase, *for you died* connotes that we died when Christ died. It happened at a point in history. In Christ's death, all believers died (2:20). Then, like a seed buried in the earth, believers' real lives are hidden from the world, just

as Christ's glory is hidden, only to be revealed when he returns
(3:3-4). The spiritual lives of believers are *hidden* inner lives that
are in union *with Christ* who has brought them to be with him *in
God.* Their new life is a mystery, a secret.

Paul often wrote about how believers already possess the life
of Christ, having died and risen with him, yet do not fully possess
the perfection and eternal body they will have upon Christ's
return. In the meantime, they are "not yet." That their lives are
"hidden" means they are concealed and safe, hidden from public
view. Just as Christ's glory was real but hidden until the Mount of
Transfiguration, so we have a glory that is hidden and will be
revealed when Christ returns. This is not only a future hope; it is
an accomplished fact. Believers' salvation is sure, so they are to
live each day for Christ and in expectation of his promises.

YOU DIED, SO LIVE!
"For you died" means that we should have as little desire for
improper worldly pleasures as a dead person would have. The
Christian's real home is where Christ lives (John 14:2-3). This
truth provides a different perspective on our lives here on earth.
To "set your mind on things above" means to look at life from
God's perspective and to seek what he desires. This provides
the antidote to materialism; we gain the proper perspective on
material goods when we take God's view of them. It also provides the antidote to sensuality. By seeking what Christ desires,
we have the power to break our obsession with pleasure and
leisure activities. But it also provides the antidote to empty religi-
osity because following Christ means loving and serving in this
world. Regard the world around you as God does; then you will
live in harmony with him.

**3:4 When Christ, who is your life, appears, then you also will
appear with him in glory.**[NIV] Christ himself gives to believers
new, divine life. He is the source, power, and goal of all Christian
growth. This life is "hidden" (3:3), and though believers are safe
and raised with him, their full potential is yet to be revealed. One
day, when Christ *appears* in his glory, believers will also *appear
with him in glory.* The divine life of Christ will be revealed fully
and will glorify us (reveal our true potential as children of God).
This verse tells further why we should orient ourselves to heaven,
not to earth. Our true glory will come from heaven. Earthly glory
is transitory and illusory; only heaven's glory will last. We will
be transformed at Christ's coming. Creation itself "waits with
eager longing for the revealing of the children of God," and we
"groan inwardly while we wait eagerly for our adoption as sons,

the redemption of our bodies" (Romans 8:19, 23 NIV). Yet we
have the promise that "those whom he justified he also glorified"
(Romans 8:30 NRSV). The apostle John wrote, "We know that
when he appears, we shall be like him, for we shall see him as he
is" (1 John 3:2 NIV). This time of glorification will be at Christ's
second coming, described in 1 Thessalonians 4:16-17.

Christians look forward to the new heaven and new earth that
God has promised, and they wait for God's new order that will
free the world of sin, sickness, and evil. "But our citizenship is in
heaven. And we eagerly await a Savior from there, the Lord Jesus
Christ" (Philippians 3:20 NIV). In the meantime, they go with
Christ into the world, where they heal people's bodies and souls
and fight the evil effects of sin. Christ gives us power to live for
him now, and he gives us hope for the future—he will return. In
the rest of this chapter Paul explains how Christians should act
now in order to be prepared for Christ's return.

CHRIST, YOUR LIFE
By realizing that Christ is our life, we can have a new attitude
about anything that happens to us. If the love of your life should
get sick or die or leave you for someone else, in all your hurt,
you know that your life is still secure in Christ. He fills the void
and loves you with love that cannot die.

If a hurricane should turn your home into toothpicks or you
get bad news from a doctor or your factory closes and jobs are
scarce, in all the mixed feelings and frustrations, your life is stable in Christ. He walks with you in the storm.

When death approaches and you wonder about the unknown,
your life will be hand in hand with Christ, who will lead you
home.

Share the Good News with someone else this week. In God's
plan, the best is yet to come.

**3:5 Put to death, therefore, whatever belongs to your earthly
nature:**NIV While Paul opposed the false teachers' asceticism and
regulations, he still forbade certain activities that had no part in
believers' lives. If the Colossian believers were to live as examples of Christ, they had to *put to death* certain aspects of the
earthly nature. "Earthly nature" refers simply to the sinful nature,
the old self. Again, Paul was describing the "already" and "not
yet" of believers' lives. Although they had died with Christ and
had been raised with him, they were still susceptible to temptation and the evils of the sinful nature. Just like diseased limbs of
a tree, these practices must be cut off. It would take conscious,
daily decisions to remove anything that supported or fed the

desires of the earthly nature and to rely, instead, on the Holy Spirit's power. Believers are not to live as they lived before. They died and were raised with Christ, so their lives must show evidence that they are new creations. (See Romans 6:11 and 8:13 for more on "put to death.")

Two sets of sins are listed. The first five refer to sexual sin; the second five to sins of speech. These first five were related to the cultural background of the Colossians and were particularly deadly to the life of the church (3:7).

Sexual immorality^{NIV} *(porneia)*. Any form of illicit sexual relationship. The term serves to spotlight forbidden sexual behavior between people or indirect participation as an audience. We derive our term "pornography" from this Greek word. In contrast to the loose morals of the ancient Greek world, believers ought to show self-discipline and obedience to God in this area.

Impurity^{NRSV} *(akatharsia)*. Moral uncleanness. Perhaps no sexual act has taken place, but the person exhibits a crudeness or insensitivity in sexual matters. Like the other characteristics mentioned on this list, impurity points to activities before knowing Christ and should have no place in a believer's life.

Lust^{NIV} *(pathos)*. Evil sexual passion that leads to excessive sexual immorality and perversion. (See Romans 1:26; 1 Thessalonians 4:5.)

Evil desire^{NRSV} *(epithumia)*. Wanting something that is sinister and vile in order to satisfy one's desires (see also Galatians 5:16). Sinful human nature cannot help but have evil desires. Thus Paul admonished the Colossian believers to get rid of the evil desires that could easily control them and which had been part of their lives before Christ.

Greed *[pleonexia]* **(which is idolatry)**^{NRSV} Relentless urge to get more for oneself. In this context, Paul may have been focusing on greed for satisfying evil desires and for sexual immorality. The greed is described as *idolatry* because its focus is on filling desires rather than on God.

3:6 On account of these the wrath of God is coming on those who are disobedient.^{NRSV} The *wrath of God* refers to God's judgment on these kinds of behavior. (The words *on those who are disobedient* are not included in some Greek manuscripts.) God does not reveal his wrath arbitrarily; his perfect moral nature will not permit sin and wickedness to go unpunished. While wrath occurs at present in the natural consequences of sinful behavior, the final

culmination of God's wrath *is coming*—with future and final punishment of evil. People may try to get around it, but there is punishment for evil for those who have not believed in Christ as
Savior. This wrath is described in other references:

- "Whoever believes in the Son has eternal life; whoever dis-
  obeys the Son will not see life, but must endure God's wrath"
  (John 3:36 NRSV).

- "But by your hard and impenitent heart you are storing up
  wrath for yourself on the day of wrath, when God's righteous
  judgment will be revealed" (Romans 2:5 NRSV).

- "When the Lord Jesus is revealed from heaven with his mighty
  angels in flaming fire, inflicting vengeance on those who do
  not know God and on those who do not obey the gospel of our
  Lord Jesus. These will suffer the punishment of eternal destruction, separated from the presence of the Lord and from the
  glory of his might" (2 Thessalonians 1:7-9 NRSV).

- "Anyone whose name was not found written in the book of life
  was thrown into the lake of fire" (Revelation 20:15 NRSV).

SEX AND SPIRITUALITY
Can a growing Christian still enjoy sex? Some Christians have
taught that sexual satisfaction is incompatible with spiritual
growth. Francis of Assisi went so far as to never look at a
woman during his adult life. Puritans are often portrayed as sex-
ually cold because they tried hard to keep stern rules.
   The warning in this verse is not against sex, but against sexual perversion. Where's the line?
   The Bible everywhere celebrates heterosexual, monoga-
mous marriage as the proper situation for sexual fulfillment.
Christian men and women should be open to true love—and to
sexual intimacy—within the commitment to lifelong fidelity. That
is God's way. The rest is dangerous and futile. Stay away. Sexual sin and perversion will drain your energies and turn your
heart away from God.

**3:7 These are the ways you also once followed, when you were liv-
ing that life.**NRSV The Colossian believers had previously been
caught up in the world, conducting their lives without concern
about the sins that Paul listed above. They had been dead in their
sins (2:13); that all changed when they came to know Christ.

3:8 But now you must get rid of all such things—NRSV Precisely
because of their new life in Christ, the believers are to put to
death the deeds and desires of the earthly nature (3:5) and *get rid*

of those things listed above and others listed below. "Get rid of" means to put off or disrobe. The old, filthy clothes must be taken off before the new clothes can be put on. The believer "removes" the old life of sin and "puts on" the new life of Christ. The Colossian believers had experienced this; Paul asked that they act it out in their lives.

Not only did they need to deal with sexual immorality in all its variations, they also needed to deal with misused anger that often spilled over into evil speech.

Anger *(orge)*. A continuous attitude of hatred that remains bottled up within. This could refer to what is under the surface, while "rage" (below) refers to what bursts out. Anger would destroy the harmony and unity Paul called for among the believers.

Rage[NIV] *(thumos)*. Outbursts of anger or quick temper for selfish reasons. This could mean continual and uncontrolled behavior.

Malice *(kakia)*. Doing evil despite the good that has been received. This word is a general term referring to an evil force that destroys relationships. It can mean anything from trouble to wickedness. It is a deliberate attempt to harm another person.

Slander[NRSV] *(blasphemia)*. Destroying another person's good reputation by lies, gossip, spreading rumors, etc. Malice often manifests itself through slander. From the Greek word we get our word "blasphemy," a term used to describe speaking against God. The Greeks used the word for defamation of character. Again, this destroys human relationships.

Filthy language[NIV] *(aisxrologia)*. Crude talk, abrasive language, expletives. Paul admonished the believers that such language must be caught and stopped before it escapes their mouths.

These behaviors have no place in any Christian or in any church. These are part of the "old life" before knowing Christ. Christians must resolutely "put off" these repulsive sins of anger and speech so that they can "put on" Christ's attitudes and actions.

Sometimes Christians and churches fall into the trap of concentrating on one of these lists to the exclusion of the other. Some churches might be horrified at sexual sin in the congregation, all the while ignoring backbiting and gossip. On the other hand, some churches want so much to keep peace and quiet that they will not confront sin, even sexual sin. But Paul doesn't leave room for any such behavior. The believers were called to get rid of it *all*.

WHISPERS
"Did you hear . . . ?"
   "Did you know . . . ?"
   "I really shouldn't say this, but . . ."
   These opening lines create more anger and hurt every day
than all the flat tires on Los Angeles freeways each year. In the
church, especially, malice and slander lead to embitterment
and dissension. Add to them an occasional temper tantrum and
the crudeness of filthy language and we get a picture of exactly
what Paul was urging the Colossians to avoid. New life in
Christ overcomes these wrongs.
   Jesus wants to clean your life and your church of sexual sin
and verbal sin. There's no place in the kingdom of God for
hedonistic sexual experimentation or gossip, rage, and backbiting. In their place, witness to the world like a lighthouse at
midnight by displaying love, faith, and hope.

3:9-10 **Do not lie to one another, seeing that you have stripped off
the old self with its practices.**^{NRSV} Because Jesus Christ is "the
truth" (John 14:6), believers ought to practice truth in all areas of
life. They should *not lie to one another.* Lying to others disrupts
unity by destroying trust. It tears down relationships and may
lead to serious conflict in a church. Lying can take place in words
said as well as words left unsaid. Believers should not exaggerate
statistics, pass on rumors or gossip, or say things to build up their
own image at others' expense. Instead, because they *have
stripped off the old self with its practices,* they should be committed to telling the truth.

What is that "old self" or "old nature"? It was each person
before he or she came to know Christ. The person was enslaved
to sin, bound to the earth, without hope. But believers **have put
on the new self, which is being renewed in knowledge in the
image of its Creator.**^{NIV} The *new self* or "new nature" from
Christ frees us from sin, sets our hearts on "things above" (3:1),
and gives us the hope of eternity. Paul was appealing to the commitment the believers had made, urging them to remain true to
their confession of faith. They were to rid themselves of the old
life and *put on* the new way of living given by Christ and guided
by the Holy Spirit.

But how can this be accomplished? How can people "put off"
and "put on"? Paul explained that they are not left alone in the
process. This new self *is being renewed in knowledge.* Every
Christian is in a continuing education program. Renewal is constantly needed in the believer's battle against sin and the old self.
The "knowledge" referred to here is personal knowledge of

Christ that is *in the image of its Creator.* The goal of the knowledge is Christlikeness. The more believers know of Christ and his work, the more they are being changed to be like him. Because this process is lifelong, we must never stop learning and obeying. There is no justification for drifting along, but there is an incentive to find the rich treasures of growing in him. It takes practice, ongoing review, patience, and concentration to keep in line with God's will.

WELCOME BROTHER, WELCOME SISTER
The gospel is color-blind because Jesus died for all races. The gospel is gender-blind because women and men in equal measure need the renewal Christ gives. The gospel is religion-blind because Jesus brings the truth of God to confront all the idols that people have fashioned.

Shaped by such a gospel, should the church reflect a preference in its welcome to new brothers and sisters in Christ?

We know that church history is full of prejudice, and we know that such bigotry is wrong. So today, do something about it. Dust off your church's welcome mat. In small group Bible study, in worship format, in elections to leadership, start showing the many faces of God's people. Let love embrace what prejudice fears.

3:11 Here there is no Greek or Jew, circumcised or uncircumcised, barbarian, Scythian, slave or free, but Christ is all, and is in all.^{NIV} *Here* (that is, "in Christ" and in the new creation, the church) there should be no barriers of nationality, race, education level, social standing, wealth, gender, religion, or power (see also Galatians 3:26-28; 6:15). Paul pointed out four groupings that were of particular importance in the Greek culture:

(1) Racial or national distinctions, such as between Greeks and Jews. The spread of the Greek culture and civilization meant that a Greek person (regardless of his or her country of origin) could feel pride in a privileged position and would look down on the Jews and their persistent clinging to an ancient culture. The Jews, meanwhile, would look down on Greeks as heathen, immoral, and outside of God's grace for the chosen nation.

(2) Religious distinctions, such as between those who have been circumcised (Jews) and those who are uncircumcised (Gentiles). The Greeks (above) would fit in among the Gentiles. Circumcision, the physical mark of the male Jew, was prized as part of the covenant of God with his chosen people. If practiced at all by Gentiles, it was as part of a heathen cult; most often, the Gen-

tiles were uncircumcised, and they mocked the seriousness of the rite for the Jews.

(3) Cultural distinctions, such as between barbarians (a contemptuous name Greeks used for people unfamiliar with Greek language and culture) and Scythians. Josephus, the ancient Jewish historian, wrote that these were wild and primitive tribal people, living near the Black Sea, who were considered little better than beasts, fit only for slavery.

(4) Economic or social distinctions, such as between slaves and free people. Slavery was common in the ancient world. Paul would have special words for the relationships between masters and slaves (3:22–4:1).

How could these barriers possibly be removed? Paul's answer: because *Christ is all, and is in all.* For all these groups of people, Christ is everything. He "is all" they need for redemption and unity. He is central and brings believers together. Christ is "in all"; he dwells in all believers so there can be no division, no prejudice. In others words, every believer is a new creation (2 Corinthians 5:17) with a new self (3:10) by the power of Christ's indwelling Holy Spirit. In Christ, human distinctions are removed. Such distinctions are no problem for him, so they should be no problem for us. Everyone is equal at the Cross.

The Colossian church was probably made up of all kinds of people. No believer should allow prejudices from pre-Christian days to be carried into the church. Christ broke down all barriers; he accepts all who come to him. Believers, as Christ's body, must do the same. Nothing should divide believers; nothing should keep them from experiencing unity. Each believer is responsible to get rid of the sinful practices of whatever life he or she led and become a new person in Christ. Then, as part of God's body of believers on earth, each person should work as part of the whole to advance God's kingdom.

NEW CLOTHES
What does it mean to "put on the new self"? It means that your conduct should match your faith. If you are a Christian, you should act like it. To be a Christian means more than just making good resolutions and having good intentions; it means taking the right actions. This is a straightforward step that is as simple as putting on your clothes. You must rid yourself of all evil practices and immorality. Then you can commit yourself to what Christ teaches. If you have made such a commitment to Christ, are you remaining true to it? What old clothes do you need to strip off?

3:12 Therefore, as God's chosen people, holy and dearly loved, clothe yourselves with . . .NIV Because believers have "put on the new self" (3:10), their clothing is pure and their lives must exhibit that purity. Why? Because they are *God's chosen people,* they are *holy,* and they are *dearly loved.*

The Greek word *eklekton* has been translated from Greek and Latin into English as the word "elect." In the Bible, God's people (the "elect") are chosen by God for a specific purpose or destiny. No one can claim to be chosen by God because of his or her heritage or good works. God freely chooses to save whomever he wills. The doctrine of election teaches that it is God's sovereign choice to save us by his goodness and mercy and not by our own merit. To have received such incredible grace from God ought to cause all believers to gladly lay aside their sinful desires in order to "put on" a nature that pleases God.

GOD'S CHOSEN PEOPLE
The concept of divine election has at times divided the Christian church. Calvinists strongly teach the idea that God chooses some people, who then become Christians. Wesleyans strongly teach the idea that all people are capable of choosing Christ, and when they do, God chooses them. It's a question of whose choice comes first. The spiritual deadness of all people apart from Christ argues that God *must* choose first. Democratic fairness argues that a huge benefit like eternal life must be equally available to anyone who freely says yes to God.

Solving this conundrum requires much study. On a much simpler level, personal and direct, all Christians should find common ground with this child's understanding of election:
"Sarah, who saves you?"
"Jesus saves me, Daddy."
"Can you help Jesus save you, Sarah?"
"I don't think so, Daddy. Jesus saves me all by himself."

How can believers be considered "holy"? The Holy Spirit is the one who helps us become holy. The Holy Spirit provides the power internally to do what God requires externally. Again this is one of the "already" but "not yet" components of our life in Christ. Believers are made holy in God's sight because of Christ's sacrifice on the cross, yet holiness is a progressive goal of salvation. Believers grow into persons who exhibit more and more of the character of Christ in the way they live.

All this happens because believers are so "dearly loved" by God. Only incredible love would cause God to do for believers all that he has done. More than anything, believers ought to

SINS VS. SIGNS OF LOVE

In Colossians 3:5 Paul tells us to put to death the things found in list one. In 3:8 he tells us to rid ourselves of the things found in list two. In 3:12 we're told to practice the things found in list three.

List one deals primarily with sins of sexual attitudes and behavior—they are particularly destructive because of what they do to destroy any group or church. List two deals with sins of speech—these are relationship breakers. List three contains relationship builders, which we are to express as members of Christ's body.

Sins of Sexual Attitude and Behavior	Sins of Speech	Signs of Love
Sexual immorality	Anger expressed	Compassion
Impurity	Rage	Kindness
Lust	Malice	Humility
Evil desires	Slander	Gentleness
Greed	Filthy language	Patience
		Forgiveness

desire to align their lives with God's will. The Colossians needed to live up to their professions of faith. They were to clothe themselves with the new attitudes and behavior exemplified by Christ (see Romans 13:14). In essence, they were to "put on Christ's clothing." In contrast to the vices listed above, Paul offered a list of virtues to be adopted as believers' strategy to live for God day by day in the social activities of life. These include

- imitating Christ's compassionate, forgiving attitude (3:12-13)

- letting love guide their lives (3:14)

- letting the peace of God rule in their hearts (3:15)

- always being thankful (3:15)

- keeping God's Word in them at all times (3:16)

- living as Jesus Christ's representative (3:17)

Compassion.[NRSV] Genuine sensitivity and heartfelt sympathy for the needs of others. This is an attribute of God, who is described as compassionate and who acted so on our behalf.

Kindness. Acting charitably, benevolently toward others, as God has done toward us. God's kindness is a continual theme in the Psalms and Prophets. Kindness takes the initiative in responding generously to others' needs. Because believers have received kindness, we ought to act that way toward others. This does not come naturally; it is a fruit of the Spirit (Galatians 5:22-23).

Humility. An attitude of self-esteem that is neither puffed up with pride, nor self-depreciating. It is a true understanding of one's position with God. As Christ humbled himself (Philippians 2:6-11), so believers ought to humble themselves in service to the Lord and Savior.

Gentleness.[NIV] Humble, considerate of others, submissive to God and his Word. Gentleness is not to be confused with weakness; instead, it means consideration for others and a willingness to give up one's rights for the sake of another. Again, Christ is our example.

Patience.[NRSV] Long-suffering, or putting up with people who irritate. The person might have the right to retaliate, but chooses patience instead. The Holy Spirit's work in us increases our endurance.

3:13 **Bear with each other and forgive whatever grievances you may have against one another. Forgive as the Lord forgave you.**[NIV] "Putting on" Christ affects how we treat others. It is only in the outworking of people's relationships with one another that compassion, kindness, humility, gentleness, and patience are worked out. The testing ground is when people have *grievances . . . against one another.* Paul called the believers to *bear with* and *forgive* one another. "Bear with" means putting up with the "extra grace required" crowd. This is only possible for those who are clothed with patience (3:12). To "forgive" implies continual, mutual forgiveness of the problems, irritations, and grievances that occur in the congregation. In order to do either one of these actions, a Christian must do both. It takes forbearance to forgive, and forgiveness means putting up with offensive people.

FORGIVE OR HATE

Formerly, when people had a grievance, they could challenge one another to a duel. That settled it, except when relatives of the loser decided to carry on the feud, sometimes for generations. Each crime against one side would escalate the motives for revenge.

Now with duels illegal, we use courts to "make ourselves whole" when someone has cheated or slandered us. It is a longer process, less bloody, more public, and civilized.

Jesus offers an even better way: forgive and forget. It's the new way of the gospel: let God worry about the wrongs you've suffered. Don't quench your life in bitter feuding; live renewed in love and joy.

Why did Paul call believers to do this? The church had enough
enemies and troubles dealing with the outside world; they didn't
need infighting or energy wasted on grievances or grudges (either
held over from pre-Christian days or arising in the church) that
could be worked out with forbearing and forgiving. The key to
forgiving others was for the believers to (1) remember how much
God had forgiven them, and (2) realize the presumption in refusing to forgive someone God had already forgiven. Remembering
God's infinite love and forgiveness should help the Colossian
believers love and forgive one another.

**3:14 Above all, clothe yourselves with love, which binds everything
together in perfect harmony.**NRSV All the virtues that Paul
encouraged the believers in Colosse to develop were perfectly
bound together by *love*. As they clothed themselves with these
virtues, the last garment to put on was love, which, like a belt,
holds all of the others in place. Literally it means "the bond of
perfection." Love pulls together the other graces in perfect, unified action. To practice any list of virtues without practicing love
will lead to distortion, fragmentation, and stagnation. In any congregation, love must be used to unify the people and build them
up. Those who would desire to be mature in Christ must make
love a top priority. Paul regularly wrote about the priority of love:

- "If I speak in the tongues . . . have prophetic powers, and understand all mysteries and all knowledge, and if I have all faith . . .
  if I give away all my possessions, and if I hand over my body
  . . . but do not have love, I gain nothing" (1 Corinthians 13:1-3
  NRSV).

- "Owe no one anything, except to love one another; for the one
  who loves another has fulfilled the law. The commandments
  . . . are summed up in this word, 'Love your neighbor as yourself.' Love does no wrong to a neighbor; therefore, love is the
  fulfilling of the law" (Romans 13:8-10 NRSV).

- "And now abide faith, hope, love, these three; but the greatest
  of these is love" (1 Corinthians 13:13 NKJV).

- "For the whole law is summed up in a single command-
  ment,'You shall love your neighbor as yourself'" (Galatians
  5:14 NRSV).

- "But the fruit of the Spirit is love" (Galatians 5:22 NIV).

- "Lead a life worthy of the calling to which you have been
  called, with all humility and gentleness, with patience, bearing
  with one another in love." (Ephesians 4:1-2 NRSV).

3:15 And let the peace of God rule in your hearts, to which also you were called in one body.^{NKJV} Putting on all the virtues, with love binding them together (3:14), would lead to peace between individuals and among the members of the body of believers. The Colossian Christians should let *the peace of God* rule their hearts. To live in peace would not mean that suddenly all differences of opinion would be eliminated, but it would require that they work together despite their differences. This kind of tranquility and cooperation can't come from mere human effort. It requires God's help to arbitrate and enable people to get along. God calms our troubled hearts; then we can better relate to others.

The word *rule* comes from the language of athletics: Paul wanted the believers to let Christ's peace be umpire or referee in their hearts. Peace would arbitrate, decide any argument, and thereby restrain any of the passions of the old nature that might threaten. Peace would settle any friction and strife so the believers could remain strong and unified. Peace must rule *hearts.* As in 3:1, the heart is the center of a person's being, the center of spiritual and moral life. If peace rules there, it rules every believer's entire life and, by extension, the life of the church.

To which refers back to "the peace of God." The believers had been called to peace. *In one body* refers to being a single organism. The unity of the body of Christ is a strong reason for peace among the members, and the peace of God enables the members to be unified.

PEACE RULES
When we exercise the traits of compassion, kindness, humility, patience, and, above all, love, we are going to face conflict. Not everyone will be playing by these rules. Not all Christians show the self-restraint needed in conflict. How can we deal with these conflicts and live as God wants? When we are hurt by others or our gracious efforts are rebuked, we must have an umpire inside that says, "Peace." We need to call a time-out on our passions and reactions; then we can think about the peace that God has won for us in Christ's death. Paul does not teach "peace at any price." Instead, he encourages believers to embrace God's peace and be under his control as they make courageous moral decisions for the truth and the right.

And be thankful. When believers have an overriding attitude of thankfulness and when they have constant gratitude in their hearts for all that God has done for them in giving salvation and making them part of Christ's body, then other virtues to which Paul called them would be much easier to live out. Such thankfulness would also make other relationships easier, as Paul explained in following verses (3:18–4:6).

3:16 Let the word of Christ dwell in you richly as you teach and admonish one another with all wisdom, and as you sing psalms, hymns and spiritual songs with gratitude in your hearts to God.[NIV] The *word of Christ* referred to the message proclaimed by Christ (the gospel). For us, this means the Bible. This teaching should *dwell* (reside permanently) in each believer by his or her study and knowledge of God's Word. The gospel must also dwell in the church, which should be the center for wise teaching of the gospel message and wise advice, encouragement, or reprimand. In our attempts to reach people with felt needs, we must keep the Bible at the core of our church ministries. (See 2 Timothy 3:16–4:2 for more on the correct use of Scripture.) *Teach and admonish* refers to the whole congregation and their responsibility to teach the Word—including the life, ministry, and teachings of Jesus Christ—as a means to warn and correct one another.

The *psalms, hymns and spiritual songs* were a vital part of this teaching and admonition. Although the early Christians had access to the Old Testament and freely used it (thus, Paul's reference to "psalms"), they did not yet have the New Testament or any other Christian books to study. Their stories and teachings about Christ were sometimes set to music to make them easier to memorize and pass on from person to person. Grounded in God's Word and correct doctrine, music can be an important part of Christian worship and education.

TANK UP ON THANKS

Thankfulness puts all we have in the right perspective; God has given us what we need for service, comfort, expression, and recreation. Greediness or discontent signals an attitude that says to God, "I'm not getting much of a bargain here."

Thankful people can worship wholeheartedly. Gratitude opens our hearts to God's peace and enables us to put on love. Discontented people constantly calculate what's wrong with their lot in life.

To increase your thankfulness, take an inventory of all you have (include your relationships, memories, abilities, and family, as well as material possessions). Use the inventory for prayers of gratitude. On Sunday, before worship, quit rushing around and take time to reflect on reasons for thanks. Early on Sunday morning, declare this your "thanks, faith, and hope" day. Celebrate God's goodness to you, and ask in prayer for all your needs for the week ahead.

While music can teach, its primary function may be to praise God. As believers sing, they ought to do so with *gratitude in their hearts* (see 4:2). Again, the word "heart" refers to a person's entire being. Gratitude to God overflows in praise.

3:17 And whatever you do in word or deed, do all in the name of the Lord Jesus, giving thanks to God the Father through Him.NKJV Earlier Paul listed a few vices and virtues to give the Colossian believers an idea of what was expected of them in their attitudes toward one another, but he did not want to regulate every area of life with a list of rules. That would be like reverting to Pharisaism. So Paul gave this general command to cover every area of life.

Everything the believers said and everything they did should be done *in the name of the Lord Jesus,* realizing his constant presence and bringing honor and glory to him in every aspect and activity of daily living. "So whether you eat or drink or whatever you do, do it all for the glory of God" (1 Corinthians 10:31 NIV). To act in someone's name is to act on his authority; believers act as Christ's representatives.

Paul echoed the need for a thankful spirit, as he had in 3:15 and 3:16. All we do for Christ should be done with the spirit of thankfulness for all he has done for us. Believers are not enslaved to rules about every word they speak or deed they do; instead, they freely put themselves under the Lord's guidance because they love him, have accepted his salvation, and live to glorify him. Their thanks can go to God through Christ because Christ is the only mediator between God and people.

HONOR AND GLORY
As a Christian, you represent Christ at all times—wherever you go and with whatever you say. Believers can go about their lives—working, playing, studying, planning—and do everything to the glory of God with thanks in their hearts. What impression do people have of Christ when they see or talk with you? What changes would you make in your life in order to honor Christ?

PRINCIPLES FOR RELATIONSHIPS / 3:18–4:6

In Paul's day, women, children, and slaves were to submit to the head of the family—slaves would submit until they were freed, male children until they grew up, and women and girls for their whole lives. Paul emphasized the equality of all believers in Christ (Galatians 3:28), but he did not suggest overthrowing

RULES OF SUBMISSION

The New Testament includes many instructions concerning relationships. Most people read these instructions for the other person and ignore the ones that apply to themselves. But you can't control another person's behavior, only your own. Start by following your own instructions and not insisting on the obedience of others first.

Wives, submit to your husbands (3:18).	*Husbands*, love your wives and don't be harsh with them (3:19).
Children, obey your parents (3:20).	*Parents*, don't embitter your children so that they become discouraged (3:21).
Slaves, obey your masters (3:22).	*Masters*, be just and fair toward your slaves (4:1).

Roman society to achieve it. Instead, he counseled all believers to submit to authority by choice. For husbands and wives, he taught mutual submission: husbands to wives and wives to husbands. This kind of mutual submission preserves order and harmony in the family while it increases love and respect among family members.

Paul gave rules for three sets of household relationships: (1) husbands and wives, (2) parents and children, and (3) masters and slaves. In each case, there is mutual responsibility to submit and love, to obey and encourage, to work hard and be fair. Examine your family and work relationships. Do you relate to others as God intended?

3:18-19 **Wives, submit to your own husbands, as is fitting in the Lord.**NKJV Why is submission of wives to husbands *fitting in the Lord?* This may have been good advice for Christian women, newly freed in Christ, who found submission difficult. Paul told them that they should willingly follow their husbands' leadership in Christ. But Paul had words for husbands as well: **Husbands, love your wives and never treat them harshly.**NRSV It may also have been true that Christian men, used to the Roman custom of giving unlimited power to the head of the family, were not used to treating their wives with respect and love. Real spiritual leadership involves service. Just as Christ served the disciples, even to the point of washing their feet, so the husband is to serve his wife. This means putting aside his own interests in order to care for his wife. A wise and Christ-honoring husband will not abuse his leadership role. At the same time, a wise and Christ-honoring wife will not try to undermine her husband's leadership. Either approach causes disunity and friction in marriage.

What does "as is fitting in the Lord" mean? Paul stressed the full equality of women and men before the Lord (Galatians 3:28). This verse provides a check and balance for selfish or tyrannical partners. Neither partner should be arrogant or domineering; there is no room for abuse. The wife must not rule her husband's life; the husband must put his wife's interests first. There must be mutual love and respect. Husband and wife must accept mutual subordination in God's hierarchy. The Lord Jesus is the criterion for our duty. He, not society, defines what is "fitting."

SUBMISSION

Wives submitting to husbands has become a cultural battle-ground because many conclude that submission means that all women should take subservient positions to all men. The stereotypes could go on forever—men should be executives, women secretaries; men should be doctors, women nurses; men should be pastors, women choir directors. Feminists resist this kind of thinking as aggressively as some Christian ministries still preach chauvinistic versions of it.

Nowhere does Paul suggest that submission requires women to be silent in the face of abuse. Abuse requires outside help and mediation, and no Christian woman should imagine that resisting abuse violates Paul's mandate.

Paul taught submission of wives to husbands, with final spiritual responsibility on a husband's shoulders, for the sake of mutual fulfillment. In Ephesians 5:25-30, Paul devoted twice as many words to telling husbands to love their wives sacrificially as to telling wives to submit to their husbands. Marriage, with two lives united as one, is difficult under any circumstances. Submit to Christ and to your spouse in order to find true happiness in your marriage.

Although some people have distorted Paul's teaching on submission by giving unlimited authority to husbands, we cannot get around it. The fact is, Paul wrote that wives should submit to their husbands. The fact that a teaching is not popular is no reason to discard it. According to the Bible, the man is the spiritual head of the family, and his wife should acknowledge his leadership. There should not be a constant battle for power in the relationship. Our concept of submission must come from the Bible, demonstrated by the church to Christ (as Christ loved the church and submitted to God, 1 Corinthians 15:28; Ephesians 5:21). We must not base it on either a feminist or chauvinist view. Christian marriage involves mutual submission (Ephesians 5:21), subordinating our personal desires for the good of the loved one, and submitting ourselves to Christ as Lord. Submission is rarely a problem in homes where both partners have a strong relationship with Christ and where each is concerned for the happiness of the other.

Submitting to another person is an often misunderstood concept. It does not mean becoming a doormat. Christ—at whose name "every knee should bow, of those in heaven, and of those on earth, and of those under the earth" (Philippians 2:10 NKJV)—submitted his will to the Father; we honor Christ by following his example. When we submit to God, we become more willing to obey his command to submit to others—that is, to subordinate our rights to theirs.

3:20-21 **Children, obey your parents in all things, for this is well pleasing to the Lord.**NKJV God's design for family relationships continues in this verse. Children (*tekna*, "young children living at home") are to obey their parents. While all young children will at times be disobedient and test their limits with their parents, as they get older and understand what they are told, God wants them to obey. Such obedience reveals an understanding of authority that can carry over into understanding God's authority and all believers' responsibility to obey him. A child's obedience to his or her parents *is well pleasing to the Lord.*

> If the home is to be a means of grace it must be a place of rules ... the alternative to rule is not freedom but the unconstitutional (and often unconscious) tyranny of the most selfish member.
> *C. S. Lewis*

Children's obedience is balanced by Paul's next command: **Fathers, do not embitter your children, or they will become discouraged.**NIV The command for children to obey does not give parents license for harsh treatment. Children must be handled with care. They need firm discipline administered in love. *Fathers* refers to both parents, although Paul's words might stress the importance of discipline administered by fathers. The Greek word *goneis* (parents) in 3:20 includes mothers; *pateres* may mean parents (as in Hebrews 11:23), but here it is head of the household. Parents must not *embitter* their children by nagging and deriding. Belittling children, or showing by words or actions that they are unimportant to the parents, should have no place in Christian families. Discipline administered in derision ultimately discourages children, destroys their self-respect, and causes them to lose heart.

The purpose of parental discipline is to help children grow, not to exasperate and provoke them to anger or discouragement. Parenting is not easy—it takes lots of patience to raise children in a loving, Christ-honoring manner. But frustration and anger should not be causes for discipline. Instead, parents should act in love, treating their children as Jesus treats the people he loves. This is vital to children's development and to their understanding of what Christ is like.

DISCIPLINE
Many people seem afraid to correct a child for fear of stifling some aspect of his or her personality or losing his or her love. Single parents or parents who cannot spend much time with a child may be prone to indulgence. Since the time together is short, they don't want to spend it correcting or punishing the child. But such children, especially, need the security of guidance and structure. Boundaries and guidelines will not embitter a child. Instead, they will set him or her free to live securely within the boundaries.

3:22 **Slaves, obey your earthly masters in everything, not only while being watched and in order to please them, but wholeheartedly, fearing the Lord.**[NRSV] Paul used the same word for *obey* here as he used in 3:20 for children to obey their parents. Slaves were also to obey the commands and desires of their masters, not just when they were being watched and hoping for a reward, but at all times. They should no longer merely work for human approval, they should work so as to gain God's approval (*fearing the Lord* means reverencing him). Believers who were slaves were not set free from serving their masters, but they were set free from slavery to sin. Their ultimate Master was God himself. Paul explained that God wanted the slaves to fulfill their responsibilities in this world even as they looked forward to the next.

Slaves played a significant part in this society, with several million in the Roman Empire at this time. Slavery was sanctioned by law and was part of the empire's social makeup. Because many slaves and slave owners had become Christians, the early church had to deal straightforwardly with the question of master/slave relations. Paul's statement neither condemns nor condones slavery. On one hand, Paul was not interested in starting a revolutionary movement to attempt to destroy the order of the empire. On the other hand, Paul *was* starting a revolutionary movement that would surely subvert all that Rome found pride in. But Paul was not a political organizer, and his movement was not political. All of Paul's revolutionary zeal was developed in the context of the

church as a new community in which selflessness and love consti-
tuted new relationships based not on power but on mutual affirmation. Would this destroy Rome's empire? Emphatically, yes.
Would it do so by armed revolt? Certainly not.

While neither condemning nor condoning slavery, Paul told
masters and slaves how to live together in Christian households.
In Paul's day, women, children, and slaves had few rights. In the
church, however, they had freedoms that society denied them.
Paul tells husbands, parents, and masters to be caring.

Although Christians may be at different levels in earthly society, we are all equal before God. He does not play favorites; no
one is more important than anyone else. Paul's letter to Philemon
stresses the same point: Philemon, the master, and Onesimus, his
slave, had become brothers in Christ. Perhaps Paul was thinking
specifically of this master and slave (see the book of Philemon).
Philemon was a slave owner in the Colossian church, and Onesimus was his slave.

WORK
Christians work first for the Lord Jesus Christ and second for
the companies that write their paychecks. No matter what the
job, our first goal is serving Jesus.

Does this verse mean that Christians should not join organized labor and, if necessary, strike for better wages? No. Justice in the workplace is also a Christian responsibility.

Does this verse refer to any kind of labor (is preaching a sermon holier than digging a ditch)? Not all jobs serve Christ. Jobs
that violate common Christian standards cannot be sanctified
by proper "attitudes." But neither are preachers holier than
laborers. All people should work with grateful hearts, using the
best of their minds and muscles to serve God.

Find the job that stretches your abilities, that makes you pray
in the morning for God's help for the day, and that sets you to
sleep at night satisfied and tired out. Then, work at it as a calling, and so witness to God's power in your life.

**3:23-24 Whatever your task, put yourselves into it, as done for the
Lord and not for your masters, since you know that from the
Lord you will receive the inheritance as your reward; you
serve the Lord Christ.**NRSV Slaves had a variety of tasks—running errands, caring for or teaching children, cleaning, preparing
meals, or doing menial work. Yet Paul gave their jobs a new dignity because these slaves would do their work for the Lord, serving the Lord Christ. Slaves had little, if any, opportunity to get
out of slavery, and they received little, if any, monetary compen-
sation for their work. Obviously, they had no inheritance in this

world, but Paul reminded the Christian slaves that they would ultimately be rewarded by Christ with their deserved inheritance as children of the true, eternal King. (See Luke 6:35 and Ephesians 6:7-8 for more on the Lord's reward.)

3:25 **For the wrongdoer will be paid back for whatever wrong has been done, and there is no partiality.**[NRSV] Echoing his words in 3:6, Paul once again explained that judgment would be coming. Whether master or slave, the *wrongdoer will be paid back,* and those who do right will receive the inheritance as their reward (3:24). At the Judgment, God will judge without partiality. Paul explained the responsibilities of the believers. Both the Christian slave with the harsh and ruthless master and the Christian master with the lazy and untrustworthy slave knew how they were to act as believers. They also knew that God would judge wrongdoing without favoritism.

4:1 **Masters, provide your slaves with what is right and fair, because you know that you also have a Master in heaven.**[NIV] Whether the master's slaves were believers or not, Christian masters were responsible to be *right and fair* to all their slaves. What would be considered "right and fair" is difficult to determine without a full picture of slavery in ancient days. We do know that slaves may have been conquered peoples from foreign lands or people sold into slavery to recover debts. It was difficult for a slave to rise from that social caste. Often slaves were treated as less than human. Without attempting to overturn the social structure of a worldwide empire, Paul applied Christ's inward transforming principles to the system (see the discussion on 3:22). Paul did not say that Christian masters should free all slaves; in fact, in some cases, setting them free might not have been humane. Instead, Paul explained that Christian masters should do what is right and fair, treating their slaves as human beings. To some masters, this would mean freeing their slaves; to others, it would mean treating the slaves better in terms of living quarters, remuneration, time to rest, and tone of voice.

Why should Paul command this of Christian slave masters? Because the slave masters themselves had someone to report to— their *Master in heaven.* The slave masters could hardly expect to be treated rightly and fairly by God if they refused right and fair treatment to those in their charge.

Masters and slaves who followed Paul's advice would be able to serve or be served in their daily routines, and yet come together to worship as brothers and sisters in the Lord without any disruption.

WHO'S WORKING FOR WHOM?
Paul's instructions encourage responsibility and integrity on the job. Christian employees should do their jobs as if Jesus Christ were their supervisor. And Christian employers should treat their employees fairly and with respect. Can you be trusted to do your best, even when the boss is not around? Do you work hard and with enthusiasm? Do you treat your employees as people, not machines? Employers should pay fair wages and treat their employees justly. Leaders should take care of their volunteers and not abuse them. If you have responsibility over others, make sure you do what is just and fair. Remember that no matter whom you work for, and no matter who works for you, the One you ultimately should want to please is your Father in heaven. You are accountable to him.

4:2 Devote yourselves to prayer, keeping alert in it with thanksgiving.[NRSV] As he began to draw his letter to a close, Paul turned his focus back to the church as a whole, reminding the Colossians of their corporate responsibilities.

The believers were responsible to pray; prayer was their lifeline to God. To *devote* themselves to prayer meant that they should be persistent and unwilling to give up, even though their prayers may seem to go unanswered. Paul's advice to the Thessalonians to "pray continually" (1 Thessalonians 5:17 NIV) has the same meaning. Their devotion to prayer did not mean that they should spend all their time on their knees, but that they should have a prayerful attitude at all times. This attitude would be built upon acknowledging their dependence on God, realizing his presence within them, and determining to obey him fully. Then they would find it natural to pray frequent, spontaneous, short prayers. A prayerful attitude is not a substitute for regular times of prayer but should be an outgrowth of those times.

They also ought to be *keeping alert* in prayer. Paul may have been referring to not dozing off, to being alert in their devotion, or to being alert for God's answers and then thankful when they came. More likely, he was focusing on the anticipation of the Lord's coming. The Lord could return at any time, so believers should be found alert and waiting.

As Paul had mentioned several times (1:3, 12; 2:7; 3:15-17), the believers ought always to be thankful. Thankfulness implies understanding all that God has done and anticipating what he promises.

TIRED OF PRAYING?
Have you ever grown tired of praying for something or someone? Paul says we should be devoted and alert in prayer. Our vigilance is an expression of our faith that God answers our prayers. Faith shouldn't die if the answers come slowly, for the delay may be God's way of working his will in our lives. When you feel tired of praying, know that God is present, always listening, always answering—maybe not in ways you had hoped, but in ways that he knows are best.

4:3 And pray for us, too, that God may open a door for our message, so that we may proclaim the mystery of Christ, for which I am in chains.^{NIV} The Colossian believers could have a part in Paul's worldwide ministry by praying for him and his coworkers. Paul requested prayer for himself and for Timothy (1:1) that God would *open a door* for their message. Perhaps Paul was implying prayer for his release so that he could continue traveling and preaching. More likely he was simply praying for opportunities to preach in spite of his imprisonment, and "open doors" of reception to the message. Although Paul was *in chains* for preaching the gospel, the chains could not stop the message. Even in prison, he would preach. The *mystery of Christ* is Christ himself as presented in the gospel—the Good News of salvation (as in 1:26-27). The whole focus of Paul's life was to tell others about Christ, explaining and preaching this wonderful mystery.

4:4 Pray that I may proclaim it clearly, as I should.^{NIV} Paul asked not only for open doors to "proclaim the mystery of Christ" (4:3), but also for the ability to proclaim that mystery *clearly*. In other words, Paul wanted to be able to "reveal" the mystery so that many could hear and believe. This was his compulsion; he had been called (Acts 9:15; 26:17-20).

KEEP IT CLEAR
God created us to love and serve him, but we have not done so because of our sin. We cannot remove this barrier of sin nor save ourselves. Only Christ can save us. He died in our place to free us to love and serve God. By trusting in Christ as Savior, we can begin this relationship with God immediately.

This is the essence of the gospel, the Good News. Paul asked for prayer that he could proclaim this good news about Christ clearly—we can ask for the same. No matter what approach to evangelism we use, whether emphasizing lifestyle and example or whether building relationships, we must keep the simple message clear.

4:5 Be wise in the way you act toward outsiders; make the most of every opportunity.^{NIV} Paul reminded the believers of their responsibility to be wise in the way they acted toward non-Christians *(outsiders)*. Paul was observing that while the Christian fellowship does (and should) make some allowances for the mistakes of its own, the world will not. Christians' behavior toward unbelievers should be above reproach. Elsewhere, Paul wrote that the believers' daily lives and hard work should win the respect of outsiders (1 Thessalonians 4:12). The believers were not to hide from the world in a secret organization; instead, they were to live in the world. They were to *make the most of every opportunity* to share the gospel with unbelievers. Paul was communicating a sense of urgency (see Galatians 6:10; Ephesians 5:15-16). The Colossians were to take full advantage of their means to win others. But their actions and their evangelistic efforts should be done wisely, strategically, and ethically.

4:6 Let your speech always be gracious, seasoned with salt, so that you may know how you ought to answer everyone.^{NRSV} The believers were to be wise in how they acted (4:5), but their witness should be more than actions alone. The spoken word would be the communication method; therefore, they should be wise in how they spoke.

Speech that is *gracious* is kind and courteous. Speech that is *seasoned with salt* is interesting (as opposed to dull), invites interaction (as opposed to refusing to listen and discuss), adds "spice" to a discussion (by penetrating to deeper levels), and is pure and wholesome (as opposed to "filthy language," 3:8). According to the parallel passage in Ephesians 4:29, the salt symbolizes that which preserves our conversation from being corrupt. Believers who are "the salt of the earth" (Matthew 5:13; Mark 9:49-50; Luke 14:34) should have speech that is tasteful. Believers should always be ready to answer questions about their faith and be ready to share words of personal testimony. As Peter wrote: "Always be prepared to give an answer to everyone who asks you to give the reason for the hope that you have. But do this with gentleness and respect, keeping a clear conscience" (1 Peter 3:15-16 NIV).

No Christian should have a dull, tiresome, know-it-all monologue of his faith. Instead, Christians, who have the most exciting news in the world to share, should be able to share that message with excitement, ability to invoke interest, an understanding of the basics, a willingness to listen and discuss, and a desire to answer everyone's questions graciously.

SALTY SPEECH
The way words are spoken is as important as the words themselves. When we tell others about Christ, we should always be
gracious in what we say. No matter how much sense the message makes, we lose our effectiveness if we are not courteous.
Just as we like to be respected, we must respect others if we
want them to listen to what we have to say.

Colossians 4:7-18

Paul often closed his letters by sending personal greetings from himself and others with him to individuals in the church to whom he wrote. After studying the intricacies of Paul's letters, we come to his final words and remember that he was writing to real people with real struggles. The names of various believers who helped and encouraged Paul give us an outline of Paul's relationships and his widespread ministry. Paul, as energetic and well known as he was, did not operate alone. Many men and women served the Lord by helping Paul in his ministry of spreading the gospel. Do you try to minister alone? How much better to use others' gifts and abilities to help get the job done.

4:7 **Tychicus will tell you all the news about me; he is a beloved brother, a faithful minister, and a fellow servant in the Lord.**[NRSV] Tychicus had accompanied Paul to Jerusalem with the collection for the church there (Acts 20:4). He later became one of Paul's personal representatives. Paul sent him to Ephesus a couple of times (Ephesians 6:21-22; 2 Timothy 4:12), and he sent him to Colosse with this letter for the Colossian church. Tychicus also may have been sent to Crete (Titus 3:12). Tychicus would

---

GREAT LEADER, GREAT FOLLOWER
Joshua Chamberlain was one of the most respected soldiers in U.S. history. A professor of rhetoric and religion, he was wounded six times and cited for bravery in action four times. He received the Congressional Medal of Honor for his command of the Twentieth Regiment, Maine Volunteers, at Gettysburg on July 2, 1863. Yet he was only a colonel, not a general. Chamberlain followed as many orders from superiors as he gave to subordinates.

Paul cited Tychicus for leadership skills, or were they "followship" skills? Tychicus followed well—with love, faithfulness, and a servant's heart. He was a team player who made an impact, but not by independent action. Like Tychicus, be as eager to follow and to serve as you are to lead.

---

give the believers news about Paul that Paul did not include in this letter. Paul trusted Tychicus, making good use of his freedom and faithfulness to continue the ministry of the gospel while Paul was imprisoned. As Paul had called himself a servant (1:23), so he called this brother a *fellow servant in the Lord*. Both men had the same Master and the same ministry.

4:8 I am sending him to you for the express purpose that you may know about our circumstances and that he may encourage your hearts.^{NIV} In spite of the fact that Paul had never been to Colosse, he and the believers there had a bond because of their unity in Christ. This letter, bearing important information needed by the church in Colosse, was entrusted to a brother who would be sure to deliver it and ensure that its contents were understood. Paul's imprisonment had theological significance; the Colossians needed to understand that what happened to Paul and to the gospel should assure them of God's sovereignty and care. Paul also sent Tychicus to tell the believers how he was doing in prison and to *encourage* them. This personal letter and Paul's continued faithfulness to spread the gospel in spite of his imprisonment would encourage and strengthen the Colossian believers.

ENCOURAGEMENT
Nobody moves an inch by standing still and pondering the future. Life offers opportunities, risks, and challenges—but if you're too afraid of losing or getting hurt, you'll probably never get in the game.

Encouragement, which seems to be the chief mission of Paul's emissary Tychicus, requires a leader willing to say, "Get going! Get moving! Follow me! Follow Christ! Keep it up! You're doing a great job. Don't lose heart!"

People all around you have potential to do more, and to be more, than they are. In Christ, who can set the limits? Perhaps your encouragement will fuel them with courage to try.

4:9 He is coming with Onesimus, the faithful and beloved brother, who is one of you. They will tell you about everything here.^{NRSV} Onesimus was a native of Colosse. He was a slave who had run away from his master, Philemon (an elder in the church at Colosse), and was saved through Paul in prison. The letter to the Colossians and the letter to Philemon were written at the same time and carried by these men back to Colosse. Paul referred to Onesimus as a dearly loved brother both here and in Philemon 16. Onesimus would accompany Tychicus and also bring news of Paul's circumstances. Tychicus probably provided moral support to Onesimus as Onesimus returned to his master in hopes of being restored. He was also returning to the church, not merely as a fellow Colossian, but also as a fellow Christian.

4:10 **Aristarchus my fellow prisoner greets you.**[NRSV] Aristarchus was from Thessalonica and had accompanied Paul on his third missionary journey. He had been arrested, along with Gaius, during the riot at Ephesus (Acts 19:29). He and Tychicus were with Paul in Greece (Acts 20:4); Aristarchus had traveled to Rome with Paul (Acts 27:2). Paul also called Epaphras a "fellow prisoner" in Philemon 23, but it is likely that his words there may have simply been a metaphor of warfare or "captivity to Christ." That Paul called Aristarchus a *fellow prisoner* may mean "captivity to Christ," or it may mean that Aristarchus was in prison with Paul.

GRACE UNDER FIRE
Strength and loyalty are the virtues behind this quick greeting from Aristarchus. He had gone to jail with Paul for Christ's sake, had stood up under the danger of riot at Ephesus, and had sailed with Paul to Rome to face imprisonment. Others might plea-bargain or claim that they acted under duress. Aristarchus would bear the cost of discipleship with cheerfulness and hope.
    Faith that cares for others, that greets people never met, that sticks close to friends in trouble—because of Jesus—is worth finding, a treasure brighter than diamonds and just as tough. Jesus promises that we'll find faith that stands firm under riots and threat of prison when we give him our whole heart.

As does Mark the cousin of Barnabas, concerning whom you have received instructions—if he comes to you, welcome him.[NRSV] Mark (also called John Mark) was not yet well known among the churches, although apparently Barnabas was (see, for example, 1 Corinthians 9:6; Galatians 2:1, 9, 13). Mark had started out with Paul and Barnabas on their first missionary journey (Acts 12:25), but had left in the middle of the trip for unknown reasons (Acts 13:13); he had returned home to Jerusalem. Barnabas was related to Mark, so when Paul refused to take Mark on another journey, Barnabas and Mark journeyed together to preach the Good News (Acts 15:37-41). Mark also had worked with Peter (Acts 12:12-13; 1 Peter 5:13). Later, Mark and Paul were reconciled (Philemon 24; see also 2 Timothy 4:11). Mark wrote the Gospel of Mark. The words *concerning whom* refer to Mark. Apparently Paul wanted the Colossians to know that he had confidence in Mark; instructions concerning Mark had already been conveyed by someone (what these instructions were is unknown). Apparently Mark was making good efforts to show himself to be an effective and productive worker. In any case, the Colossians were to welcome Mark if he were to arrive at their church.

4:11 **And Jesus who is called Justus greets you.**^{NRSV} *Jesus* was a common Jewish name, as was the name *Justus* (which means "righteous"). But the phrase, *who is called,* serves to distinguish this Jesus from others with the same name.

These are the only ones of the circumcision among my co-workers for the kingdom of God, and they have been a comfort to me.^{NRSV} It may be that Aristarchus, Mark, and Justus were the only ones among Paul's fellow workers who were Jewish (as the NIV translates this). Or the meaning could be more vague—that these men were "from the circumcised," referring not to ethnic background, but to a special group of Jewish Christian missionaries called "the circumcision party" (see Acts 10:45; 11:2; 15:1-5; Galatians 2:12). Since Paul severely criticized the circumcision party, his words here may mean that these men came from that background. When they had joined with Paul in the ministry of the gospel, they had kept their zeal to reach the Jews for Christ.

SERVING ACROSS BORDERS
Jesus Justus was a Jew. Apparently he had kept up the mission to reach Jews, but still was supporting Paul, who reached Gentiles. Any good Jew of Paul's day regarded Gentiles as low-lifes, dogs, dirt. Jews did not associate with those Gentiles. It was not proper. To like them was to be a pervert. The same could have been said at one time about Jews in Europe or blacks in the South or Indians on the western frontier. "Good people" kept their distance. Yet Jesus Justus was both a coworker and a comfort to Paul.

Who are your equivalent outcasts today? It's "incorrect" to have any, but most people don't live in the perfect social world of political correctness. Christ changes everything. In Christ, we love across boundaries and minister to people with habits and lifestyle preferences quite unlike our own. That's how the church grows.

Could God be calling you to love and serve people you once abhorred, as Paul did the Gentiles? Might God want you to work at friendships with those not of your background or school of thought?

These men had proven to be *a comfort* to Paul. The word for "comfort" *(paregoria)* is used only here in the New Testament. It means comfort, relief, or consolation. Paul had been called as a

missionary to the Gentiles, yet he had kept his concern for the
lost of his own nation, Israel. Yet Paul's very mission to the Gentiles had alienated him from many of his fellow Jews; thus, the
hard work on behalf of the gospel by these faithful Jewish Christians was especially comforting to Paul.

**4:12 Epaphras, who is one of you, a servant of Christ Jesus, greets
you.**^{NRSV} Like Onesimus (4:9), Epaphras was *one of you,* that is, a
Colossian. Epaphras may have been converted in Ephesus under
Paul's teaching, for Paul had stayed in Ephesus for three years,
teaching and preaching (Acts 20:31). Epaphras, then, had
returned to Colosse, his hometown, where he had founded the
church there and probably the churches in Hieropolis and Laodicea as well (1:7; Acts 19:10). Later, he apparently visited Paul in
Rome, perhaps to get the apostle's advice on dealing with the
false teachers. His report to Paul caused Paul to write this letter.
Like Paul (1:23) and Tychicus (4:7), Epaphras was *a servant of
Christ Jesus,* who had been responsible for the missionary out-
reach to these cities.

**He is always wrestling in his prayers on your behalf, so that
you may stand mature and fully assured in everything that
God wills.**^{NRSV} Epaphras was a hero of the Colossian church, one
of the believers who had helped keep the church together despite
growing troubles. His earnest prayers for the believers show his
deep love and concern for them. The word for *wrestling* is the
same word used in 1:29 and 2:1. It describes physical striving
and conflict, as with an athlete in an arena. Just as Paul was struggling for the church in ministry, so Epaphras was struggling in
intercessory prayer. Such descriptions indicate that prayer was
not a one-time event, but a long-term labor requiring complete
energy. Although away from the church, his ministry was always
before him as he prayed for the congregation. He was doing what
Paul had taught in 4:2-4. Epaphras's prayers focused on the
Colossian believers' growth in the faith—that they would *stand
mature* ("complete") spiritually (as in 1:28; 2:2; 3:14) and be
fully assured (filled with everything that is God's will). We have
already been filled with Christ, but we must go on to fulfill what
has been given us. Such strength and assurance of faith will help
believers of any time period stand against false teaching.

**4:13 For I testify for him that he has worked hard for you and for
those in Laodicea and in Hierapolis.**^{NRSV} Epaphras wrestled in
prayer, not only for the believers in Colosse, but also for those in
the other cities in the Lycus Valley. Laodicea was located a few
miles northwest of Colosse, also on the Lycus River, and was a

stopover along the main road from the East to Ephesus. The city was named for Laodice, queen of Antiochus II. Hierapolis was about five miles north of Laodicea. Epaphras was truly a zealous missionary in this particular portion of the Roman Empire.

PRAYER WARRIOR
If you think prayer is too passive for such an energetic person as yourself, think of Epaphras, the prayer warrior.

If you think prayer is too isolated and individualistic for such a social creature as yourself, think of Epaphras.

If you think prayer accomplishes little more than venting frustrations to some cosmic ear, think of Epaphras, who wrestled in prayer.

This strong leader spent energy in prayer for people he loved, and God enriched their lives as a result.

Your prayers count. Don't ignore the Christian's unique invitation to address the heart of almighty God to pray for others. Pray often. Pray with passion.

4:14 **Luke the beloved physician and Demas greet you.**^{NKJV} Luke had spent much time with Paul. He had accompanied Paul on most of the third missionary journey. He also remained beside Paul through this imprisonment, as well as Paul's final imprisonment (see 2 Timothy 4:11). The good doctor certainly had helped with Paul's health (especially after the beatings Paul received during his travels, as well as other ailments that plagued Paul in prison). Luke was also a prolific writer, authoring the Gospel of Luke and the book of Acts. Since Paul had explained that the only three Jewish Christians with him were Aristarchus, Mark, and Justus, it has been assumed that Luke was a Gentile or a Greek-speaking Jew.

Apparently Demas was faithful at this time (see also Philemon 24), but later he deserted Paul "because he loved this world" (2 Timothy 4:10 NIV).

4:15 **Give my greetings to the brothers and sisters in Laodicea, and to Nympha and the church in her house.**^{NRSV} Paul turned his attention from sending everyone else's greetings to sending his own. He asked that the Colossian church relay his greetings to the church (that is, to the *brothers and sisters*) in Laodicea (ten miles to the west). This gives an interesting sidelight to church life in the first century—it seems that the churches had fellowship with one another, as the sending of greetings and sharing of letters would indicate (4:16; 1 Thessalonians 5:27). Another sidelight is the picture of believers meeting in private homes. It wasn't until the middle of the third century that churches began to own property and build public places of worship. So during this time, individual believers opened their homes for worship services. Here Paul greeted those who met in Nympha's home. In Colosse, the believers met in Philemon's house (Philemon 2). Lydia opened her home to the believers in Philippi (Acts 16:40). Gaius offered his home to the believers in Corinth (Romans 16:23). Aquila and Priscilla, a husband and wife team, opened their home while they lived in Rome (Romans 16:5) and in Ephesus (1 Corinthians 16:19).

This verse has posed some interesting questions. The first question focuses on Nympha's name. The sex cannot be determined from the Greek form of the name, but scholars conclude that Nympha probably was a woman because the feminine pronoun *autais* ("her") appears in some ancient manuscripts. However, if Paul were greeting the brothers and sisters in Laodicea (thus, the church there), and if the church had been meeting in Nympha's house, why would he make a point to greet the church in Nympha's house? This would have been greeting the same people twice.

One answer is that within any particular local church, there were several smaller assemblies of believers meeting in various homes. Paul thus may have been greeting the entire church in Laodicea and then singling out one person (Nympha). This would be important as he laid the groundwork for a relationship with these believers whom he did not know. It is significant that the only other letter in which Paul named various believers in this manner is the letter to the Romans—also a church that Paul had not visited.

4:16 After this letter has been read to you, see that it is also read in the church of the Laodiceans and that you in turn read the letter from Laodicea.NIV After this letter had *been read* to all the believers in Colosse in a worship service, they were to send it on to Laodicea. Apparently the heresy was a problem for that church as well, and they needed Paul's advice and encouragement. This is another interesting sidelight to the life of the early church. At this time, no New Testaments had been assembled—indeed, most of the New Testament books were still being written. So the churches circulated these letters from Paul (1 Thessalonians 5:27), Peter (1 Peter 1:1), James (James 1:1), and other key Christian leaders.

The Colossians, in turn, were to read *the letter from Laodicea.* This was not a letter written by the Laodiceans; rather, it was a letter written to them that they were to pass on to Colosse. Most scholars suggest that the letter may have been the book of Ephesians because the letter to the Ephesians was to be circulated to all the churches in Asia Minor. It is also possible that there was a special letter to the Laodiceans, which we do not have. Paul wrote several letters that have been lost (for example, we know that there were probably four letters to the Corinthians, only two of which appear in the Bible). Or the letter may not have survived to be included in the New Testament because the church in Laodicea was later chastised for being "lukewarm" (Revelation 3:14-22). In any case, the important point is that Paul intended his letters to carry his apostolic authority. Thus they were carefully kept and eventually compiled with the complete New Testament.

4:17 And say to Archippus, "See that you complete the task that you have received in the Lord."NRSV Paul's letter to Philemon is also addressed to Archippus (Philemon 2), where Paul called him a "fellow soldier." Archippus may have been a Roman soldier who had become a member of the Colossian church, or he may have been Philemon's son. In any case, Paul called upon the members of the church to encourage Archippus to complete some task that he had been given. Archippus may have been ministering to the church in Epaphras's absence and needed special encouragement in the job as he dealt with the false teaching. He may have been ministering in some specific capacity and needed to be nudged. Or he may have been involved in the acceptance of Onesimus on this newly converted slave's return to Philemon's household. In any case, Paul singled out Archippus for making sure his job was completed. Paul saw nothing wrong in challenging believers to attempt more in ministry and to go beyond their current level of achievement.

GET IT DONE
Paul encouraged Archippus to make sure that he completed the work he had received in the Lord. There are many ways for us to leave our work unfinished. We can easily get sidetracked morally, we can become exhausted and stop, we can get mad and quit, or we can let it slide and leave it up to others. We should see to it that we finish God's assignments, completing the work we have received.

4:18 I, Paul, write this greeting with my own hand.NRSV Paul usually dictated his letters to a scribe, and he often ended with a short note in his own handwriting (see also 1 Corinthians 16:21; Galatians 6:11; 2 Thessalonians 3:17; Philemon 19). This assured the recipients that false teachers were not writing letters in Paul's name (as apparently had been a problem, see 2 Thessalonians 2:2; 3:17). It also gave the letters a personal touch, especially to this congregation Paul had never visited.

Remember my chains.^{NRSV} Paul asked that the believers continue to pray for him during his imprisonment (see also 4:3, 10). This reference also reminded the believers that the letter had been written to them while he was in prison. Paul had been remembering them; he wanted them to remember that he was a prisoner for the gospel's sake, a gospel he would not stop preaching regardless of his chains. Indeed he had to continue, for his calling and apostolic authority would not allow him to stop. Paul was in prison because he refused to set aside one iota of his faith; he hoped that the Colossian believers would remember that when they encountered the false teachings.

Grace be with you. Just as Paul had begun his letter with "grace" (1:2), so he ended it with the benediction that the believers would continue to experience God's unmerited favor. Ultimately, God's grace would strengthen and defend the church.

To understand the letter to the Colossians, we need to realize that the church was facing pressure from a heresy that promised deeper spiritual life through secret knowledge. The false teachers were destroying faith in Christ by undermining Christ's humanity and divinity.

Paul makes it clear in this letter to the Colossian believers that Christ alone is the source of our spiritual life, the Head of the body of believers. Christ is Lord of both the physical and spiritual worlds. The path to deeper spiritual life is not through religious duties, special knowledge, or secrets; it is only through a clear connection with the Lord Jesus Christ. We must never let anything come between us and our Savior.

PHILEMON

INTRODUCTION TO PHILEMON

Invisible walls divide people into the "ins and outs," the "haves and have nots," and an endless assortment of groups, cliques, and castes. Determined by race, skin color, nationality, money, background, education, status, religion, sex, or ability, individuals are judged, categorized, and put in their place. When those social barriers are crossed, usually it is at a great price.

But Jesus broke the barriers that divide men and women from each other and from God. In a male-dominated society, he spoke freely with women (Matthew 9:18-26; Luke 8:1-3). In the face of holier-than-thou hypocrites, he partied with sinners (Matthew 9:10-13). Ignoring years of prejudice and discrimination, he associated with Samaritans (John 4:1-42) and Gentiles (Luke 7:1-10; 8:26-39). And he continually sought to bring outcasts and the powerless into his fold: the crippled and lame (Luke 6:1-11), the desperately ill (Matthew 8:1-4; Luke 17:11-19), the blind (Luke 18:35-42; Mark 8:22-26; John 9:1-7), children (Mark 10:13-16), swindlers and cheaters (Mark 11:13-17; Luke 19:1-10), and the poor (Mark 3:7-12; Luke 21:1-4).

Following in the footsteps of his Lord, Paul became the apostle to the Gentiles as he traveled extensively and shared Christ's message with all types of people. In fact, writing to the Galatians, Paul declared: "There is neither Jew nor Greek, slave nor free, male nor female, for you are all one in Christ Jesus" (Galatians 3:28 NIV).

Perhaps the greatest example of the barrier-shattering power of the gospel is here in Philemon, where Paul reunites a rich slave-owner and his runaway slave, now both members of God's family.

As you read this personal letter of reconciliation, consider what divides you from your brothers and sisters in Christ. Ask God to obliterate those walls and bring you together.

AUTHOR

Paul (See the introduction to this volume.)

The very first word of this letter names Paul as the writer. In Colossians, Paul explained that, along with his letter to the believers in Colosse, he would be sending Onesimus (4:9). Tychicus would deliver both. This letter to Philemon focuses on this same Onesimus. Clearly, then, Paul wrote both letters at about the same time and sent them together.

SETTING

Written from a Roman prison in about A.D. 60 (See the introduction to Philippians.)

This letter was written at about the same time as Ephesians and Colossians. Paul wrote that he was a prisoner (vv. 1, 9, 23) and in chains (vv. 10, 13), so clearly he was in prison. And the reference in Colossians 4:9 implies that he would send this letter to Philemon along with his runaway slave, Onesimus.

AUDIENCE

Philemon and the church at large

Philemon was a leader in the church at Colosse—the church met at his house (v. 2). Evidently Philemon was a wealthy slaveholder who had been converted to Christ under Paul's ministry (v. 19). Slaveholders had absolute power over their slaves. Whether or not Philemon was a kind owner, Onesimus had run away and could be beaten, jailed, or even killed for his offense according to Roman law.

People could become slaves by being born to a woman who was a slave, as punishment for a crime, by being kidnapped from another land, and by being conquered by another nation (slave dealers would buy captured prisoners and send them to the slave markets to be sold for a profit). Sometimes, however, parents would sell their children into slavery. And some would voluntarily become slaves in order to pay a debt.

Slavery was taken for granted in the first century—85 to 90 percent of the inhabitants of Italy were slaves. Usually those with financial means would own slaves. Under Roman law, a slave could expect to be set free in seven years. How slave owners treated their slaves could vary greatly, depending on the temperament of the owner and the performance of the slave. Owners could inflict cruel punishments upon slaves, considered as their property, usually by whipping or beating with a stick. Like thieves, runaway slaves were branded on the forehead. Others were imprisoned. Many slaves died from mistreatment or impris-

onment, but it was illegal to take the life of a slave without a
court order. Philemon had the power; Onesimus was powerless.

OCCASION AND PURPOSE FOR WRITING

Onesimus had come to faith in Christ while in Rome and was
returning to Colosse, to his master, Philemon.

Because of his unique imprisonment in a rented house, Paul
was able to have a steady stream of visitors and to freely preach
and teach the Word for two years (Acts 28:17-31). During that
time, the young man Onesimus heard the gospel and became a
follower of Christ (v. 10). Onesimus had stolen money from his
master, Philemon, and had fled to Rome. Now, as a new Christian, he was preparing to return to Colosse and to Philemon.

Paul wrote this letter on behalf of Onesimus, urging Philemon
to see the young man not as a slave but as a "brother in the Lord"
(v. 16 NIV). Thus Paul hoped that Philemon would welcome him
(v. 17), forgive him (vv. 18-19), and perhaps even free him (v. 21).

Paul's appeal is based on their common love for Christ (v. 9),
on their relationship (vv. 17-19), and on his authority as an apostle (v. 8). Philemon's response is unknown, but it would be difficult to imagine him not welcoming Onesimus as his new brother
in Christ.

One of the lessons of this short letter is the example of Paul.
He wrote as the advocate of Onesimus, trusting him to return, to
submit to Philemon, and to live with the consequences of his
actions. Paul believes in Onesimus, that he is a true brother in the
faith. Paul does more than write and endorse this runaway slave,
he also backs up his words with his money—Paul offers to pay
for anything Onesimus may have broken or stolen (v. 18).

Another lesson concerns the power of the gospel to bring
people together. At an opposite pole in the society stood Philemon and Onesimus, yet they became unified brothers through
their common faith in Christ. God can reconcile people, regardless of their differences or offenses.

With whom do you need to be reconciled? What new Christian
needs your affirmation and support?

MESSAGE

Forgiveness, Barriers, Respect

Forgiveness (vv. 17-21). Philemon was Paul's friend, but he also
was the legal owner of the slave Onesimus. He could have punished Onesimus severely, as a runaway and as a thief. Paul asked

this dear friend not only to withhold punishment, but to forgive
Onesimus and to accept him as a new Christian brother, welcoming him into his home as he would welcome Paul (v. 17).

Importance for Today. Many factors divide people today,
including disagreements, politics, arguments, and personal
offenses. Yet Christians are to be unified, demonstrating the love
of Christ by their love for each other (John 13:34-35). Thus Christian relationships must be filled with forgiveness and acceptance.

Who has wronged you? With what brother or sister in Christ
do you feel estranged, distant, or angry? Who do you need to forgive? Build bridges, not walls.

Barriers (vv. 10-16). Slavery was widespread in the Roman
Empire, but no one is lost to God or beyond his love, not even the
poorest slave. Slavery was a thick barrier, but God can break
through anything that divides people. And God tells us, as those
committed to Christ, to love all kinds of people. Christian love
and fellowship should overcome all barriers.

Importance for Today. In Christ, we are one family. No walls
of racial, economic, political, or social differences should separate us. Christ wants to work through us to remove barriers between brothers and sisters.

What can you do to fellowship with Christians of other races?
How can you reach out to those from different cultures and social
standing?

Respect (vv. 4-9, 21-25). Paul was a friend of both Philemon and
Onesimus. He had the authority as an apostle to tell Philemon
what to do (v. 8). Yet Paul chose to appeal to his friend in Christian love rather than to order him what to do. Paul clearly made
his desires known, but he treated Philemon with respect, as a peer
and fellow believer.

Importance for Today. Tactful persuasion will accomplish
much more than strong commands when dealing with people. No
one appreciates being bossed around or ordered what to do.
Remember to be courteous and to treat people with respect.

VITAL STATISTICS

Purpose: To convince Philemon to forgive his runaway slave, Onesimus, and to accept him as a brother in the faith

Author: Paul

To whom written: Philemon, who was probably a wealthy member of the Colossian church, and all believers

Date written: About A.D. 60, during Paul's first imprisonment in Rome, at about the same time Ephesians and Colossians were written

Setting: Slavery was very common in the Roman Empire, and evidently some Christians had slaves. Paul does not condemn the institution of slavery in his writings, but he makes a radical statement by calling this slave Philemon's brother in Christ.

Key verses: "Perhaps the reason he was separated from you for a little while was that you might have him back for good—no longer as a slave, but better than a slave, as a dear brother. He is very dear to me but even dearer to you, both as a man and as a brother in the Lord" (15-16 NIV).

OUTLINE OF PHILEMON

1. Paul's appreciation of Philemon (1-7)

2. Paul's appeal for Onesimus (8-25)

Philemon

Paul wrote Philemon, along with Ephesians, Philippians, and Colossians, from prison in Rome (see Acts 28:30-31). Onesimus, a domestic slave, belonged to Philemon, a wealthy man and a member of the church in Colosse. Onesimus had run away from Philemon and had made his way to Rome, where he had met Paul, who apparently had led him to Christ (v. 10). Paul convinced Onesimus that running from his problems wouldn't solve them, and he persuaded Onesimus to return to his master. In Colossians 4:9, Paul regarded Onesimus as a trusted associate. Paul wrote this letter to Philemon to ask him to be reconciled to his runaway slave.

Reconciliation may not be easy. Often it requires the help of a mature Christian worker. It always requires love and God's grace. In this short book, look for ways to help you solve disputes and break down barriers.

1 Paul, a prisoner of Christ Jesus. Letters in Paul's day often would begin with the writer's name instead of adding it at the end. Thus Paul always identified himself at the beginning of his letters. Paul wrote many letters—some during his time of imprisonment, others during his travels. He wrote to congregations to settle disputes, deal with problems, or give necessary doctrinal teaching. He wrote to friends (such as in 1 and 2 Timothy and Titus), to church congregations that he knew well (such as Ephesians and Philippians), and to believers whom he had never met (such as Romans and Colossians).

In some letters Paul would identify himself as an "apostle" of Jesus Christ for the sake of those who had never met him and/or were doubting his authority. In other letters, he would call himself a "servant" of Jesus Christ. Although neither Paul nor Timothy had visited the church in Colosse, they had, during their earlier travels, met individual Colossians such as Epaphras, Philemon, Archippus, and Apphia who, after their conversion, had returned with the gospel to their native city. So Philemon was a friend and fellow believer. But this letter does not present doctrine or give commands; instead, it is a request on behalf of another believer. Paul chose to introduce himself in this letter as *a prisoner of Christ Jesus.* This is the only one of Paul's letters where he used such an introduction. Paul was indeed a prisoner, captive in Rome for preaching the gospel—the Good News of Christ Jesus (see Philippians 1:13).

(For more about the apostle Paul, see the introduction to this volume.)

And Timothy our brother. Timothy's name is included with Paul's in 2 Corinthians, 1 and 2 Thessalonians, Philippians, Colossians, and Philemon. Timothy was one of Paul's trusted companions; Paul wrote two letters to him (1 and 2 Timothy).

Timothy visited Paul frequently during his imprisonment (see also Colossians 1:1) and was with Paul in Rome when he wrote this letter. Timothy was not imprisoned with Paul, but he had stayed in Rome to encourage Paul and to help with ministry needs. Timothy had grown up in Lystra, a city in the province of Galatia. Paul and Barnabas had visited Lystra on Paul's first missionary journey (see Acts 14:8-21). Most likely, Paul had met the young Timothy and his mother, Eunice, and grandmother Lois (see 2 Timothy 1:5), during that visit. He may have stayed in their home.

On Paul's second missionary journey, he and Silas had returned to several cities that Paul had already visited, including Lystra. There Paul met Timothy (see Acts 16:1-3). Timothy probably had come to believe in Christ through Paul, for Paul later would call him "my true son in the faith" (1 Timothy 1:2 NIV). Paul and Timothy had developed a special bond, like father and son (Philippians 2:22). Timothy became Paul's assistant and emissary—traveling with him and sometimes for him.

Although mentioned in the salutation, Timothy is not considered a coauthor. Paul wrote in the first person throughout this letter (the same is true for the letter to the Philippians).

To Philemon our dear friend and fellow worker.[NIV] Philemon was a wealthy Greek landowner living in Colosse. He had been converted under Paul's ministry (v. 19), perhaps in Ephesus or some other city where he had met and talked with Paul. During Paul's years of ministry in nearby Ephesus, Philemon had been building up the Colossian church, which would meet in his home (v. 2). Thus Paul considered him not only a *dear friend* but also a *fellow worker* on behalf of the gospel. (Paul also referred to him as "brother" in vv. 7 and 20.) Like most wealthy landowners of ancient times, Philemon owned slaves. Onesimus, the subject of this letter, was one of those slaves.

2 To Apphia our sister.^{NRSV} Apphia probably was Philemon's wife or another close relative who helped manage his household; otherwise, she would not have been greeted with Philemon in a letter concerning a domestic matter. At this time, women handled the day-to-day responsibilities of the slaves. Thus, the final decision about Onesimus would have been as much her choice as Philemon's. Paul greeted Apphia as *our sister,* that is, a sister in the Christian faith. Like Philemon, Apphia was a believer.

To Archippus our fellow soldier.^{NRSV} Archippus may have been Philemon's son, or perhaps an elder in the Colossian church (at the end of the letter to the Colossians, Paul had given special encouragement to a man named Archippus; see Colossians 4:17). In either case, Paul included him as a recipient of the letter, possibly so that Archippus would read the letter with Philemon and encourage him to take Paul's advice.

Paul described Archippus as *our fellow soldier.* Paul often used military metaphors for serving Christ (see, for example, Romans 7:23; 2 Corinthians 6:7; 10:3-5; Ephesians 6:10-18; Philippians 2:25; 1 Timothy 1:18; 2 Timothy 2:3-4). Soldiers must be disciplined, committed, and unified. So, too, believers must lead disciplined lives, stand strongly committed to the faith, and work to remain unified because they fight the same battle—that of bringing the gospel to an unbelieving and increasingly hostile world. Paul was in chains for preaching the gospel; apparently Archippus was fighting the battle well as he also worked to spread the gospel.

And to the church that meets in your home.^{NIV} The early churches always met in people's homes. Because of sporadic persecutions and the great expense involved, church buildings were not constructed at this time (church buildings were not built until the third century). Many congregations were small enough that the entire church could meet in one home.

Because Philemon was one of those who had worked to begin the church at Colosse, it was natural that believers would meet in his home. *The church* could refer to the entire body of believers, although it seems unlikely because Paul had been writing a letter to the entire Colossian church at this same time. It may have been that, as in any large city even today, smaller groups of believers met regularly in various private homes. One group met in Philemon's home; some in other believers' homes, such as Nympha's. Paul had greeted Nympha and the church in her house in Colossians 4:15. (For references to other house churches, see Romans 16:5 and 1 Corinthians 16:19-20.)

Because of the personal nature of this letter, Paul apparently chose not to include his instructions to Philemon in his general letter to the Colossians. Paul greeted the believers who met in Philemon's home because Paul knew that not only would this group know about the runaway slave, but they would also become Onesimus's "family" upon his return as a new believer. The church would need to understand Paul's request and Philemon's response to it. Then there would be no gossip, and they could immediately and lovingly accept Onesimus into their fellowship.

OPEN HOUSE
Philemon opened his home for church meetings and for Christians who traveled through that region. Hospitality honors Christ. When we share our homes and our food, we honor our guests as those created in the image of God and loved by the Lord. Meeting another person's need for food or shelter was and still is one of the most immediate and practical ways to obey God. It helps build relationships, offers time for talking, and gives children the opportunity to learn about how God uses other people in a variety of situations and cultures. As God has blessed you, share your provision with others. Open your home and invite others in.

---

3 Grace to you and peace from God our Father and the Lord Jesus Christ. Paul used *grace* and *peace* as a standard greeting in all his letters. "Grace" is God's undeserved favor—his lovingkindness shown to sinners whereby he saves them and gives them strength to live for him; *peace* refers to the peace that Christ made between sinners and God through his death on the cross. "Peace" refers to that inner assurance and tranquility that God places in a person, producing confidence and contentment in Christ. Only God can grant such wonderful gifts.

The phrase *God our Father* focuses on the family relationship among all believers as God's children. In the context of this letter, Paul was emphasizing the family relationship that the master, Philemon, and the slave, Onesimus, had because both were believers.

By using the phrase, *Lord Jesus Christ,* Paul was pointing to Jesus as a full person of the Godhead and was recognizing Jesus' full deity. God the Father and Christ the Lord are coequal in providing grace and peace.

4 When I remember you in my prayers, I always thank my God.^{NRSV} Most ancient letters included a thanksgiving for the addressee immediately after the salutation. With these words, Paul was expressing his love for Philemon (the word *you* is singular, as it is through the entire letter, except in vv. 22 and 25). Paul constantly prayed for churches and for individual believers who had specific needs (see the chart "Prayer in Paul's Life and Letters" in Philippians 1:4).

THANKS FOR THE MEMORIES
Every time Paul prayed for Philemon, he would thank God for him. Paul's prayers of intercession flowed from loving and grateful memories. When you think of people to pray for, do you also express thanks to God for them? As you pray for people, thank God for their salvation and for the good work that God has done in their lives. Like Paul, make thanksgiving a regular part of your prayer life (see Colossians 3:16-17).

---

5 Because I hear of your love for all the saints and your faith toward the Lord Jesus.^{NRSV} Philemon had been converted under Paul's ministry and then had returned to Colosse. Although Paul had never visited Colosse, he had heard (perhaps from Onesimus or Epaphras) about Philemon's continued faith and love for the believers. Paul was saying that if Philemon truly loved *all* the believers, then he certainly would be willing to include another believer—Onesimus—in that love.

The NIV reverses the words "faith" and "love" to match all of Paul's letters where he thanked God for believers' faith and love. However, other versions (as NRSV above) place the word "love" before "faith" as it is in the Greek text. Some scholars think that Paul purposely reversed his typical words of greeting because he would appeal to Philemon's love later in this letter. In the Greek text, the phrase is "I hear of your love and faith which you have to the Lord Jesus and to all the saints." The Greek word *pistis* can be translated "faith," "faithfulness," or "loyalty." Loyalty may be a more natural meaning for Paul's usage here. Paul always thanked God for Philemon because of his faith and love that had ministered to many believers in Colosse and, Paul hoped, would continue to be true with Onesimus.

The phrases *love for the saints* and *faith toward the Lord Jesus* are often connected in the New Testament epistles because faith in Christ brings us into a new community based on love. Love is required to unify the community of believers. Love and faith reinforce each other.

**6 I pray that you may be active in sharing your faith, so that
you will have a full understanding of every good thing we
have in Christ.**^{NIV} This verse describes Paul's prayer (the NIV
adds the words *I pray that* to make this clear; they are not in the
Greek text) and introduces the request that Paul will make to Philemon in this letter. The word *you* is singular (as in v. 4)—this
was what Paul prayed for Philemon himself.

Yet the identification of what Paul prayed for Philemon is very
difficult to determine from his words. Consider how this verse is
rendered in other Bible versions:

Literal translation of the Greek text: "So that the sharing of
your faith may become effective in the acknowledgment of all
the good in us for Christ."

NRSV: "I pray that the sharing of your faith may become effective when you perceive all the good that we may do for Christ."

TEV: "My prayer is that our fellowship with you as believers
will bring about a deeper understanding of every blessing which
we have in our life in union with Christ."

The Greek word *koinonia* is rendered in these verses as "sharing" or "fellowship." To us, "sharing" usually means evangelism,
and "fellowship" can mean potluck suppers or small-group meetings. Neither of these were in Paul's thoughts as he prayed for
Philemon. *Koinonia* is a difficult word to translate, but it incorporates the true outworking of Christian love in the body of Christ—
fellowship that causes individual believers to belong to one
another, willingly rejoicing with those who rejoice and weeping
with those who weep (Romans 12:15). The word focused on Philemon's relationship with other Christians. Paul prayed that Philemon's faith would show itself in *koinonia* among the believers,
especially those that would meet in his home (v. 2). The "faith"
that Philemon was called to share was both the content of what
he believed (doctrine) and the practical demonstration of his
devotion to Christ. The word "fellowship" also anticipated Paul's
coming request on behalf of a new believer who would become
part of that group. Paul prayed that Philemon would be *active* in
this *koinonia,* this fellowship and sharing. Paul would later ask
Philemon to welcome Onesimus as if he were Paul, and that Philemon should charge any of Onesimus's debts to Paul (vv. 17-19).
This is true *koinonia,* Christians giving to one another and caring
for one another because they belong to one another.

Some scholars believe that *koinonia* refers to Philemon's sharing of his resources or a spirit of liberality stemming from his
faith in Christ (see 2 Corinthians 9:6-8). The great evangelist
Paul, the wealthy master Philemon, and the runaway slave Onesi-

mus belonged to one another in the body of Christ because of their faith in him.

The NIV translates the Greek *en* as "so that you will have," sounding as if the second clause is a result of the first (actively sharing your faith results in having a full understanding of the good things). Yet it could just as easily be the case that the first clause is a result of the second (having a full understanding of the good things results in actively sharing your faith). Either one could be true, although some force can be given to the NRSV translation based on Paul's view that knowledge precedes good works (see Colossians 1:9-10). In any case, Paul prayed that Philemon would *have a full understanding of every good thing we have in Christ*. Paul also prayed for this "full understanding" (*epignosei*, also translated "knowledge") for other believers (see Ephesians 1:18; Philippians 1:9; Colossians 1:9). Every "good thing" refers to what God does for believers through Christ and looks forward to the "good deed" Philemon would do for Onesimus (v. 14). Finally, the words "in Christ" explain that, as for all believers, everything Philemon was, had, and would become was because of Christ; everything he did, then, ought to glorify Christ.

ACTIVE SHARING
Paul's prayer for Philemon was setting the stage for the request Paul would make in this letter. As Philemon was active in his faith and in sharing its blessings, as he learned more about God and his ways, and as he gained fuller understanding of all that Christ had done on his behalf, this knowledge should cause him to respond appropriately to Paul's request regarding Onesimus. Are you active and effective in sharing with others your faith, your resources, and your love?

---

7 Your love has given me great joy and encouragement, because you, brother, have refreshed the hearts of the saints.[NIV] The love that Philemon showed to all the saints (v. 5) refreshed their hearts and gave Paul joy and encouragement. Philemon probably had acted out his faith among the believers in many ways beyond sharing his home for church meetings. But Paul was concerned less about Philemon's actions than about the spirit in which he was performing them. Paul hoped that Philemon's loving spirit—which had given others joy, encouragement, and refreshment—would also show itself in his dealings with Onesimus.

Paul had written to the Colossian church: "Epaphras . . . told us of your love in the Spirit" (Colossians 1:7-8 NIV). The outpouring of love among believers is a sure sign of the Spirit's work among them (Galatians 5:22). Philemon's love *refreshed the hearts of the saints*. The word "refreshed" (*anapepautai,* see also v. 20) is the same word that Jesus used in Matthew 11:28 to describe the rest ("refreshment") he would give those who came to him. Philemon had the ability to give refreshment to people. The word "hearts" is *splangchna;* it refers to the inner parts of the body. The Greeks used the word to describe the place of deepest emotions. Paul also used *splangchna* in verse 12, calling Onesimus his "very heart." Paul's use of the word showed his intense emotion about the situation. Paul knew Philemon's response to his request about Onesimus would then, in turn, "refresh" him (v. 20).

REFRESHMENTS

Like iced tea on a hot day or cold water on a long hike, this Christian brother Philemon knew how to be refreshing. He was able to revive and restore his brothers and sisters in the faith. His love and generosity had replenished and stimulated them. Philemon also encouraged Paul by his love and loyalty. Are you a refreshing influence on others, or does your attitude and temperament add to the burden they carry? Instead of draining others' energy and motivation with complaints and problems, replenish their spirits by encouragement, love, and a helpful attitude.

PAUL'S APPEAL FOR ONESIMUS / 8-25

While in prison, Paul had led Onesimus to the Lord. So he asked Philemon to forgive his runaway slave who had become a Christian and, even going beyond forgiveness, to accept Onesimus as a brother. As Christians, we should forgive as we have been forgiven (Matthew 6:12; Ephesians 4:31-32). True forgiveness means that we treat the one we've forgiven as we would want to be treated. Is there someone you say you have forgiven, but who still needs your kindness?

8 Therefore, although in Christ I could be bold and order you to do what you ought to do.^{NIV} The word *therefore* carries on the thought from verse 7—the love Philemon had shown to the saints ought to be extended to include Onesimus. Such a request would be *bold* indeed; in the Roman Empire, a master had the right to kill a disobedient slave. In any other situation, Onesimus's action of running away would have signed his death warrant. But Onesimus had met Paul, and Paul knew Philemon, so Paul mediated because of their common brotherhood in Christ.

Paul first described his right to make this appeal to Philemon. Paul was Philemon's friend and spiritual father (v. 19), but Paul was also an elder and an apostle with authority *in Christ*. Paul was subtly reminding Philemon of his authority. Paul could have used his authority with Philemon and ordered him to deal kindly with his runaway slave. But Paul based his request not on his own authority, but on his friendship with Philemon and Philemon's Christian commitment. Paul wanted Philemon's heartfelt, not grudging, obedience. Paul would explain to Philemon *what he ought to do* but would not enforce it, hoping, instead, that Philemon would act on his own volition (v. 14).

RELATIONSHIPS RECONCILED AND REBUILT
Paul provides a good example of how to deal with conflict between Christians. When reconciling a separation or mediating a dispute, trust must be rebuilt between the conflicting parties. Notice the steps that Paul used to help rebuild the trust:
- Paul identified with the people. He called Philemon "brother" and Onesimus "my son."
- Paul requested, not ordered, Philemon.
- Paul sought Philemon's voluntary consent, not his submission to rules or authority.
- Paul appealed to Christian love, not to power or authority.
- Paul agreed to absorb the loss and pay any cost for restoration.
   Instead of overusing power or position, use Paul's approach to rebuild a trusting relationship.

---

9 Yet I would rather appeal to you on the basis of love—and I, Paul, do this as an old man, and now also as a prisoner of Christ Jesus.^{NRSV} Although Paul certainly had the authority to tell Philemon what to do, he preferred not to use his authority in this particular situation. He wanted Philemon to make the final decision. The love to which Paul referred may have been Paul's love for Philemon, Paul's love for Onesimus, Philemon's well-known love for the believers (vv. 4-5, 7), or the virtue of Christian love in general. In any case, Paul would make his appeal for Onesimus *on the basis of love*. Paul appealed to Philemon not so he could exercise his authority; instead, he appealed from his heart because of his concern for this new believer's future.

Yet Paul's authority was not to be completely forgotten. Philemon ought to be motivated to follow Paul's advice, not only because Paul was a friend and spiritual mentor, but because Paul was, first, *an old man*. The Greek word for "old man" *(presbutes)* could easily be confused for the Greek word for "ambassador" *(presbeutes);* so some scholars and translators (see RSV and NEB) have translated this "ambassador." However, there is no textual evidence for this rendering. By referring to himself as an old man, Paul was asking for Philemon's respect.

Second, Paul described himself as *a prisoner of Christ Jesus*. Paul was a representative of Christ whose commitment to his calling had landed him in prison. Paul could do nothing more than write this note to help Onesimus—he couldn't go with him back to Colosse. Paul's authority in his appeal to Philemon came not from position or popularity, but from Christ alone.

10 I appeal to you for my son Onesimus, who became my son while I was in chains.[NIV] In the Greek text, Onesimus's name is the last word in this verse. Paul skillfully crafted this letter, with its introduction and sincere compliments to Philemon, here beginning to state his appeal but only giving Onesimus's name at the last possible moment, and then never getting to the actual appeal until verse 17. Paul approached Philemon with tact and humility.

Philemon probably had been angered that his slave had disappeared (in Roman times, it was like losing a piece of valuable property). Thus, Paul first explained that his appeal was on behalf of someone who had become his *son* during Paul's imprisonment— that is, someone Paul had led to Christ from prison. Philemon would be dealing with a fellow believer. "And, by the way," Paul added, "it's Onesimus. Remember him?" That Paul called Onesimus a "son" reveals their close relationship. Paul used *tou emou teknou* (my child) elsewhere only of Timothy and Titus (see 1 Timothy 1:2; Titus 1:4), although he often used the father/child analogy for those he had led to Christ (see, for example, 1 Corinthians 4:14-15; 2 Corinthians 6:13; Galatians 4:19; Philippians 2:22).

What incredible providence had brought this runaway slave to the door of Paul's prison—Paul, who also had led this slave's master to the Lord! That Paul appealed *for* Onesimus has been taken by some to mean that Paul was asking to keep Onesimus with him. However, verse 15 reveals that Paul had planned for Onesimus to return to his master. The word "for" should be read as "on behalf of."

11 Formerly he was useless to you, but now he has become useful both to you and to me.[NIV] Onesimus's name in Greek means "useful." The name was a common name for slaves and is found in many ancient inscriptions. A nameless slave might receive this name in the hopes that he would live up to it in serving his master.

Paul used a play on words, saying that Onesimus had formerly been *useless (achreston)* to Philemon but had become very *useful (euchreston)* both to Paul and, potentially, to Philemon. Under Philemon's service, Onesimus had failed to live up to his name. Phrygian slaves were referred to stereotypically as useless and undependable. Paul was confident, however, that this new man with his new life in Christ would live up to his name if Philemon would take him back. In Colossians 4:9, Paul called Onesimus a "faithful and dear brother" (NIV). Onesimus had become known for his faithfulness.

It is interesting to note that Paul did not ask Philemon to free Onesimus. Paul didn't condemn or condone slavery, but he worked to transform relationships. The gospel begins to change social structures by changing the *people* within those structures. There were several million slaves in the Roman Empire at this time. Slavery was sanctioned by law and was part of the empire's social makeup. Because many slaves and slave owners had become Christians, the early church had to deal straightforwardly with the question of master/slave relations. In other letters, Paul simply was stating that slaves should serve well and that masters should be fair (1 Corinthians 7:20-24; Ephesians 6:5-9; Colossians 3:22–4:1). Paul was not interested in trying to change Roman culture; he wanted to build the church as a new community. In the church, relationships should be based on love, not on power or position.

12-13 I am sending him—who is my very heart—back to you.NIV Although Paul would have liked to have kept Onesimus with him, he was sending Onesimus back, requesting that Philemon accept him not only as a forgiven runaway servant, but also as a brother in Christ. This verse suggests that Onesimus himself would deliver this letter to Philemon, so Philemon would need to make his decision as he stood face-to-face with his slave.

Paul described Onesimus as *my very heart,* once again using the Greek *splangchna* as in verse 7, referring to the place of deepest emotions. Paul loved Onesimus dearly, as a father loves a child (v. 10). Paul was willing to give away "his very heart," a part of himself, in order to return Onesimus permanently to Philemon. Onesimus had become part of Paul's ministry team. This was a sacrifice on Paul's part, who said, **I wanted to keep him with me, so that he might be of service to me in your place during my imprisonment for the gospel.**NRSV Onesimus had truly become "useful" (v. 11)—so useful that Paul would have liked to have kept him in Rome so that Onesimus could *be of service* to him. Paul knew that if Philemon were available to be with Paul, he would have helped him in any way he could; therefore, if Paul had kept Onesimus, Philemon would have been helping

Paul vicariously. Paul implied that he trusted Onesimus so much that Onesimus's service could be considered in place of Philemon's; therefore, Philemon should be able to trust him as well. Paul, imprisoned *for the gospel,* longed for his friends; how difficult it was for him to send away this dear "son." Yet Paul knew it was his duty to do so—Roman law demanded that a deserting slave be returned to his legal owner (although Deuteronomy 23:15-16 states the opposite). Because Onesimus belonged to Philemon, Paul chose to send him back.

WHO CAN YOU SEND?
Paul described Onesimus as much more than just a useful servant. Paul called him his "very heart." Paul took the risk in faith that Philemon would respond in true Christian character and receive Onesimus as a Christian. Paul had such a good relationship with Onesimus that it hurt him deeply to send him back. Do you have anyone who is your very heart and soul that you could send on a mission? Are your children preparing to leave you for the mission field? It may tear your heart to see them go, yet you must send them to do God's work.

Christianity must be more than a practical, functional experience. At times it is painful, but believers must develop relationships that are warm, genuine, and deep with feeling. Seek to be a heart-to-heart type of friend.

---

14 But I preferred to do nothing without your consent, in order that your good deed might be voluntary and not something forced.NRSV Paul would have liked to have kept Onesimus with him (v. 13). However, he decided not to try to talk Philemon into allowing Onesimus to return to Rome to serve Paul; Paul might have felt that this was taking undue advantage of his relationship with Philemon. Only if Philemon were to give his *consent* for this would it have been *voluntary.*

Whether Onesimus was sent back to Paul is unknown. Paul had willingly returned Onesimus to Philemon, preferring that Philemon make the final decision in the matter. The *good deed* probably was not allowing Onesimus to return to Paul, because the Greek structure of the sentence does not imply that Paul was asking this. Rather, Paul simply did not want to do anything about Onesimus without Philemon's consent. Paul wanted to place no constraint on Philemon other than to deal in Christian kindness and love toward his slave. Paul hoped that Philemon would do a "good deed" in pardoning his slave from severe punishment, especially since Onesimus had become a new person in Christ.

Philemon had to think of Onesimus not as a piece of property, but as a brother in the fellowship.

15 Perhaps the reason he was separated from you for a little while was that you might have him back for good.NIV Paul considered that all that had happened—Onesimus's desertion and subsequent conversion to Christ—had been part of God's providence. God can overrule and bring good out of human sin and folly. Onesimus had caused trouble and heartache, but he had become a new person, and Philemon would soon *have him back*. The Greek means, "have him for yourself in full possession." The *little while* of Onesimus's absence would be overshadowed by the devotion that would bind him to his master *for good*. They would be together for eternity, but Paul also wanted Philemon to take Onesimus back into his service permanently now.

Paul may still have hoped that Onesimus would be returned to him. However, he knew that true reconciliation could only occur if (1) Onesimus himself went back to Philemon willing to return to service, and (2) if Philemon willingly accepted Onesimus back.

PROVIDENCE
Paul acknowledged that God was at work behind the scenes in this separation of Onesimus and Philemon. God carried out his hidden purpose even in the apparent turmoil of human events.

Crysostom, a father of the ancient Greek church, drew a parallel between the lives of Joseph and Onesimus. Joseph had been sold into slavery by his brothers, only to become their benefactor when famine hit Egypt (Genesis 45:4-8). Joseph told his brothers, "So then, it was not you who sent me here, but God" (Genesis 45:8 NIV). When Joseph's father, Jacob, died, Joseph reassured his brothers, "You intended to harm me, but God intended it for good to accomplish what is now being done, the saving of many lives" (Genesis 50:20 NIV). Although Philemon lost Onesimus, it was only for a time. Philemon eventually regained his slave, but even more, he gained a new brother in Christ.

When we face painful separations or difficult times in relationships with loved ones, we must trust in God's loving care and in his wisdom and power over all events. God may be using the difficulty to bring people to himself, to develop character, and to help us grow. Can you trust God enough to leave the situation in his hands?

16 No longer as a slave, but better than a slave, as a dear brother. He is very dear to me but even dearer to you, both as a man and as a brother in the Lord.NIV For Philemon to accept Onesimus back, he would have to do so with the understanding that Onesimus had a new status—he was a person (that is, not merely a possession), and he was also *a brother in the Lord.*

The phrase *no longer as a slave* has caused much debate. Was this Paul's way of asking Philemon to free Onesimus? Or was it his way of stating that there should be a new relationship of brother to brother even though they still would be master and slave? According to 1 Corinthians 7:21, Paul encouraged slaves to gain freedom if they could. Thus, it would be consistent for Paul to ask for Onesimus's freedom in this case. Paul's asking for Onesimus to be part of his team would be equal to freeing him permanently. But since Paul didn't ask for the freedom directly, we can't be sure what he meant. If Onesimus was supposed to return to Philemon as his slave, Philemon would be expected to treat his slave in accordance with their relationship in Christ. Paul had given guidelines for slaves and masters in other letters (1 Corinthians 7:20-24; Ephesians 6:5-9; Colossians 3:22–4:1). Onesimus's new status as a believer did not negate his responsibilities to Philemon.

Paul knew how difficult it might be for Philemon to deal with Onesimus as a *dear brother* after the trouble he had caused. Paul made it clear that he not only trusted Onesimus (v. 13) but that he considered Onesimus a brother in Christ. With these words, Paul deftly placed himself, Philemon, and Onesimus all at the same level. While this prisoner, landowner, and slave had very different social positions, they were equals in Christ.

While Onesimus had become very dear to Paul, he was *even dearer* to Philemon because Onesimus's former relationship with Philemon had laid the groundwork for a lasting relationship between them.

STATUS UN-CONSCIOUS
What a difference Onesimus's status as a Christian made in his relationship to Philemon. He was no longer merely a slave, he was also a brother. That meant that both Onesimus and Philemon were members of God's family—equals in Christ. A Christian's status as a member of God's family transcends all other distinctions among believers. Do you look down on any fellow Christians? Remember, they are your equals before Christ (Galatians 3:28). How you treat your brothers and sisters in Christ's family reflects your true Christian commitment.

---

17 So if you consider me your partner, welcome him as you would welcome me.[NRSV] In this verse Paul stated his request: *welcome him.* Like the father of the prodigal son in Jesus' parable,

Philemon should open his arms to welcome Onesimus back to his household
and, as a new believer, to the church.
God had welcomed Onesimus; so
should Philemon.

> Justification by faith must result in fellowship by faith. This latter means the settled determination to share fully in mutual fellowship with all those who share the faith, however awkward or angular or muddled or misguided, or simply *different,* they may be, or appear to be. *N. T. Wright*

The word *partner* is *koinonon* from
the word *koinonia,* meaning fellowship
or sharing. Philemon and Paul shared
the *koinonia* described in verse 6. Paul
wanted Philemon's attitude toward Onesimus to be based on his attitude toward
Paul. If Paul and Philemon had fellowship, then Philemon would have to
include Onesimus as well. Paul was
relying on his relationship with Philemon (their fellowship and
partnership) to cause Philemon to welcome Onesimus as he
would welcome Paul (v. 12).

PARTNERS
Paul called Philemon his "partner," but he did not mean a partner in the business sense of the word. Philemon was a partner
in grace. Paul and Philemon shared the same experience in
Jesus Christ of being saved; in that sense, they were equals.
Too often our relationships in the church don't possess true
partnership but reflect merely tolerance of one another. Do you
have room in your heart to welcome other believers warmly?
Treat them as companions in God's grace and love, not just fellow workers. Let your common interests in Christ and your common feeling of gratitude for Christ's love knit you together with
others.

**18 If he has done you any wrong or owes you anything, charge it
to me.**[NIV] Onesimus may have confessed some such act to Paul.
The only way Onesimus could have financed his flight was to
have stolen from his master money or possessions that he could
sell. Even if not, he still would be in debt for the work that had
not been performed in his absence. This would cause Onesimus
to be extremely afraid to return to his master. It was bad enough
that he had run away, but if he had also stolen money or possessions or had wronged his master in any other way, he would be in
deep trouble. Thus Paul's letter served as a buffer—giving Onesimus courage to return and giving Philemon the entire picture so
that he might deal kindly with his slave.

Any money or possessions that Onesimus had taken certainly
were long gone. Onesimus had no means to repay. Paul asked

THE WORK OF RECONCILIATION
What Paul did for Onesimus parallels what Christ did for us.

Onesimus had wronged Philemon and thus was separated from him.	Sinners have wronged God and are thus separated from him (Romans 3:23).
Paul had not been involved with Onesimus's guilt.	Jesus was sinless, separated from sinners (Hebrews 4:15).
Paul wrote this letter to reconcile Onesimus and Philemon.	Jesus' work on the cross reconciled sinners and the holy God (2 Corinthians 5:17-21).
The debt Onesimus had with Philemon had to be paid.	The penalty for sin had to be paid.
Paul took on a debt that was not his own by promising to repay Philemon.	Jesus took on the debt of sin that was not his own (the sins of the whole world) and paid it by his death (John 1:29; Romans 5:8-9; Hebrews 7:27; 9:26, 28).

that any money stolen be charged (*elloga* is an accounting term) to his own account; in other words, Onesimus no longer would owe Philemon anything, but Paul would. Paul was not suggesting to Philemon that he simply forgive Onesimus's debt; the wrong needed to be righted. Instead, Paul took on that debt on Onesimus's behalf. (For a discussion of Paul's source of funds, see Philippians 1:1 and 4:18.) Onesimus would never know whether the debt was actually demanded and repaid. All he knew was that a debt needed to be paid because of his wrong actions—but that someone else was going to pay it for him. Onesimus got a dose of true Christian love through Paul's action.

WORTHY INVESTMENTS
Paul genuinely loved Onesimus. Paul showed his love by personally guaranteeing payment for any stolen goods or wrongs for which Onesimus might be responsible. Paul's investment in the life of this new believer certainly encouraged and strengthened Onesimus's faith. Are there young believers who need you to demonstrate such self-sacrifice toward them? Be grateful when you can invest in people, helping them with Bible study, prayer, encouragement, support, and friendship.

19 I, Paul, am writing this with my own hand: I will repay it.^{NRSV}
Often Paul would use a secretary to write his letters as he dictated them (see Romans 16:22). But sometimes at the end of the let-

ters, he would take the pen and write a few words in order to
authenticate the letters (see, for example, Galatians 6:11; Colossians 4:18). Most likely this entire letter was written in his own
hand, for it was a personal letter to a personal friend. This letter
was short, not filled with doctrinal teachings; it would be more
effective if written by Paul. For Paul to write again the words *I
will repay it* emphasized that he was placing himself under legal
obligation to do so. Paul was not "just saying" this to placate Philemon; he meant to do so by putting it in writing. If Philemon had
demanded repayment, Paul would have had to do it.

I say nothing about your owing me even your own self.^{NRSV} It

I say nothing about your owing me even your own self.[NRSV] It
seems that Paul knew his friend well enough to know that he
would not demand repayment (vv. 19-21), but this does not less-
en Paul's generous action toward Onesimus, who knew only that
someone else was paying for his wrongdoing. While Paul told
Philemon to put Onesimus's charge on Paul's "page" in the
accounting book, Paul also reminded Philemon that he (Paul) had
a huge credit already, in that Philemon owed himself (that is, his
conversion, his true *self* in Christ) to Paul. Once Onesimus's debt
was put on Paul's page, it would be cancelled. As Philemon's spiritual father, Paul was hoping that Philemon would feel a debt of
gratitude that would cause him to accept Onesimus with a spirit
of forgiveness.

REFRESH THEIR HEARTS
Have you benefited from the ministry of others? Has there
been a pastor, youth worker, or Sunday school teacher whose
guidance and faithfulness stimulated you to grow in Christ?
Consider how you may refresh their hearts with some word of
encouragement or some thoughtful gift. Let them know that you
have followed their examples by being faithful to Christ.

**20 I do wish, brother, that I may have some benefit from you in
the Lord; refresh my heart in Christ.**[NIV] Again Paul called Philemon *brother*. In the matters of ledgers and debts, once Onesimus's debt was repaid, Paul would still have a credit, for who can
ever repay someone for bringing him or her to eternal life? Thus
Paul asked that the balance be paid in kindness to Onesimus. The
Greek word translated *some benefit* is *onaimen,* a word sounding
much like Onesimus. Onesimus had benefited Paul (v. 11); Paul
hoped that Philemon would do likewise. And as Philemon had
refreshed the hearts of the saints (v. 7), he could hardly do other
than refresh Paul's heart as well. The word *my* is emphatic in the

Greek. It is as if Paul were saying, "It is *my* turn to be refreshed by you."

21 Confident of your obedience, I write to you, knowing that you will do even more than I ask.NIV Paul's use of the word *obedience* seems strong in contrast to how he had carefully worded his request throughout this letter. He may have been alluding to his apostolic authority at which he had hinted previously in the letter but had chosen not to use (v. 8), preferring instead to let Philemon's act be voluntary (v. 14). But the word "obedience" is more flexible in Greek than in English and does not mean that Paul had been issuing orders. Instead, "obedience" here indicates a person's response to God's will. Paul wanted Philemon to obey in the sense of following God's will.

Paul was not only confident that Philemon would welcome Onesimus back, but that Philemon would also *do even more* than Paul asked. This may have been a hint that Philemon would willingly free Onesimus so that he could return to Paul or be freed when Paul got to Colosse. We can be sure that Philemon welcomed Onesimus, but the "even more" is left unknown.

22 One thing more—prepare a guest room for me, for I am hoping through your prayers to be restored to you.NRSV That Paul would ask Philemon to prepare a guest room in his home indicates that Paul expected to be released (see also Philippians 2:23-24). Some feel that this was Paul's way of reminding Philemon of his apostolic authority. Or it may have been a tongue-in-cheek way of securing a kindly reception for Onesimus because Paul hoped to eventually arrive to check up on what had occurred. It is more likely that Paul was simply hoping to eventually visit these friends who had been praying for him.

His freedom would be secured through these prayers. The words *your* and *you* are plural, focusing on Philemon, Apphia, Archippus, and the church in Philemon's house. Paul had never been to Colosse; the word *restored* in Greek simply means "granted" or "given as a gift" (the root of the word is *charis*, "grace"). For Philemon and the church in his home to have their prayers answered with a visit from Paul would indeed be a gift of grace. Paul was released from prison soon after writing this letter, but the Bible doesn't say whether he went to Colosse.

23 Epaphras, my fellow prisoner in Christ Jesus, greets you.NKJV The *you* in this verse is singular. These are personal greetings to Philemon. Epaphras was well known to the Colossians because he had founded the church there (Colossians 1:7), perhaps while Paul was living in Ephesus (Acts 19:10). Epaphras may have been converted in Ephesus and then had returned to Colosse, his hometown. He was a hero to this church, helping to hold it together in spite of growing persecution and struggles with false doctrine. His report to Paul about the problems in Colosse had prompted Paul to write his letter to the Colossians. Epaphras's greetings to and prayers for the Colossian Christians reveal his deep love for them (Colossians 4:12-13).

It is unclear whether Epaphras was actually in prison with Paul. Paul's words *fellow prisoner in Christ Jesus* may have been a metaphor of warfare or "captivity to Christ." It is more likely that Epaphras was with Paul voluntarily and would return to Colosse.

24 And so do Mark, Aristarchus, Demas, and Luke, my fellow workers.^{NRSV} Mark, Aristarchus, Demas, and Luke are also mentioned in Colossians 4:10, 14. Mark had accompanied Paul and Barnabas on their first missionary journey (Acts 12:25ff.) and eventually wrote the Gospel of Mark. Luke had accompanied Paul on his third missionary journey and was the writer of the Gospel of Luke and the book of Acts. Demas had been faithful to Paul for a while but then had deserted him (see 2 Timothy 4:10). Paul had sent greetings from these same people in the letter to the Colossians. But in that letter, a man "Jesus who is called Justus" also had sent greetings to Colosse. Much speculation has been done as to why his greetings were not included here, but it may simply have been that he was absent on the day Paul wrote this letter to Philemon.

25 The grace of the Lord Jesus Christ be with your spirit.^{NRSV} The word *your* is plural, indicating that Paul sent this final blessing not to Philemon only, but to the entire church that regularly met in his home (v. 2). As Paul had begun his letter with "grace" (v. 3), so he ended it with the benediction that the believers would continue to experience God's unmerited favor. The grace of the Lord Jesus Christ is with Christians' spirits because the Spirit of Jesus Christ indwells the spirits (the inner selves) of believers (see Romans 8:9-11).

While this is Paul's standard benediction, it certainly had special meaning to Philemon. It would take God's grace working in Philemon to enable him to do something difficult, something unnatural—forgiving, welcoming, and accepting into the fellowship as a brother a slave who had, at least at a previous time, proven himself to be unfaithful and untrustworthy. It would be through God's grace alone that this reconciliation would be possible. Yet the grace was available; Philemon only had to act upon it. If the entire letter was meant to be read to the church that met in Philemon's home, then they too would, by God's grace, also need to welcome and accept Onesimus. God's grace, working in the spirits of believers, makes true fellowship and reconciliation possible within any body of believers.

TRANSFORMATION
Paul urged Philemon to be reconciled to his slave, receiving him as a brother and fellow member of God's family. "Reconciliation" means reestablishing relationship. Christ has reconciled us to God and to others. Many barriers come between people—race, social status, sex, personality differences—but Christ can break down these barriers. Jesus Christ changed Onesimus's relationship with Philemon from slave to brother. Christ can transform our most hopeless relationships into deep and loving friendships.

BIBLIOGRAPHY

Beers, V. Gilbert. *The Victor Handbook of Bible Knowledge*. Wheaton, Ill.: Victor, 1981.

Bruce, F. F. *The Epistles to the Colossians, to Philemon, and to the Ephesians* (in the New International Commentary on the New Testament series). Grand Rapids: Eerdmans, 1984.

————*Philippians* (in the New International Biblical Commentary series). Peabody, Mass.: Hendrickson Publishers, 1989.

Douglas, J. D., and Philip W. Comfort, eds. *New Commentary on the Whole Bible: New Testament Volume*. Wheaton, Ill.: Tyndale House, 1990.

Hawthorne, Gerald F. *Philippians* (in the Word Biblical Commentary series). Waco, Texas: Word, 1983.

Hawthorne, Gerald F., Ralph P. Martin, Daniel Reid, eds. *Dictionary of Paul and His Letters*. Downers Grove, Ill.: InterVarsity Press, 1993.

Kent, Homer A. "Philippians" in *The Expositor's Bible Commentary*. Vol. 11, edited by Frank E. Gaebelein. Grand Rapids: Zondervan, 1978.

Martin, Ralph. *Colossians and Philemon*. Greenwood, S.C.: The Attic Press, Inc., 1974.

————*Philippians* (in the Tyndale New Testament Commentary series). Grand Rapids: Eerdmans, 1987.

O'Brien, Peter T. *Colossians, Philemon* (in the Word Biblical Commentary series). Waco, Texas: Word, 1982.

Patzia, Arthur G. *Ephesians, Colossians, Philemon* (in the New International Biblical Commentary series). Peabody, Mass.: Hendrickson Publishers, 1990.

Rupprecht, Arthur A. "Philemon" in *The Expositor's Bible Commentary*. Vol. 11, edited by Frank E. Gaebelein. Grand Rapids: Zondervan, 1978.

Tenney, Merrill C. *New Testament Survey*. Grand Rapids: Eerdmans, 1976.

Vaughn, Curtis. "Colossians" in *The Expositor's Bible Commentary*. Vol. 11, edited by Frank E. Gaebelein. Grand Rapids: Zondervan, 1978.

Wall, Robert W. *Colossians & Philemon* (in the IVP New Testament Commentary series). Downers Grove, Ill.: InterVarsity Press, 1993.

Walvoord, John F., and Roy B. Zuck. *Bible Knowledge Commentary: New Testament Edition*. Wheaton, Ill.: Victor, 1983.

Wright, N. T. *Colossians and Philemon* (in the Tyndale New Testament Commentary series). Grand Rapids: Eerdmans, 1988.

INDEX